SO-BSC-394

Philosophy of Human Nature: Readings
Selections from primary sources

Selected by Dr. Astrid O'Brien

Course: Philosophy of Human Nature

THOMSON

WADSWORTH

Australia · Canada · Mexico · Singapore · Spain · United Kingdom · United States

Philosophy of Human Nature: Readings

Custom Editor:
Pete Nasta

Project Development Editor:
Brian Schaefer

Marketing Coordinators:
Sara Mercurio and Lindsay Annett

Production/Manufacturing Supervisor:
Donna M. Brown

Project Coordinator:
Susannah Maynard

Pre-Media Services Supervisor:
Dan Plofchan

Senior Prepress Specialist:
Joel Brennecke

Cover Design:
Krista Pierson

Cover Image:
© Photo/Yvo

Printer:
RR Donnelley

© 2006 Wadsworth, a part of the Thomson Corporation. Thomson, the Star logo and Wadsworth are trademarks used herein under license.

ALL RIGHTS RESERVED. No part of this work covered by the copyright hereon may be reproduced or used in any form or by any means — graphic, electronic, or mechanical, including photocopying, recording, taping, Web distribution or information storage and retrieval systems — without the written permission of the publisher.

Printed in the United States of America
1 2 3 4 5 6 7 8 9 10 11 12 13 14 09 08 07 06 05

For information about our products, contact us at:
Thomson Learning Academic Resource Center
(800) 423-0563

For permission to use material from this text or product, submit a request online at **http://www.thomsonrights.com**. Any additional questions about permissions can be submitted by email to **thomsonrights@thomson.com**.

The Adaptable Courseware Program consists of products and additions to existing Wadsworth products that are produced from camera-ready copy. Peer review, class testing, and accuracy are primarily the responsibility of the author(s).

Student Edition: ISBN 978-0-495-20569-2
(0-495-20569-9)

Thomson Custom Solutions
5191 Natorp Boulevard
Mason, OH 45040
www.thomsoncustom.com

Thomson Higher Education
10 Davis Drive
Belmont, CA 94002-3098
USA

Asia (Including India):
Thomson Learning
60 Albert Street, #15-01
Albert Complex
Singapore 189969
Tel 65 336-6411
Fax 65 336-7411

Australia/New Zealand:
Thomson Learning Australia
102 Dodds Street
Southbank, Victoria 3006
Australia

Latin America:
Thomson Learning
Seneca 53
Colonia Polano
11560 Mexico, D.F., Mexico
Tel (525) 281-2906
Fax (525) 281-2656

Canada:
Thomson Nelson
1120 Birchmount Road
Toronto, Ontario
Canada M1K 5G4
Tel (416) 752-9100
Fax (416) 752-8102

UK/Europe/Middle East/Africa:
Thomson Learning
High Holborn House
50-51 Bedford Row
London, WC1R 4LS
United Kingdom
Tel 44 (020) 7067-2500
Fax 44 (020) 7067-2600

Spain (Includes Portugal):
Thomson Paraninfo
Calle Magallanes 25
28015 Madrid
España
Tel 34 (0)91 446-3350
Fax 34 (0)91 445-6218

Acknowledgements

The content of this text has been adapted from the following product(s):

Complete Works (Ed. John M. Cooper, Assoc. Ed. D.S. Hutchinson)
Plato (0-87220-349-2)

Philosophical Essays and Correspondence (Ed. Roger Ariew)
Descartes (0-87220-502-9)

Table Of Contents

1

APOLOGY

*T*his work is universally known as Plato's 'Apology' of Socrates, in deference to the word apologia that stands in its Greek title. Actually, the word means not an apology but a defense speech in a legal proceeding, and that is what we get—certainly, Socrates does not apologize for anything! This is not really a dialogue. Except for an interlude when he engages one of his accusers in the sort of question-and-answer discussion characteristic of Plato's 'Socratic' dialogues, we see Socrates delivering a speech before his jury of 501 fellow male Athenians. At the age of seventy he had been indicted for breaking the law against 'impiety'—for offending the Olympian gods (Zeus, Apollo, and the rest) recognized in the city's festivals and other official activities. The basis of the charge, such as it was, lay in the way that, for many years, Socrates had been carrying on his philosophical work in Athens. It has often been thought that the real basis for it lay in 'guilt by association': several of Socrates' known associates had been prominent malfeasants in Athens' defeat in the Peloponnesian War only a few years earlier and the oligarchic reign of terror that followed; but an amnesty had forbidden suits based on political offenses during that time. However much those associations may have been in the minds of his accusers—and his jurors, too—Plato makes him respond sincerely to the charges as lodged. After all, these would be the ultimate basis on which he should or should not be found guilty of anything. So he takes the occasion to explain and defend his devotion to philosophy, and the particular ways he has pursued that in discussions with select young men and with people prominent in the city—discussions like those we see in Plato's other 'Socratic' works. He argues that, so far from offending the gods through his philosophizing, or showing disbelief in them, he has piously followed their lead (particularly that of Apollo, through his oracle at Delphi) in making himself as good a person as he can and encouraging (even goading) others to do the same. The gods want, more than anything else, that we shall be good, and goodness depends principally upon the quality of our understanding of what to care about and how to behave in our lives: philosophy, through Socratic discussion, is the pursuit of that understanding.

This is, of course, no record of the actual defense Socrates mounted at his trial in 399 B.C., but a composition of Plato's own—we have no way of knowing how closely, if at all, it conforms to Socrates' real speech. In it Plato gives us the best, most serious, response to the charges that, on his own knowledge of Socrates, Socrates was entitled to give. Was Socrates nonetheless guilty as charged? In deciding this, readers should notice that, however sincere Plato's Socrates may be in claiming a pious motivation for his philosophical work, he does set up human reason in his own person as the final arbiter of what is right and wrong, and so of what the gods want us to do: he interprets Apollo, through his oracle at Delphi, to have told him to do *that! As we see also from* Euthyphro, *he has no truck with the authority of myths or ancient poets or religious tradition and 'divination' to tell us what to think about the gods and their commands or wishes as regards ourselves.*

In democratic Athens, juries were randomly selected subsets—representatives—of the whole people. Hence, as Socrates makes clear, he is addressing the democratic people of Athens, and when the jury find him guilty and condemn him to death, they act as and for the Athenian people. Did Socrates bring on his own condemnation, whether wittingly or not, by refusing to say the sorts of things and to comport himself in the sort of way that would have won his acquittal? Perhaps. True to his philosophical calling, he requires that the Athenians think, *honestly and dispassionately, and decide the truth of the charges by reasoning from the facts as they actually were. This was his final challenge to them to care more for their souls—their minds, their power of reason—than for their peace and comfort, undisturbed by the likes of him. Seen in that light, as Plato wants us to see it, the failure was theirs.*

J.M.C.

17   I do not know, men of Athens, how my accusers affected you; as for me, I was almost carried away in spite of myself, so persuasively did they speak. And yet, hardly anything of what they said is true. Of the many lies they told, one in particular

b   surprised me, namely that you should be careful not to be deceived by an accomplished speaker like me. That they were not ashamed to be immediately proved wrong by the facts, when I show myself not to be an accomplished speaker at all, that I thought was most shameless on their part—unless indeed they call an accomplished speaker the man who speaks the truth. If they mean that, I would agree

c   that I am an orator, but not after their manner, for indeed, as I say, practically nothing they said was true. From me you will hear the whole truth, though not, by Zeus, gentlemen, expressed in embroidered and stylized phrases like theirs, but things spoken at random and expressed in the first words that come to mind, for I put my trust in the justice of what I say, and let none of you expect anything else. It would not be fitting at my age, as it might be for a young man, to toy with words when I appear before you.

One thing I do ask and beg of you, gentlemen: if you hear me making my defense in the same kind of language as I am accustomed to use in the marketplace by the

d   bankers' tables, where many of you have heard me, and elsewhere, do not be surprised or create a disturbance on that account. The position is this: this is my first appearance in a lawcourt, at the age of seventy; I am therefore simply a stranger to the manner of speaking here. Just as if I were really a stranger, you would certainly

18   excuse me if I spoke in that dialect and manner in which I had been brought up, so too my present request seems a just one, for you to pay no attention to my manner

Translated by G.M.A. Grube.

of speech—be it better or worse—but to concentrate your attention on whether what I say is just or not, for the excellence of a judge lies in this, as that of a speaker lies in telling the truth.

It is right for me, gentlemen, to defend myself first against the first lying accusations made against me and my first accusers, and then against the later accusations and the later accusers. There have been many who have accused me to   b
you for many years now, and none of their accusations are true. These I fear much more than I fear Anytus and his friends, though they too are formidable. These earlier ones, however, are more so, gentlemen; they got hold of most of you from childhood, persuaded you and accused me quite falsely, saying that there is a man called Socrates, a wise man, a student of all things in the sky and below the earth, who makes the worse argument the stronger. Those who spread that rumor, gentlemen,   c
are my dangerous accusers, for their hearers believe that those who study these things do not even believe in the gods. Moreover, these accusers are numerous, and have been at it a long time; also, they spoke to you at an age when you would most readily believe them, some of you being children and adolescents, and they won their case by default, as there was no defense.

What is most absurd in all this is that one cannot even know or mention their names unless one of them is a writer of comedies.[1] Those who maliciously and   d
slanderously persuaded you—who also, when persuaded themselves then persuaded others—all those are most difficult to deal with: one cannot bring one of them into court or refute him; one must simply fight with shadows, as it were, in making one's defense, and cross-examine when no one answers. I want you to realize too that my accusers are of two kinds: those who have accused me recently, and the old ones I mention; and to think that I must first defend myself against the latter, for you have also heard their accusations first, and to a much greater extent than the more recent.   e

Very well then, men of Athens. I must surely defend myself and attempt to uproot from your minds in so short a time the slander that has resided there so long. I wish   19
this may happen, if it is in any way better for you and me, and that my defense may be successful, but I think this is very difficult and I am fully aware of how difficult it is. Even so, let the matter proceed as the god may wish, but I must obey the law and make my defense.

Let us then take up the case from its beginning. What is the accusation from which arose the slander in which Meletus trusted when he wrote out the charge   b
against me? What did they say when they slandered me? I must, as if they were my actual prosecutors, read the affidavit they would have sworn. It goes something like this: Socrates is guilty of wrongdoing in that he busies himself studying things in the sky and below the earth; he makes the worse into the stronger argument, and he teaches these same things to others. You have seen this yourself in the comedy of   c
Aristophanes, a Socrates swinging about there, saying he was walking on air and talking a lot of other nonsense about things of which I know nothing at all. I do not speak in contempt of such knowledge, if someone is wise in these things—lest

---

[1] This is Aristophanes. Socrates refers below (19c) to the character Socrates in his *Clouds* (225 ff.), first produced in 423 B.C.

Meletus bring more cases against me—but, gentlemen, I have no part in it, and on this point I call upon the majority of you as witnesses. I think it right that all those
d   of you who have heard me conversing, and many of you have, should tell each other if anyone of you has ever heard me discussing such subjects to any extent at all. From this you will learn that the other things said about me by the majority are of the same kind.

Not one of them is true. And if you have heard from anyone that I undertake to
e   teach people and charge a fee for it, that is not true either. Yet I think it a fine thing to be able to teach people as Gorgias of Leontini does, and Prodicus of Ceos, and Hippias of Elis.[2] Each of these men can go to any city and persuade the young, who
20   can keep company with anyone of their own fellow citizens they want without paying, to leave the company of these, to join with themselves, pay them a fee, and be grateful to them besides. Indeed, I learned that there is another wise man from Paros who is visiting us, for I met a man who has spent more money on Sophists than everybody else put together, Callias, the son of Hipponicus. So I asked him—he has two sons—"Callias," I said, "if your sons were colts or calves, we could find and
b   engage a supervisor for them who would make them excel in their proper qualities, some horse breeder or farmer. Now since they are men, whom do you have in mind to supervise them? Who is an expert in this kind of excellence, the human and social kind? I think you must have given thought to this since you have sons. Is there such a person," I asked, "or is there not?" "Certainly there is," he said. "Who is he?" I asked, "What is his name, where is he from? and what is his fee?" "His name,
c   Socrates, is Evenus, he comes from Paros, and his fee is five minas." I thought Evenus a happy man, if he really possesses this art, and teaches for so moderate a fee. Certainly I would pride and preen myself if I had this knowledge, but I do not have it, gentlemen.

One of you might perhaps interrupt me and say: "But Socrates, what is your occupation? From where have these slanders come? For surely if you did not busy yourself with something out of the common, all these rumors and talk would not
d   have arisen unless you did something other than most people. Tell us what it is, that we may not speak inadvisedly about you." Anyone who says that seems to be right, and I will try to show you what has caused this reputation and slander. Listen then. Perhaps some of you will think I am jesting, but be sure that all that I shall say is true. What has caused my reputation is none other than a certain kind of wisdom. What kind of wisdom? Human wisdom, perhaps. It may be that I really possess this,
e   while those whom I mentioned just now are wise with a wisdom more than human; else I cannot explain it, for I certainly do not possess it, and whoever says I do is lying and speaks to slander me. Do not create a disturbance, gentlemen, even if you think I am boasting, for the story I shall tell does not originate with me, but I will refer you to a trustworthy source. I shall call upon the god at Delphi as witness to the

---

2   These were all well-known Sophists. For Gorgias and Hippias see Plato's dialogues named after them; both Hippias and Prodicus appear in *Protagoras*.

existence and nature of my wisdom, if it be such. You know Chaerephon. He was my   21
friend from youth, and the friend of most of you, as he shared your exile and your
return. You surely know the kind of man he was, how impulsive in any course of
action. He went to Delphi at one time and ventured to ask the oracle—as I say,
gentlemen, do not create a disturbance—he asked if any man was wiser than I, and
the Pythian replied that no one was wiser. Chaerephon is dead, but his brother will
testify to you about this.

Consider that I tell you this because I would inform you about the origin of the   b
slander. When I heard of this reply I asked myself: "Whatever does the god mean?
What is his riddle? I am very conscious that I am not wise at all; what then does he
mean by saying that I am the wisest? For surely he does not lie; it is not legitimate
for him to do so." For a long time I was at a loss as to his meaning; then I very
reluctantly turned to some such investigation as this; I went to one of those reputed
wise, thinking that there, if anywhere, I could refute the oracle and say to it: "This   c
man is wiser than I, but you said I was." Then, when I examined this man there is no
need for me to tell you his name, he was one of our public men—my experience was
something like this: I thought that he appeared wise to many people and especially
to himself, but he was not. I then tried to show him that he thought himself wise, but
that he was not. As a result he came to dislike me, and so did many of the bystanders.   d
So I withdrew and thought to myself: "I am wiser than this man; it is likely that
neither of us knows anything worthwhile, but he thinks he knows something when
he does not, whereas when I do not know, neither do I think I know; so I am likely
to be wiser than he to this small extent, that I do not think I know what I do not
know." After this I approached another man, one of those thought to be wiser than
he, and I thought the same thing, and so I came to be disliked both by him and by   e
many others.

After that I proceeded systematically. I realized, to my sorrow and alarm, that I
was getting unpopular, but I thought that I must attach the greatest importance to the
god's oracle, so I must go to all those who had any reputation for knowledge to
examine its meaning. And by the dog, men of Athens—for I must tell you the truth—   22
I experienced something like this: in my investigation in the service of the god I
found that those who had the highest reputation were nearly the most deficient, while
those who were thought to be inferior were more knowledgeable. I must give you an
account of my journeyings as if they were labors I had undertaken to prove the oracle
irrefutable. After the politicians, I went to the poets, the writers of tragedies and   b
dithyrambs and the others, intending in their case to catch myself being more
ignorant than they. So I took up those poems with which they seemed to have taken
most trouble and asked them what they meant, in order that I might at the same time
learn something from them. I am ashamed to tell you the truth, gentlemen, but I
must. Almost all the bystanders might have explained the poems better than their   c
authors could. I soon realized that poets do not compose their poems with
knowledge, but by some inborn talent and by inspiration, like seers and prophets
who also say many fine things without any understanding of what they say. The poets
seemed to me to have had a similar experience. At the same time I saw that, because

of their poetry, they thought themselves very wise men in other respects, which they were not. So there again I withdrew, thinking that I had the same advantage over them as I had over the politicians.

d   Finally I went to the craftsmen, for I was conscious of knowing practically nothing, and I knew that I would find that they had knowledge of many fine things. In this I was not mistaken; they knew things I did not know, and to that extent they were wiser than I. But, men of Athens, the good craftsmen seemed to me to have the same fault as the poets: each of them, because of his success at his craft, thought

e   himself very wise in other most important pursuits, and this error of theirs overshadowed the wisdom they had, so that I asked myself, on behalf of the oracle, whether I should prefer to be as I am, with neither their wisdom nor their ignorance, or to have both. The answer I gave myself and the oracle was that it was to my advantage to be as I am.

           As a result of this investigation, men of Athens, I acquired much unpopularity,
23   of a kind that is hard to deal with and is a heavy burden; many slanders came from these people and a reputation for wisdom, for in each case the bystanders thought that I myself possessed the wisdom that I proved that my interlocutor did not have. What is probable, gentlemen, is that in fact the god is wise and that his oracular

b   response meant that human wisdom is worth little or nothing, and that when he says this man, Socrates, he is using my name as an example, as if he said: "This man among you, mortals, is wisest who, like Socrates, understands that his wisdom is worthless." So even now I continue this investigation as the god bade me—and I go around seeking out anyone, citizen or stranger, whom I think wise. Then if I do not think he is, I come to the assistance of the god and show him that he is not wise. Because of this occupation, I do not have the leisure to engage in public affairs to any extent, nor indeed to look after my own, but I live in great poverty because of my service to the god.

c   Furthermore, the young men who follow me around of their own free will, those who have most leisure, the sons of the very rich, take pleasure in hearing people questioned; they themselves often imitate me and try to question others. I think they find an abundance of men who believe they have some knowledge but know little or nothing. The result is that those whom they question are angry, not with themselves

d   but with me. They say: "That man Socrates is a pestilential fellow who corrupts the young." If one asks them what he does and what he teaches to corrupt them, they are silent, as they do not know, but, so as not to appear at a loss, they mention those accusations that are available against all philosophers, about "things in the sky and things below the earth," about "not believing in the gods" and "making the worse the stronger argument"; they would not want to tell the truth, I'm sure, that they have been proved to lay claim to knowledge when they know nothing. These people are ambitious, violent and numerous; they are continually and convincingly talking

e   about me; they have been filling your ears for a long time with vehement slanders against me. From them Meletus attacked me, and Anytus and Lycon, Meletus being vexed on behalf of the poets, Anytus on behalf of the craftsmen and the politicians, Lycon on behalf of the orators, so that, as I started out by saying, I should be

24   surprised if I could rid you of so much slander in so short a time. That, men of

Athens, is the truth for you. I have hidden or disguised nothing. I know well enough that this very conduct makes me unpopular, and this is proof that what I say is true, that such is the slander against me, and that such are its causes. If you look into this   b either now or later, this is what you will find.

Let this suffice as a defense against the charges of my earlier accusers. After this I shall try to defend myself against Meletus, that good and patriotic man, as he says he is, and my later accusers. As these are a different lot of accusers, let us again take up their sworn deposition. It goes something like this: Socrates is guilty of corrupting the young and of not believing in the gods in whom the city believes, but in other new spiritual things? Such is their charge. Let us examine it point by point.   c

He says that I am guilty of corrupting the young, but I say that Meletus is guilty of dealing frivolously with serious matters, of irresponsibly bringing people into court, and of professing to be seriously concerned with things about none of which he has ever cared, and I shall try to prove that this is so. Come here and tell me, Meletus. Surely you consider it of the greatest importance that our young men be as   d good as possible?—Indeed I do.

Come then, tell these men who improves them. You obviously know, in view of your concern. You say you have discovered the one who corrupts them, namely me, and you bring me here and accuse me to these men. Come, inform them and tell them who it is. You see, Meletus, that you are silent and know not what to say. Does this not seem shameful to you and a sufficient proof of what I say, that you have not been concerned with any of this? Tell me, my good sir, who improves our young men?—   e The laws.

That is not what I am asking, but what person who has knowledge of the laws to begin with?—These jurymen, Socrates.

How do you mean, Meletus? Are these able to educate the young and improve them?—Certainly.

All of them, or some but not others?—All of them.

Very good, by Hera. You mention a great abundance of benefactors. But what   25 about the audience? Do they improve the young or not?—They do, too.

What about the members of Council?—The Councillors, also.

But, Meletus, what about the assembly? Do members of the assembly corrupt the young, or do they all improve them?—They improve them.

All the Athenians, it seems, make the young into fine good men, except me, and I alone corrupt them. Is that what you mean?—That is most definitely what I mean.

You condemn me to a great misfortune. Tell me: does this also apply to horses do   b you think? That all men improve them and one individual corrupts them? Or is quite the contrary true, one individual is able to improve them, or very few, namely, the horse breeders, whereas the majority, if they have horses and use them, corrupt them? Is that not the case, Meletus, both with horses and all other animals? Of course it is, whether you and Anytus say so or not. It would be a very happy state of affairs if only one person corrupted our youth, while the others improved them.

You have made it sufficiently obvious, Meletus, that you have never had any   c concern for our youth; you show your indifference clearly; that you have given no thought to the subjects about which you bring me to trial.

And by Zeus, Meletus, tell us also whether it is better for a man to live among good or wicked fellow citizens. Answer, my good man, for I am not asking a difficult question. Do not the wicked do some harm to those who are ever closest to them, whereas good people benefit them?—Certainly.

d　　　And does the man exist who would rather be harmed than benefited by his associates? Answer, my good sir, for the law orders you to answer. Is there any man who wants to be harmed?—Of course not.

Come now, do you accuse me here of corrupting the young and making them worse deliberately or unwillingly?—Deliberately.

e　　　What follows, Meletus? Are you so much wiser at your age than I am at mine that you understand that wicked people always do some harm to their closest neighbors while good people do them good, but I have reached such a pitch of ignorance that I do not realize this, namely that if I make one of my associates wicked I run the risk of being harmed by him so that I do such a great evil deliberately, as you say? I do

26　not believe you, Meletus, and I do not think anyone else will. Either I do not corrupt the young or, if I do, it is unwillingly, and you are lying in either case. Now if I corrupt them unwillingly, the law does not require you to bring people to court for such unwilling wrongdoings, but to get hold of them privately, to instruct them and exhort them; for clearly, if I learn better, I shall cease to do what I am doing unwillingly. You, however, have avoided my company and were unwilling to instruct me, but you bring me here, where the law requires one to bring those who are in need of punishment, not of instruction.

b　　　And so, men of Athens, what I said is clearly true: Meletus has never been at all concerned with these matters. Nonetheless tell us, Meletus, how you say that I corrupt the young; or is it obvious from your deposition that it is by teaching them not to believe in the gods in whom the city believes but in other new spiritual things? Is this not what you say I teach and so corrupt them?—That is most certainly what I do say.

c　　　Then by those very gods about whom we are talking, Meletus, make this clearer to me and to these men: I cannot be sure whether you mean that I teach the belief that there are some gods—and therefore I myself believe that there are gods and am not altogether an atheist, nor am I guilty of that—not, however, the gods in whom the city believes, but others, and that this is the charge against me, that they are others. Or whether you mean that I do not believe in gods at all, and that this is what I teach to others.—This is what I mean, that you do not believe in gods at all.

d　　　You are a strange fellow, Meletus. Why do you say this? Do I not believe, as other men do, that the sun and the moon are gods?—No, by Zeus, gentlemen of the jury, for he says that the sun is stone, and the moon earth.

My dear Meletus, do you think you are prosecuting Anaxagoras? Are you so contemptuous of these men and think them so ignorant of letters as not to know that the books of Anaxagoras of Clazomenae are full of those theories, and further, that

e　　　the young men learn from me what they can buy from time to time for a drachma, at most, in the bookshops, and ridicule Socrates if he pretends that these theories are his own, especially as they are so absurd? Is that, by Zeus, what you think of me, Meletus, that I do not believe that there are any gods?—That is what I say, that you do not believe in the gods at all.

You cannot be believed, Meletus, even, I think, by yourself. The man appears to me, men of Athens, highly insolent and uncontrolled. He seems to have made this deposition out of insolence, violence and youthful zeal. He is like one who composed a riddle and is trying it out: "Will the wise Socrates realize that I am jesting and contradicting myself, or shall I deceive him and others?" I think he contradicts himself in the affidavit, as if he said: "Socrates is guilty of not believing in gods but believing in gods," and surely that is the part of a jester!

Examine with me, gentlemen, how he appears to contradict himself, and you, Meletus, answer us. Remember, gentlemen, what I asked you when I began, not to create a disturbance if I proceed in my usual manner.

Does any man, Meletus, believe in human activities who does not believe in humans? Make him answer, and not again and again create a disturbance. Does any man who does not believe in horses believe in horsemen's activities? Or in flute-playing activities but not in flute-players? No, my good sir, no man could. If you are not willing to answer, I will tell you and these men. Answer the next question, however. Does any man believe in spiritual activities who does not believe in spirits?—No one.

Thank you for answering, if reluctantly, when these gentlemen made you. Now you say that I believe in spiritual things and teach about them, whether new or old, but at any rate spiritual things according to what you say, and to this you have sworn in your deposition. But if I believe in spiritual things I must quite inevitably believe in spirits. Is that not so? It is indeed. I shall assume that you agree, as you do not answer. Do we not believe spirits to be either gods or the children of gods? Yes or no?—Of course.

Then since I do believe in spirits, as you admit, if spirits are gods, this is what I mean when I say you speak in riddles and in jest, as you state that I do not believe in gods and then again that I do, since I do believe in spirits. If on the other hand the spirits are children of the gods, bastard children of the gods by nymphs or some other mothers, as they are said to be, what man would believe children of the gods to exist, but not gods? That would be just as absurd as to believe the young of horses and asses, namely mules, to exist, but not to believe in the existence of horses and asses. You must have made this deposition, Meletus, either to test us or because you were at a loss to find any true wrongdoing of which to accuse me. There is no way in which you could persuade anyone of even small intelligence that it is possible for one and the same man to believe in spiritual but not also in divine things, and then again for that same man to believe neither in spirits nor in gods nor in heroes.

I do not think, men of Athens, that it requires a prolonged defense to prove that I am not guilty of the charges in Meletus' deposition, but this is sufficient. On the other hand, you know that what I said earlier is true, that I am very unpopular with many people. This will be my undoing, if I am undone, not Meletus or Anytus but the slanders and envy of many people. This has destroyed many other good men and will, I think, continue to do so. There is no danger that it will stop at me.

27

b

c

d

e

28

b

Someone might say: "Are you not ashamed, Socrates, to have followed the kind of occupation that has led to your being now in danger of death?" However, I should be right to reply to him: "You are wrong, sir, if you think that a man who is any good at all should take into account the risk of life or death; he should look to this only in

c   his actions, whether what he does is right or wrong, whether he is acting like a good or a bad man." According to your view, all the heroes who died at Troy were inferior people, especially the son of Thetis who was so contemptuous of danger compared with disgrace.[3] When he was eager to kill Hector, his goddess mother warned him, as I believe, in some such words as these: "My child, if you avenge the death of your comrade, Patroclus, and you kill Hector, you will die yourself, for your death is to follow immediately after Hector's." Hearing this, he despised death and danger and

d   was much more afraid to live a coward who did not avenge his friends. "Let me die at once," he said, "when once I have given the wrongdoer his deserts, rather than remain here, a laughingstock by the curved ships, a burden upon the earth." Do you think he gave thought to death and danger?

This is the truth of the matter, men of Athens: wherever a man has taken a position that he believes to be best, or has been placed by his commander, there he must I think remain and face danger, without a thought for death or anything else, rather

e   than disgrace. It would have been a dreadful way to behave, men of Athens, if, at Potidaea, Amphipolis and Delium, I had, at the risk of death, like anyone else, remained at my post where those you had elected to command had ordered me, and then, when the god ordered me, as I thought and believed, to live the life of a philosopher, to examine myself and others, I had abandoned my post for fear of

29   death or anything else. That would have been a dreadful thing, and then I might truly have justly been brought here for not believing that there are gods, disobeying the oracle, fearing death, and thinking I was wise when I was not. To fear death, gentlemen, is no other than to think oneself wise when one is not, to think one knows what one does not know. No one knows whether death may not be the greatest of all blessings for a man, yet men fear it as if they knew that it is the greatest of evils. And

b   surely it is the most blameworthy ignorance to believe that one knows what one does not know. It is perhaps on this point and in this respect, gentlemen, that I differ from the majority of men, and if I were to claim that I am wiser than anyone in anything, it would be in this, that, as I have no adequate knowledge of things in the underworld, so I do not think I have. I do know, however, that it is wicked and shameful to do wrong, to disobey one's superior, be he god or man. I shall never fear or avoid things of which I do not know, whether they may not be good rather than

c   things that I know to be bad. Even if you acquitted me now and did not believe Anytus, who said to you that either I should not have been brought here in the first place, or that now I am here, you cannot avoid executing me, for if I should be acquitted, your sons would practice the teachings of Socrates and all be thoroughly corrupted; if you said to me in this regard: "Socrates, we do not believe Anytus now; we acquit you, but only on condition that you spend no more time on this investigation and do not practice philosophy, and if you are caught doing so you will

[3] See *Iliad* xviii.94 ff.

die;" if, as I say, you were to acquit me on those terms, I would say to you: "Men of   d
Athens, I am grateful and I am your friend, but I will obey the god rather than you,
and as long as I draw breath and am able, I shall not cease to practice philosophy, to
exhort you and in my usual way to point out to any one of you whom I happen to
meet: Good Sir, you are an Athenian, a citizen of the greatest city with the greatest
reputation for both wisdom and power; are you not ashamed of your eagerness to
possess as much wealth, reputation and honors as possible, while you do not care for   e
nor give thought to wisdom or truth, or the best possible state of your soul?" Then,
if one of you disputes this and says he does care, I shall not let him go at once or
leave him, but I shall question him, examine him and test him, and if I do not think
he has attained the goodness that he says he has, I shall reproach him because he   30
attaches little importance to the most important things and greater importance to
inferior things. I shall treat in this way anyone I happen to meet, young and old,
citizen and stranger, and more so the citizens because you are more kindred to me.
Be sure that this is what the god orders me to do, and I think there is no greater
blessing for the city than my service to the god. For I go around doing nothing but
persuading both young and old among you not to care for your body or your wealth   b
in preference to or as strongly as for the best possible state of your soul, as I say to
you: "Wealth does not bring about excellence, but excellence makes wealth and
everything else good for men, both individually and collectively."[4]

  Now if by saying this I corrupt the young, this advice must be harmful, but if
anyone says that I give different advice, he is talking nonsense. On this point I would
say to you, men of Athens: "Whether you believe Anytus or not, whether you acquit   c
me or not, do so on the understanding that this is my course of action, even if I am
to face death many times." Do not create a disturbance, gentlemen, but abide by my
request not to cry out at what I say but to listen, for I think it will be to your
advantage to listen, and I am about to say other things at which you will perhaps cry
out. By no means do this. Be sure that if you kill the sort of man I say I am, you will
not harm me more than yourselves. Neither Meletus nor Anytus can harm me in any   d
way; he could not harm me, for I do not think it is permitted that a better man be
harmed by a worse; certainly he might kill me, or perhaps banish or disfranchise me,
which he and maybe others think to be great harm, but I do not think so. I think he
is doing himself much greater harm doing what he is doing now, attempting to have
a man executed unjustly. Indeed, men of Athens, I am far from making a defense now
on my own behalf, as might be thought, but on yours, to prevent you from   e
wrongdoing by mistreating the god's gift to you by condemning me; for if you kill
me you will not easily find another like me. I was attached to this city by the god—
though it seems a ridiculous thing to say—as upon a great and noble horse which was
somewhat sluggish because of its size and needed to be stirred up by a kind of gadfly.
It is to fulfill some such function that I believe the god has placed me in the city. I
never cease to rouse each and every one of you, to persuade and reproach you all day   31
long and everywhere I find myself in your company.

---

4 Alternatively, this sentence could be translated: "Wealth does not bring about excellence, but
  excellence brings about wealth and all other public and private blessings for men."

Another such man will not easily come to be among you, gentlemen, and if you believe me you will spare me. You might easily be annoyed with me as people are when they are aroused from a doze, and strike out at me; if convinced by Anytus you could easily kill me, and then you could sleep on for the rest of your days, unless the god, in his care for you, sent you someone else. That I am the kind of person to be a

b   gift of the god to the city you might realize from the fact that it does not seem like human nature for me to have neglected all my own affairs and to have tolerated this neglect now for so many years while I was always concerned with you, approaching each one of you like a father or an elder brother to persuade you to care for virtue. Now if I profited from this by charging a fee for my advice, there would be some sense to it, but you can see for yourselves that, for all their shameless accusations, my accusers have not been able in their impudence to bring forward a witness to say

c   that I have ever received a fee or ever asked for one. I, on the other hand, have a convincing witness that I speak the truth, my poverty.

It may seem strange that while I go around and give this advice privately and interfere in private affairs, I do not venture to go to the assembly and there advise the city. You have heard me give the reason for this in many places. I have a divine or

d   spiritual sign which Meletus has ridiculed in his deposition. This began when I was a child. It is a voice, and whenever it speaks it turns me away from something I am about to do, but it never encourages me to do anything. This is what has prevented me from taking part in public affairs, and I think it was quite right to prevent me. Be sure, men of Athens, that if I had long ago attempted to take part in politics, I should

e   have died long ago, and benefited neither you nor myself. Do not be angry with me for speaking the truth; no man will survive who genuinely opposes you or any other crowd and prevents the occurrence of many unjust and illegal happenings in the city.

32   A man who really fights for justice must lead a private, not a public, life if he is to survive for even a short time.

I shall give you great proofs of this, not words but what you esteem, deeds. Listen to what happened to me, that you may know that I will not yield to any man contrary to what is right, for fear of death, even if I should die at once for not yielding. The things I shall tell you are commonplace and smack of the lawcourts, but they are true.

b   I have never held any other office in the city, but I served as a member of the Council, and our tribe Antiochis was presiding at the time when you wanted to try as a body the ten generals who had failed to pick up the survivors of the naval battle.[5] This was illegal, as you all recognized later. I was the only member of the presiding committee to oppose your doing something contrary to the laws, and I voted against it. The orators were ready to prosecute me and take me away, and your shouts were egging them on, but I thought I should run any risk on the side of law and justice rather than

c   join you, for fear of prison or death, when you were engaged in an unjust course.

---

5 This was the battle of Arginusae (south of Lesbos) in 406 B.C., the last Athenian victory of the Peloponnesian war. A violent storm prevented the Athenian generals from rescuing their survivors.

This happened when the city was still a democracy. When the oligarchy was established, the Thirty[6] summoned me to the Hall, along with four others, and ordered us to bring Leon from Salamis, that he might be executed. They gave many such orders to many people, in order to implicate as many as possible in their guilt. Then I showed again, not in words but in action, that, if it were not rather vulgar to say so, death is something I couldn't care less about, but that my whole concern is   d
not to do anything unjust or impious. That government, powerful as it was, did not frighten me into any wrongdoing. When we left the Hall, the other four went to Salamis and brought in Leon, but I went home. I might have been put to death for this, had not the government fallen shortly afterwards. There are many who will   e
witness to these events.

Do you think I would have survived all these years if I were engaged in public affairs and, acting as a good man must, came to the help of justice and considered this the most important thing? Far from it, men of Athens, nor would any other man.   33
Throughout my life, in any public activity I may have engaged in, I am the same man as I am in private life. I have never come to an agreement with anyone to act unjustly, neither with anyone else nor with any one of those who they slanderously say are my pupils. I have never been anyone's teacher. If anyone, young or old, desires to listen to me when I am talking and dealing with my own concerns, I have never begrudged this to anyone, but I do not converse when I receive a fee and not when I do not. I   b
am equally ready to question the rich and the poor if anyone is willing to answer my questions and listen to what I say. And I cannot justly be held responsible for the good or bad conduct of these people, as I never promised to teach them anything and have not done so. If anyone says that he has learned anything from me, or that he heard anything privately that the others did not hear, be assured that he is not telling the truth.

Why then do some people enjoy spending considerable time in my company? You   c
have heard why, men of Athens, I have told you the whole truth. They enjoy hearing those being questioned who think they are wise, but are not. And this is not unpleasant. To do this has, as I say, been enjoined upon me by the god, by means of oracles and dreams, and in every other way that a divine manifestation has ever ordered a man to do anything. This is true, gentlemen, and can easily be established.

If I corrupt some young men and have corrupted others, then surely some of them   d
who have grown older and realized that I gave them bad advice when they were young should now themselves come up here to accuse me and avenge themselves. If they were unwilling to do so themselves, then some of their kindred, their fathers or brothers or other relations should recall it now if their family had been harmed by me. I see many of these present here, first Crito, my contemporary and fellow   e
demesman, the father of Critobulus here; next Lysanias of Sphettus, the father of Aeschines here; also Antiphon the Cephisian, the father of Epigenes; and others whose brothers spent their time in this way; Nicostratus, the son of Theozotides,

---

6 This was the harsh oligarchy that was set up after the final defeat of Athens in 404 B.C. and ruled Athens
   for some nine months in 404–3 before the democracy was restored.

34   brother of Theodotus, and Theodotus has died so he could not influence him; Paralius here, son of Demodocus, whose brother was Theages; there is Adeimantus, son of Ariston, brother of Plato here; Acantidorus, brother of Apollodorus here.

     I could mention many others, some one of whom surely Meletus should have brought in as witness in his own speech. If he forgot to do so, then let him do it now; I will yield time if he has anything of the kind to say. You will find quite the contrary, gentlemen. These men are all ready to come to the help of the corruptor, the man who

b   has harmed their kindred, as Meletus and Anytus say. Now those who were corrupted might well have reason to help me, but the uncorrupted, their kindred who are older men, have no reason to help me except the right and proper one, that they know that Meletus is lying and that I am telling the truth.

     Very well, gentlemen. This, and maybe other similar things, is what I have to say

c   in my defense. Perhaps one of you might be angry as he recalls that when he himself stood trial on a less dangerous charge, he begged and implored the jurymen with many tears, that he brought his children and many of his friends and family into court to arouse as much pity as he could, but that I do none of these things, even though I may seem to be running the ultimate risk. Thinking of this, he might feel resentful

d   toward me and, angry about this, cast his vote in anger. If there is such a one among you—I do not deem there is, but if there is—I think it would be right to say in reply: My good sir, I too have a household and, in Homer's phrase, I am not born "from oak or rock" but from men, so that I have a family, indeed three sons, men of Athens, of whom one is an adolescent while two are children. Nevertheless, I will not beg you to acquit me by bringing them here. Why do I do none of these things? Not

e   through arrogance, gentlemen, nor through lack of respect for you. Whether I am brave in the face of death is another matter, but with regard to my reputation and yours and that of the whole city, it does not seem right to me to do these things, especially at my age and with my reputation. For it is generally believed, whether it be true or false, that in certain respects Socrates is superior to the majority of men.

35   Now if those of you who are considered superior, be it in wisdom or courage or whatever other virtue makes them so, are seen behaving like that, it would be a disgrace. Yet I have often seen them do this sort of thing when standing trial, men who are thought to be somebody, doing amazing things as if they thought it a terrible thing to die, and as if they were to be immortal if you did not execute them. I think

b   these men bring shame upon the city so that a stranger, too, would assume that those who are outstanding in virtue among the Athenians, whom they themselves select from themselves to fill offices of state and receive other honors, are in no way better than women. You should not act like that, men of Athens, those of you who have any reputation at all, and if we do, you should not allow it. You should make it very clear that you will more readily convict a man who performs these pitiful dramatics in court and so makes the city a laughingstock, than a man who keeps quiet.

c   Quite apart from the question of reputation, gentlemen, I do not think it right to supplicate the jury and to be acquitted because of this, but to teach and persuade them. It is not the purpose of a juryman's office to give justice as a favor to whoever seems good to him, but to judge according to law, and this he has sworn to do. We should not accustom you to perjure yourselves, nor should you make a habit of it. This is irreverent conduct for either of us.

Do not deem it right for me, men of Athens, that I should act towards you in a way that I do not consider to be good or just or pious, especially, by Zeus, as I am being prosecuted by Meletus here for impiety; clearly, if I convinced you by my supplication to do violence to your oath of office, I would be teaching you not to believe that there are gods, and my defense would convict me of not believing in them. This is far from being the case, gentlemen, for I do believe in them as none of my accusers do. I leave it to you and the god to judge me in the way that will be best for me and for you.

d

[*The jury now gives its verdict of guilty, and Meletus asks for the penalty of death.*]

There are many other reasons for my not being angry with you for convicting me, men of Athens, and what happened was not unexpected. I am much more surprised at the number of votes cast on each side for I did not think the decision would be by so few votes but by a great many. As it is, a switch of only thirty votes would have acquitted me. I think myself that I have been cleared on Meletus' charges, and not only this, but it is clear to all that, if Anytus and Lycon had not joined him in accusing me, he would have been fined a thousand drachmas for not receiving a fifth of the votes.

e
36

b

He assesses the penalty at death. So be it. What counter-assessment should I propose to you, men of Athens? Clearly it should be a penalty I deserve, and what do I deserve to suffer or to pay because I have deliberately not led a quiet life but have neglected what occupies most people: wealth, household affairs, the position of general or public orator or the other offices, the political clubs and factions that exist in the city? I thought myself too honest to survive if I occupied myself with those things. I did not follow that path that would have made me of no use either to you or to myself, but I went to each of you privately and conferred upon him what I say is the greatest benefit, by trying to persuade him not to care for any of his belongings before caring that he himself should be as good and as wise as possible, not to care for the city's possessions more than for the city itself, and to care for other things in the same way. What do I deserve for being such a man? Some good, men of Athens, if I must truly make an assessment according to my deserts, and something suitable. What is suitable for a poor benefactor who needs leisure to exhort you? Nothing is more suitable, gentlemen, than for such a man to be fed in the Prytaneum,[7] much more suitable for him than for any one of you who has won a victory at Olympia with

c

d

---

[7] The Prytaneum was the magistrates' hall or town hall of Athens in which public entertainments were given, particularly to Olympian victors on their return home.

a pair or a team of horses. The Olympian victor makes you think yourself happy; I
make you be happy. Besides, he does not need food, but I do. So if I must make a
just assessment of what I deserve, I assess it as this: free meals in the Prytaneum.

When I say this you may think, as when I spoke of appeals to pity and entreaties,
that I speak arrogantly, but that is not the case, men of Athens; rather it is like this: I
am convinced that I never willingly wrong anyone, but I am not convincing you of
this, for we have talked together but a short time. If it were the law with us, as it is
elsewhere, that a trial for life should not last one but many days, you would be
convinced, but now it is not easy to dispel great slanders in a short time. Since I am
convinced that I wrong no one, I am not likely to wrong myself, to say that I deserve
some evil and to make some such assessment against myself. What should I fear?
That I should suffer the penalty Meletus has assessed against me, of which I say I do
not know whether it is good or bad? Am I then to choose in preference to this
something that I know very well to be an evil and assess the penalty at that?
Imprisonment? Why should I live in prison, always subjected to the ruling
magistrates, the Eleven? A fine, and imprisonment until I pay it? That would be the
same thing for me, as I have no money. Exile? for perhaps you might accept that
assessment.

I should have to be inordinately fond of life, men of Athens, to be so
unreasonable as to suppose that other men will easily tolerate my company and
conversation when you, my fellow citizens, have been unable to endure them, but
found them a burden and resented them so that you are now seeking to get rid of
them. Far from it, gentlemen. It would be a fine life at my age to be driven out of
one city after another, for I know very well that wherever I go the young men will
listen to my talk as they do here. If I drive them away, they will themselves persuade
their elders to drive me out; if I do not drive them away, their fathers and relations
will drive me out on their behalf.

Perhaps someone might say: But Socrates, if you leave us will you not be able to
live quietly, without talking? Now this is the most difficult point on which to
convince some of you. If I say that it is impossible for me to keep quiet because that
means disobeying the god, you will not believe me and will think I am being ironical.
On the other hand, if I say that it is the greatest good for a man to discuss virtue every
day and those other things about which you hear me conversing and testing myself
and others, for the unexamined life is not worth living for men, you will believe me
even less.

What I say is true, gentlemen, but it is not easy to convince you. At the same time,
I am not accustomed to think that I deserve any penalty. If I had money, I would
assess the penalty at the amount I could pay, for that would not hurt me, but I have
none, unless you are willing to set the penalty at the amount I can pay, and perhaps
I could pay you one mina of silver.[8] So that is my assessment.

---

[8] One mina was the equivalent of 100 drachmas. In the late fifth century one drachma was the standard
daily wage of a laborer. A mina, then, was a considerable sum.

Plato here, men of Athens, and Crito and Critobulus and Apollodorus bid me put the penalty at thirty minas, and they will stand surety for the money. Well then, that is my assessment, and they will be sufficient guarantee of payment.

[The jury now votes again and sentences Socrates to death.]

It is for the sake of a short time, men of Athens, that you will acquire the   c
reputation and the guilt, in the eyes of those who want to denigrate the city, of having killed Socrates, a wise man, for they who want to revile you will say that I am wise even if I am not. If you had waited but a little while, this would have happened of its own accord. You see my age, that I am already advanced in years and close to death.   d
I am saying this not to all of you but to those who condemned me to death, and to these same ones I say: Perhaps you think that I was convicted for lack of such words as might have convinced you, if I thought I should say or do all I could to avoid my sentence. Far from it. I was convicted because I lacked not words but boldness and shamelessness and the willingness to say to you what you would most gladly have heard from me, lamentations and tears and my saying and doing many things that I   e
say are unworthy of me but that you are accustomed to hear from others. I did not think then that the danger I ran should make me do anything mean, nor do I now regret the nature of my defense. I would much rather die after this kind of defense than live after making the other kind. Neither I nor any other man should, on trial or   39
in war, contrive to avoid death at any cost. Indeed it is often obvious in battle that one could escape death by throwing away one's weapons and by turning to supplicate one's pursuers, and there are many ways to avoid death in every kind of danger if one will venture to do or say anything to avoid it. It is not difficult to avoid   b
death, gentlemen; it is much more difficult to avoid wickedness, for it runs faster than death. Slow and elderly as I am, I have been caught by the slower pursuer, whereas my accusers, being clever and sharp, have been caught by the quicker, wickedness. I leave you now, condemned to death by you, but they are condemned by truth to wickedness and injustice. So I maintain my assessment, and they maintain theirs. This perhaps had to happen, and I think it is as it should be.

Now I want to prophesy to those who convicted me, for I am at the point when   c
men prophesy most, when they are about to die. I say gentlemen, to those who voted to kill me, that vengeance will come upon you immediately after my death, a vengeance much harder to bear than that which you took in killing me. You did this in the belief that you would avoid giving an account of your life, but I maintain that quite the opposite will happen to you. There will be more people to test you, whom   d
I now held back, but you did not notice it. They will be more difficult to deal with as they will be younger and you will resent them more. You are wrong if you believe that by killing people you will prevent anyone from reproaching you for not living in the right way. To escape such tests is neither possible nor good, but it is best and easiest not to discredit others but to prepare oneself to be as good as possible. With this prophecy to you who convicted me, I part from you.

I should be glad to discuss what has happened with those who voted for my   e
acquittal during the time that the officers of the court are busy and I do not yet have

to depart to my death. So, gentlemen, stay with me awhile, for nothing prevents us
from talking to each other while it is allowed. To you, as being my friends, I want to
40   show the meaning of what has occurred. A surprising thing has happened to me,
jurymen—you. I would rightly call jurymen. At all previous times my familiar
prophetic power, my spiritual manifestation, frequently opposed me, even in small
matters, when I was about to do something wrong, but now that, as you can see for
yourselves, I was faced with what one might think, and what is generally thought to
be, the worst of evils, my divine sign has not opposed me, either when I left home at
b   dawn, or when I came into court, or at any time that I was about to say something
during my speech. Yet in other talks it often held me back in the middle of my
speaking, but now it has opposed no word or deed of mine. What do I think is the
reason for this? I will tell you. What has happened to me may well be a good thing,
and those of us who believe death to be an evil are certainly mistaken. I have
c   convincing proof of this, for it is impossible that my familiar sign did not oppose me
if I was not about to do what was right.

Let us reflect in this way, too, that there is good hope that death is a blessing, for
it is one of two things: either the dead are nothing and have no perception of
anything, or it is, as we are told, a change and a relocating for the soul from here to
d   another place. If it is complete lack of perception, like a dreamless sleep, then death
would be a great advantage. For I think that if one had to pick out that night during
which a man slept soundly and did not dream, put beside it the other nights and days
of his life, and then see how many days and nights had been better and more pleasant
than that night, not only a private person but the great king would find them easy to
e   count compared with the other days and nights. If death is like this I say it is an
advantage, for all eternity would then seem to be no more than a single night. If, on
the other hand, death is a change from here to another place, and what we are told is
true and all who have died are there, what greater blessing could there be, gentlemen
41   of the jury? If anyone arriving in Hades will have escaped from those who call
themselves jurymen here, and will find those true jurymen who are said to sit in
judgment there, Minos and Rhadamanthus and Aeacus and Triptolemus and the other
demi-gods who have been upright in their own life, would that be a poor kind of
change? Again, what would one of you give to keep company with Orpheus and
Musaeus, Hesiod and Homer? I am willing to die many times if that is true. It would
be a wonderful way for me to spend my time whenever I met Palamedes and Ajax,
b   the son of Telamon, and any other of the men of old who died through an unjust
conviction, to compare my experience with theirs. I think it would be pleasant. Most
important, I could spend my time testing and examining people there, as I do here,
as to who among them is wise, and who thinks he is, but is not.
c   What would one not give, gentlemen of the jury, for the opportunity to examine
the man who led the great expedition against Troy, or Odysseus, or Sisyphus, and
innumerable other men and women one could mention. It would be an extraordinary
happiness to talk with them, to keep company with them and examine them. In any
case, they would certainly not put one to death for doing so. They are happier there
than we are here in other respects, and for the rest of time they are deathless, if
indeed what we are told is true.

You too must be of good hope as regards death, gentlemen of the jury, and keep   d
this one truth in mind, that a good man cannot be harmed either in life or in death,
and that his affairs are not neglected by the gods. What has happened to me now has
not happened of itself, but it is clear to me that it was better for me to die now and
to escape from trouble. That is why my divine sign did not oppose me at any point.
So I am certainly not angry with those who convicted me, or with my accusers. Of
course that was not their purpose when they accused and convicted me, but they
thought they were hurting me, and for this they deserve blame. This much I ask from   e
them: when my sons grow up, avenge yourselves by causing them the same kind of
grief that I caused you, if you think they care for money or anything else more than
they care for virtue, or if they think they are somebody when they are nobody.
Reproach them as I reproach you, that they do not care for the right things and think
they are worthy when they are not worthy of anything. If you do this, I shall have   42
been justly treated by you, and my sons also.

Now the hour to part has come. I go to die, you go to live. Which of us goes to
the better lot is known to no one, except the god.

2

PHAEDO

Phaedo, *known to the ancients also by the descriptive title* On the Soul, *is a drama about Socrates' last hours and his death in the jail at Athens. On the way back home to Elis, one of his intimates, Phaedo, who was with him then, stops off at Phlius, in the Peloponnese. There he reports it all to a group of Pythagoreans settled there since their expulsion from Southern Italy. The Pythagorean connection is carried further in the dialogue itself, since Socrates' two fellow discussants, Simmias and Cebes—from Thebes, the other city where expelled members of the brotherhood settled—are associates of Philolaus, the leading Pythagorean there. Pythagoreans were noted for their belief in the immortality of the soul and its reincarnation in human or animal form and for the consequent concern to keep one's soul pure by avoiding contamination with the body, so as to win the best possible next life. Socrates weaves all these themes into his own discussion of the immortality of the soul.*

It is noteworthy that these Pythagorean elements are lacking from the Apology, *where Socrates expresses himself noncommittally and unconcernedly about the possibility of immortality—and from* Crito, *as well as the varied discussions of the soul's virtues in such dialogues as* Euthyphro, Laches, *and* Protagoras. *Those dialogues are of course not records of discussions the historical Socrates actually held, but Plato seems to take particular pains to indicate that* Phaedo *does not give us Socrates' actual last conversation or even one that fits at all closely his actual views. He takes care to tell us that he was not present on the last day:* Phaedo *says he was ill. Socrates makes much of the human intellect's affinity to eternal Forms of Beauty, Justice, and other normative notions, and of mathematical properties and objects, such as Oddness and Evenness and the integers Two, Three, and the rest, as well as physical forces such as Hot and Cold, all existing in a nonphysical realm accessible only to abstract thought. None of this comports well with Socrates' description of his philosophical interests in the* Apology *or with the way he conducts his inquiries in Plato's 'Socratic' dialogues. It is generally agreed that both the Pythagorean motifs of immortality and purification and the theory of eternal Forms that is linked with them in this dialogue are Plato's own contribution. Indeed, the* Phaedo's *affinities in philosophical theory go not toward the Socratic dialogues, but to* Symposium *and* Republic. *There is an unmistakable reference to* Meno's *theory of theoretical knowledge (of geometry, and also of the nature of human virtue) as coming by recollection of objects known before birth. But now the claim is made that this recollection is of Forms.*

Phaedo *concludes with a myth, describing the fate of the soul after death. Concluding myths in other dialogues, with which this one should be compared, are those in* Gorgias *and* Republic. *It should also be compared with the myth in Socrates' second speech in the* Phaedrus.

Despite the Platonic innovations in philosophical theory, the Phaedo *presents a famously moving picture of Socrates' deep commitment to philosophy and the philosophical life even, or especially, in the face of an unjustly imposed death.*

J.M.C.

57   ECHECRATES: Were you with Socrates yourself, Phaedo, on the day when he drank the poison in prison, or did someone else tell you about it?

PHAEDO: I was there myself, Echecrates.

ECHECRATES: What are the things he said before he died? And how did he die?

b   I should be glad to hear this. Hardly anyone from Phlius visits Athens nowadays, nor has any stranger come from Athens for some time who could give us a clear account of what happened, except that he drank the poison and died, but nothing more.

58   PHAEDO: Did you not even hear how the trial went?

ECHECRATES: Yes, someone did tell us about that, and we wondered that he seems to have died a long time after the trial took place. Why was that, Phaedo?

PHAEDO: That was by chance, Echecrates. The day before the trial, as it happened, the prow of the ship that the Athenians send to Delos had been crowned with garlands.

ECHECRATES: What ship is that?

PHAEDO: It is the ship in which, the Athenians say, Theseus once sailed to Crete,

b   taking with him the two lots of seven victims.[1] He saved them and was himself saved. They vowed then to Apollo, so the story goes, that if they were saved they would send a mission to Delos every year. And from that time to this they send such an annual mission to the god. They have a law to keep the city pure while it lasts, and no execution may take place once the mission has begun until the ship has made its journey to Delos and returned to Athens, and this can sometimes take a long time

c   if the winds delay it. The mission begins when the priest of Apollo crowns the prow of the ship, and this happened, as I say, the day before Socrates' trial. That is why Socrates was in prison a long time between this trial and his execution.

ECHECRATES: What about his actual death, Phaedo? What did he say? What did he do? Who of his friends were with him? Or did the authorities not allow them to be present and he died with no friends present?

d   PHAEDO: By no means. Some were present, in fact, a good many.

ECHECRATES: Please be good enough to tell us all that occurred as fully as possible, unless you have some pressing business.

PHAEDO: I have the time and I will try to tell you the whole story, for nothing gives me more pleasure than to call Socrates to mind, whether talking about him myself, or listening to someone else do so.

ECHECRATES: Your hearers will surely be like you in this, Phaedo. So do try to tell us every detail as exactly as you can.

Translated by G.M.A. Grube.

[1] Legend says that Minos, king of Crete, compelled the Athenians to send seven youths and seven maidens every year to be sacrificed to the Minotaur until Theseus saved them and killed the monster.

PHAEDO: I certainly found being there an astonishing experience. Although I was witnessing the death of one who was my friend, I had no feeling of pity, for the man appeared happy both in manner and words as he died nobly and without fear, Echecrates, so that it struck me that even in going down to the underworld he was going with the gods' blessing and that he would fare well when he got there, if anyone ever does. That is why I had no feeling of pity, such as would seem natural in my sorrow, nor indeed of pleasure, as we engaged in philosophical discussion as we were accustomed to do—for our arguments were of that sort—but I had a strange feeling, an unaccustomed mixture of pleasure and pain at the same time as I reflected that he was just about to die. All of us present were affected in much the same way, sometimes laughing, then weeping; especially one of us, Apollodorus—you know the man and his ways.

ECHECRATES: Of course I do.

PHAEDO: He was quite overcome; but I was myself disturbed, and so were the others.

ECHECRATES: Who, Phaedo, were those present?

PHAEDO: Among the local people there was Apollodorus, whom I mentioned, Critobulus and his father,[2] also Hermogenes, Epigenes, Aeschines and Antisthenes. Ctesippus of Paeania was there, Menexenus and some others. Plato, I believe, was ill.

ECHECRATES: Were there some foreigners present?

PHAEDO: Yes, Simmias from Thebes with Cebes and Phaedondes, and from Megara, Euclides and Terpsion.

ECHECRATES: What about Aristippus and Cleombrotus? Were they there?

PHAEDO: No. They were said to be in Aegina.

ECHECRATES: Was there anyone else?

PHAEDO: I think these were about all.

ECHECRATES: Well then, what do you say the conversation was about?

PHAEDO: I will try to tell you everything from the beginning. On the previous days also both the others and I used to visit Socrates. We foregathered at daybreak at the court where the trial took place, for it was close to the prison, and each day we used to wait around talking until the prison should open, for it did not open early. When it opened we used to go in to Socrates and spend most of the day with him. On this day we gathered rather early, because when we left the prison on the previous evening we were informed that the ship from Delos had arrived, and so we told each other to come to the usual place as early as possible. When we arrived the gatekeeper who used to answer our knock came out and told us to wait and not go in until he

---

[2] The father of Critobulus is Crito, after whom the dialogue *Crito* is named. Several of the other friends of Socrates mentioned here also appear in other dialogues. Hermogenes is one of the speakers in *Cratylus*. Epigenes is mentioned in *Apology* 33d, as is Aeschines, who was a writer of Socratic dialogues. Menexenus has a part in *Lysis* and has a dialogue named after him; Ctesippus appears in both *Lysis* and *Euthydemus*. Euclides and Terpsion are speakers in the introductory conversation of *Theaetetus*, and Euclides too wrote Socratic dialogues. Simmias and Cebes are mentioned in *Crito*, 45b, as having come to Athens with enough money to secure Socrates' escape.

told us to. "The Eleven,"[3] he said, "are freeing Socrates from his bonds and telling
60   him how his death will take place today." After a short time he came and told us to
go in. We found Socrates recently released from his chains, and Xanthippe—you
know her—sitting by him, holding their baby. When she saw us, she cried out and
said the sort of thing that women usually say: "Socrates, this is the last time your
friends will talk to you and you to them." Socrates looked at Crito. "Crito," he said,
b   "let someone take her home." And some of Crito's people led her away lamenting
and beating her breast.

Socrates sat up on the bed, bent his leg and rubbed it with his hand, and as he
rubbed he said: "What a strange thing that which men call pleasure seems to be, and
how astonishing the relation it has with what is thought to be its opposite, namely
pain! A man cannot have both at the same time. Yet if he pursues and catches the one,
he is almost always bound to catch the other also, like two creatures with one head.
c   I think that if Aesop had noted this he would have composed a fable that a god
wished to reconcile their opposition but could not do so, so he joined their two heads
together, and therefore when a man has the one, the other follows later. This seems
to be happening to me. My bonds caused pain in my leg, and now pleasure seems to
be following."

Cebes intervened and said: "By Zeus, yes, Socrates, you did well to remind me.
d   Evenus[4] asked me the day before yesterday, as others had done before, what induced
you to write poetry after you came to prison, you who had never composed any
poetry before, putting the fables of Aesop into verse and composing the hymn to
Apollo. If it is of any concern to you that I should have an answer to give to Evenus
when he repeats his question, as I know he will, tell me what to say to him."

Tell him the truth, Cebes, he said, that I did not do this with the idea of rivaling
him or his poems, for I knew that would not be easy, but I tried to find out the
e   meaning of certain dreams and to satisfy my conscience in case it was this kind of
art they were frequently bidding me to practice. The dreams were something like
this: the same dream often came to me in the past, now in one shape now in another,
but saying the same thing: "Socrates," it said, "practice and cultivate the arts." In the
past I imagined that it was instructing and advising me to do what I was doing, such
61   as those who encourage runners in a race, that the dream was thus bidding me do the
very thing I was doing, namely, to practice the art of philosophy, this being the
highest kind of art, and I was doing that.

But now, after my trial took place, and the festival of the god was preventing my
execution, I thought that, in case my dream was bidding me to practice this popular
art, I should not disobey it but compose poetry. I thought it safer not to leave here
b   until I had satisfied my conscience by writing poems in obedience to the dream. So
I first wrote in honor of the god of the present festival. After that I realized that a
poet, if he is to be a poet, must compose fables, not arguments. Being no teller of
fables myself, I took the stories I knew and had at hand, the fables of Aesop, and I

---

3 The Eleven were the police commissioners of Athens.
4 Socrates refers to Evenus as a Sophist and teacher of the young in *Apology* 20a, c.

versified the first ones I came across. Tell this to Evenus, Cebes, wish him well and
bid him farewell, and tell him, if he is wise, to follow me as soon as possible. I am
leaving today, it seems, as the Athenians so order it.   c

Said Simmias: "What kind of advice is this you are giving to Evenus, Socrates? I
have met him many times, and from my observation he is not at all likely to follow
it willingly."

How so, said he, is Evenus not a philosopher?

I think so, Simmias said.

Then Evenus will be willing, like every man who partakes worthily of philosophy.
Yet perhaps he will not take his own life, for that, they say, is not right. As he said
this, Socrates put his feet on the ground and remained in this position during the rest   d
of the conversation.

Then Cebes asked: "How do you mean Socrates, that it is not right to do oneself
violence, and yet that the philosopher will be willing to follow one who is dying?"

Come now, Cebes, have you and Simmias, who keep company with Philolaus,[5]
not heard about such things?

Nothing definite, Socrates.

Indeed, I too speak about this from hearsay, but I do not mind telling you what I
have heard, for it is perhaps most appropriate for one who is about to depart yonder
to tell and examine tales about what we believe that journey to be like. What else   e
could one do in the time we have until sunset?

But whatever is the reason, Socrates, for people to say that it is not right to kill
oneself? As to your question just now, I have heard Philolaus say this when staying
in Thebes and I have also heard it from others, but I have never heard anyone give a
clear account of the matter.

Well, he said, we must do our best, and you may yet hear one. And it may well   62
astonish you if this subject, alone of all things, is simple, and it is never, as with
everything else, better at certain times and for certain people to die than to live. And
if this is so, you may well find it astonishing that those for whom it is better to die are
wrong to help themselves, and that they must wait for someone else to benefit them.

And Cebes, lapsing into his own dialect, laughed quietly and said: "Zeus knows
it is."

Indeed, said Socrates, it does seem unreasonable when put like that, but perhaps   b
there is reason to it. There is the explanation that is put in the language of the
mysteries, that we men are in a kind of prison, and that one must not free oneself or
run away. That seems to me an impressive doctrine and one not easy to understand
fully. However, Cebes, this seems to me well expressed, that the gods are our
guardians and that men are one of their possessions. Or do you not think so?

I do, said Cebes.

And would you not be angry if one of your possessions killed itself when you had   c
not given any sign that you wished it to die, and if you had any punishment you could
inflict, you would inflict it?

Certainly, he said.

---

[5] See Introductory Note.

Perhaps then, put in this way, it is not unreasonable that one should not kill oneself before a god had indicated some necessity to do so, like the necessity now put upon us.

d   That seems likely, said Cebes. As for what you were saying, that philosophers should be willing and ready to die, that seems strange, Socrates, if what we said just now is reasonable, namely, that a god is our protector and that we are his possessions. It is not logical that the wisest of men should not resent leaving this service in which they are governed by the best of masters, the gods, for a wise man cannot believe that he will look after himself better when he is free. A foolish man might easily think so, e   that he must escape from his master; he would not reflect that one must not escape from a good master but stay with him as long as possible, because it would be foolish to escape. But the sensible man would want always to remain with one better than himself. So, Socrates, the opposite of what was said before is likely to be true; the wise would resent dying, whereas the foolish would rejoice at it.

I thought that when Socrates heard this he was pleased by Cebes' argumentation. 63   Glancing at us, he said: "Cebes is always on the track of some arguments; he is certainly not willing to be at once convinced by what one says."

Said Simmias: "But actually, Socrates, I think myself that Cebes has a point now. Why should truly wise men want to avoid the service of masters better than themselves, and leave them easily? And I think Cebes is aiming his argument at you, because you are bearing leaving us so lightly, and leaving those good masters, as you say yourself, the gods."

b   You are both justified in what you say, and I think you mean that I must make a defense against this, as if I were in court.

You certainly must, said Simmias.

Come then, he said, let me try to make my defense to you more convincing than it was to the jury. For, Simmias and Cebes, I should be wrong not to resent dying if I did not believe that I should go first to other wise and good gods, and then to men who have died and are better than men are here. Be assured that, as it is, I expect to c   join the company of good men. This last I would not altogether insist on, but if I insist on anything at all in these matters, it is that I shall come to gods who are very good masters. That is why I am not so resentful, because I have good hope that some future awaits men after death, as we have been told for years, a much better future for the good than for the wicked.

Well now, Socrates, said Simmias, do you intend to keep this belief to yourself as d   you leave us, or would you share it with us? I certainly think it would be a blessing for us too, and at the same time it would be your defense if you convince us of what you say.

I will try, he said, but first let us see what it is that Crito here has, I think, been wanting to say for quite a while.

What else, Socrates, said Crito, but what the man who is to give you the poison has been telling me for some time, that I should warn you to talk as little as possible. People get heated when they talk, he says, and one should not be heated when taking e   the poison, as those who do must sometimes drink it two or three times.

Socrates replied: "Take no notice of him; only let him be prepared to administer it twice or, if necessary, three times."

I was rather sure you would say that, Crito said, but he has been bothering me for some time.

Let him be, he said. I want to make my argument before you, my judges, as to why I think that a man who has truly spent his life in philosophy is probably right to be of good cheer in the face of death and to be very hopeful that after death he will attain the greatest blessings yonder. I will try to tell you, Simmias and Cebes, how   64 this may be so. I am afraid that other people do not realize that the one aim of those who practice philosophy in the proper manner is to practice for dying and death. Now if this is true, if would be strange indeed if they were eager for this all their lives and then resent it when what they have wanted and practiced for a long time comes upon them.

Simmias laughed and said: "By Zeus, Socrates, you made me laugh, though I was in no laughing mood just now. I think that the majority, on hearing this, will think   b that it describes the philosophers very well, and our people in Thebes would thoroughly agree that philosophers are nearly dead and that the majority of men is well aware that they deserve to be.

And they would be telling the truth, Simmias, except for their being aware. They are not aware of the way true philosophers are nearly dead, nor of the way they   c deserve to be, nor of the sort of death they deserve. But never mind them, he said, let us talk among ourselves. Do we believe that there is such a thing as death?

Certainly, said Simmias.

Is it anything else than the separation of the soul from the body? Do we believe that death is this, namely, that the body comes to be separated by itself apart from the soul, and the soul comes to be separated by itself apart from the body? Is death anything else than that?

No, that is what it is, he said.

Consider then, my good sir, whether you share my opinion, for this will lead us to   d a better knowledge of what we are investigating. Do you think it is the part of a philosopher to be concerned with such so-called pleasures as those of food and drink?

By no means.

What about the pleasures of sex?

Not at all.

What of the other pleasures concerned with the service of the body? Do you think such a man prizes them greatly, the acquisition of distinguished clothes and shoes and the other bodily ornaments? Do you think he values these or despises them,   e except in so far as one cannot do without them?

I think the true philosopher despises them.

Do you not think, he said, that in general such a man's concern is not with the body but that, as far as he can, he turns away from the body towards the soul?

I do.

So in the first place, such things show clearly that the philosopher more than other   65 men frees the soul from association with the body as much as possible?

Apparently.

A man who finds no pleasure in such things and has no part in them is thought by the majority not to deserve to live and to be close to death; the man, that is, who does not care for the pleasures of the body.

What you say is certainly true.

Then what about the actual acquiring of knowledge? Is the body an obstacle when b   one associates with it in the search for knowledge? I mean, for example, do men find any truth in sight or hearing, or are not even the poets forever telling us that we do not see or hear anything accurately, and surely if those two physical senses are not clear or precise, our other senses can hardly be accurate, as they are all inferior to these. Do you not think so?

I certainly do, he said.

When then, he asked, does the soul grasp the truth? For whenever it attempts to examine anything with the body, it is clearly deceived by it.

c   True.

Is it not in reasoning if anywhere that any reality becomes clear to the soul?

Yes.

And indeed the soul reasons best when none of these senses troubles it, neither hearing nor sight, nor pain nor pleasure, but when it is most by itself, taking leave of the body and as far as possible having no contact or association with it in its search for reality.

That is so.

d   And it is then that the soul of the philosopher most disdains the body, flees from it and seeks to be by itself?

It appears so.

What about the following, Simmias? Do we say that there is such a thing as the Just itself, or not?

We do say so, by Zeus.

And the Beautiful, and the Good?

Of course.

And have you ever seen any of these things with your eyes?

In no way, he said.

Or have you ever grasped them with any of your bodily senses? I am speaking of all things such as Bigness, Health, Strength and, in a word the reality of all other things, that which each of them essentially is. Is what is most true in them e   contemplated through the body, or is this the position: whoever of us prepares himself best and most accurately to grasp that thing itself which he is investigating will come closest to the knowledge of it?

Obviously.

Then he will do this most perfectly who approaches the object with thought alone, 66 without associating any sight with his thought, or dragging in any sense perception with his reasoning, but who, using pure thought alone, tries to track down each reality pure and by itself, freeing himself as far as possible from eyes and ears, and in a word, from the whole body, because the body confuses the soul and does not allow it to acquire truth and wisdom whenever it is associated with it. Will not that man reach reality, Simmias, if anyone does?

What you say, said Simmias, is indeed true.

All these things will necessarily make the true philosophers believe and say to   b
each other something like this: "There is likely to be something such as a path to guide us out of our confusion, because as long as we have a body and our soul is fused with such an evil we shall never adequately attain what we desire, which we affirm to be the truth. The body keeps us busy in a thousand ways because of its need for nurture. Moreover, if certain diseases befall it, they impede our search for the truth. It fills us with wants, desires, fears, all sorts of illusions and much nonsense,   c
so that, as it is said, in truth and in fact no thought of any kind ever comes to us from the body. Only the body and its desires cause war, civil discord and battles, for all wars are due to the desire to acquire wealth, and it is the body and the care of it, to which we are enslaved, which compel us to acquire wealth, and all this makes us too   d
busy to practice philosophy. Worst of all, if we do get some respite from it and turn to some investigation, everywhere in our investigations the body is present and makes for confusion and fear, so that it prevents us from seeing the truth.

"It really has been shown to us that, if we are ever to have pure knowledge, we   e
must escape from the body and observe things in themselves with the soul by itself. It seems likely that we shall, only then, when we are dead, attain that which we desire and of which we claim to be lovers, namely, wisdom, as our argument shows, not while we live; for if it is impossible to attain any pure knowledge with the body, then one of two things is true: either we can never attain knowledge or we can do so after death. Then and not before, the soul is by itself apart from the body. While we live,   67
we shall be closest to knowledge if we refrain as much as possible from association with the body and do not join with it more than we must, if we are not infected with its nature but purify ourselves from it until the god himself frees us. In this way we shall escape the contamination of the body's folly; we shall be likely to be in the company of people of the same kind, and by our own efforts we shall know all that is pure, which is presumably the truth, for it is not permitted to the impure to attain   b
the pure."

Such are the things, Simmias, that all those who love learning in the proper manner must say to one another and believe. Or do you not think so?

I certainly do, Socrates.

And if this is true, my friend, said Socrates, there is good hope that on arriving where I am going, if anywhere, I shall acquire what has been our chief preoccupation   c
in our past life, so that the journey that is now ordered for me is full of good hope, as it is also for any other man who believes that his mind has been prepared and, as it were, purified.

It certainly is, said Simmias.

And does purification not turn out to be what we mentioned in our argument some time ago, namely, to separate the soul as far as possible from the body and

d   accustom it to gather itself and collect itself out of every part of the body and to
      dwell by itself as far as it can both now and in the future, freed, as it were, from the
      bonds of the body?

      Certainly, he said.

      And that freedom and separation of the soul from the body is called death?

      That is altogether so.

      It is only those who practice philosophy in the right way, we say, who always
      most want to free the soul; and this release and separation of the soul from the body
      is the preoccupation of the philosophers?

      So it appears.

      Therefore, as I said at the beginning, it would be ridiculous for a man to train
e   himself in life to live in a state as close to death as possible, and then to resent it
      when it comes?

      Ridiculous, of course.

      In fact, Simmias, he said, those who practice philosophy in the right way are in
      training for dying and they fear death least of all men. Consider it from this point of
      view: if they are altogether estranged from the body and desire to have their soul by
      itself, would it not be quite absurd for them to be afraid and resentful when this
      happens? If they did not gladly set out for a place, where, on arrival, they may hope
      to attain that for which they had yearned during their lifetime, that is, wisdom, and
68   where they would be rid of the presence of that from which they are estranged?

      Many men, at the death of their lovers, wives or sons, were willing to go to the
      underworld, driven by the hope of seeing there those for whose company they
      longed, and being with them. Will then a true lover of wisdom, who has a similar
      hope and knows that he will never find it to any extent except in Hades, be resentful
      of dying and not gladly undertake the journey thither? One must surely think so, my
      friend, if he is a true philosopher, for he is firmly convinced that he will not find pure
b   knowledge anywhere except there. And if this is so, then, as I said just now, would
      it not be highly unreasonable for such a man to fear death?

      It certainly would, by Zeus, he said.

      Then you have sufficient indication, he said, that any man whom you see
c   resenting death was not a lover of wisdom but a lover of the body, and also a lover
      of wealth or of honors, either or both.

      It is certainly as you say.

      And, Simmias, he said, does not what is called courage belong especially to men
      of this disposition?

      Most certainly.

      And the quality of moderation which even the majority call by that name, that is,
      not to get swept off one's feet by one's passions, but to treat them with disdain and
d   orderliness, is this not suited only to those who most of all despise the body and live
      the life of philosophy?

      Necessarily so, he said.

      If you are willing to reflect on the courage and moderation of other people, you
      will find them strange.

In what way, Socrates?

You know that they all consider death a great evil?

Definitely, he said.

And the brave among them face death, when they do, for fear of greater evils?

That is so.

Therefore, it is fear and terror that make all men brave, except the philosophers. Yet it is illogical to be brave through fear and cowardice.

It certainly is.   e

What of the moderate among them? Is their experience not similar? Is it license of a kind that makes them moderate? We say this is impossible, yet their experience of this unsophisticated moderation turns out to be similar: they fear to be deprived of other pleasures which they desire, so they keep away from some pleasures because they are overcome by others. Now to be mastered by pleasure is what they call license, but what happens to them is that they master certain pleasures   69 because they are mastered by others. This is like what we mentioned just now, that in some way it is a kind of license that has made them moderate.

That seems likely.

My good Simmias, I fear this is not the right exchange to attain virtue, to exchange pleasures for pleasures, pains for pains and fears for fears, the greater for   b the less like coins, but that the only valid currency for which all these things should be exchanged is wisdom. With this we have real courage and moderation and justice and, in a word, true virtue, with wisdom, whether pleasures and fears and all such things be present or absent. Exchanged for one another without wisdom such virtue is only an illusory appearance of virtue; it is in fact fit for slaves, without soundness or truth, whereas, in truth, moderation and courage and justice are a purging away of   c all such things, and wisdom itself is a kind of cleansing or purification. It is likely that those who established the mystic rites for us were not inferior persons but were speaking in riddles long ago when they said that whoever arrives in the underworld uninitiated and unsanctified will wallow in the mire, whereas he who arrives there purified and initiated will dwell with the gods. There are indeed, as those concerned with the mysteries say, many who carry the thyrsus but the Bacchants are few.[6]   d These latter are, in my opinion, no other than those who have practiced philosophy in the right way. I have in my life left nothing undone in order to be counted among these as far as possible, as I have been eager to be in every way. Whether my eagerness was right and we accomplished anything we shall, I think, know for certain in a short time, god willing, on arriving yonder.

This is my defense, Simmias and Cebes, that I am likely to be right to leave you   e and my masters here without resentment or complaint, believing that there, as here, I shall find good masters and good friends. If my defense is more convincing to you than to the Athenian jury, it will be well.

---

[6] That is, the true worshippers of Dionysus, as opposed to those who only carry the external symbols of his worship.

70   When Socrates finished, Cebes intervened: Socrates, he said, everything else you said is excellent, I think, but men find it very hard to believe what you said about the soul. They think that after it has left the body it no longer exists anywhere, but that it is destroyed and dissolved on the day the man dies, as soon as it leaves the body; and that, on leaving it, it is dispersed like breath or smoke, has flown away and gone and is no longer anything anywhere. If indeed it gathered itself together and existed

b   by itself and escaped those evils you were recently enumerating, there would then be much good hope, Socrates, that what you say is true; but to believe this requires a good deal of faith and persuasive argument, to believe that the soul still exists after a man has died and that it still possesses some capability and intelligence."

        What you say is true, Cebes, Socrates said, but what shall we do? Do you want to discuss whether this is likely to be true or not?

        Personally, said Cebes, I should like to hear your opinion on the subject.

        I do not think, said Socrates, that anyone who heard me now, not even a comic

c   poet, could say that I am babbling and discussing things that do not concern me, so we must examine the question thoroughly, if you think we should do so. Let us examine it in some such a manner as this: whether the souls of men who have died exist in the underworld or not. We recall an ancient theory that souls arriving there come from here, and then again that they arrive here and are born here from the dead. If that is true, that the living come back from the dead, then surely our souls must

d   exist there, for they could not come back if they did not exist, and this is a sufficient proof that these things are so if it truly appears that the living never come from any other source than from the dead. If this is not the case we should need another argument.

        Quite so, said Cebes.

        Do not, he said, confine yourself to humanity if you want to understand this more readily, but take all animals and all plants into account, and, in short, for all things

e   which come to be, let us see whether they come to be in this way, that is, from their opposites if they have such, as the beautiful is the opposite of the ugly and the just of the unjust, and a thousand other things of the kind. Let us examine whether those that have an opposite must necessarily come to be from their opposite and from nowhere else, as for example when something comes to be larger it must necessarily become larger from having been smaller before.

        Yes.

        Then if something smaller comes to be, it will come from something larger

71   before, which became smaller?

        That is so, he said.

        And the weaker comes to be from the stronger, and the swifter from the slower?

        Certainly.

        Further, if something worse comes to be, does it not come from the better, and the juster from the more unjust?

        Of course.

        So we have sufficiently established that all things come to be in this way, opposites from opposites?

        Certainly.

There is a further point, something such as this, about these opposites: between each of those pairs of opposites there are two processes: from the one to the other and then again from the other to the first; between the larger and the smaller there is increase and decrease, and we call the one increasing and the other decreasing?   b

Yes, he said.

And so too there is separation and combination, cooling and heating, and all such things, even if sometimes we do not have a name for the process, but in fact it must be everywhere that they come to be from one another, and that there is a process of becoming from each into the other?

Assuredly, he said.

Well then, is there an opposite to living, as sleeping is the opposite of   c
being awake?

Quite so, he said.

What is it?

Being dead, he said.

Therefore, if these are opposites, they come to be from one another, and there are two processes of generation between the two?

Of course.

I will tell you, said Socrates, one of the two pairs I was just talking about, the pair itself and the two processes, and you will tell me the other. I mean, to sleep and to   d
be awake; to be awake comes from sleeping, and to sleep comes from being awake. Of the two processes one is going to sleep, the other is waking up. Do you accept that, or not?

Certainly.

You tell me in the same way about life and death. Do you not say that to be dead is the opposite of being alive?

I do.

And they come to be from one another?

Yes.

What comes to be from being alive?

Being dead.

And what comes to be from being dead?

One must agree that it is being alive.

Then, Cebes, living creatures and things come to be from the dead?

So it appears, he said.   e

Then our souls exist in the underworld.

That seems likely.

Then in this case one of the two processes of becoming is clear, for dying is clear enough, is it not?

It certainly is.

What shall we do then? Shall we not supply the opposite process of becoming? Is nature to be lame in this case? Or must we provide a process of becoming opposite to dying?

We surely must.

And what is that?

Coming to life again.

72   Therefore, he said, if there is such a thing as coming to life again, it would be a process of coming from the dead to the living?

Quite so.

It is agreed between us then that the living come from the dead in this way no less than the dead from the living and, if that is so, it seems to be a sufficient proof that the souls of the dead must be somewhere whence they can come back again.

I think, Socrates, he said, that this follows from what we have agreed on.

Consider in this way, Cebes, he said, that, as I think, we were not wrong to agree. If the two processes of becoming did not always balance each other as if they were going round in a circle, but generation proceeded from one point to its opposite in a straight line and it did not turn back again to the other opposite or take any turning, do you realize that all things would ultimately be in the same state, be affected in the same way, and cease to become?

How do you mean? he said.

It is not hard to understand what I mean. If, for example, there was such a process as going to sleep, but no corresponding process of waking up, you realize that in the end everything would show the story of Endymion[7] to have no meaning. There would be no point to it because everything would have the same experience as he, be asleep. And if everything were combined and nothing separated, the saying of Anaxagoras[8] would soon be true, "that all things were mixed together." In the same way, my dear Cebes, if everything that partakes of life were to die and remain in that state and not come to life again, would not everything ultimately have to be dead and nothing alive? Even if the living came from some other source, and all that lived died, how could all things avoid being absorbed in death?

It could not be, Socrates, said Cebes, and I think what you say is altogether true.

I think, Cebes, said he, that this is very definitely the case and that we were not deceived when we agreed on this: coming to life again in truth exists, the living come to be from the dead, and the souls of the dead exist.

Furthermore, Socrates, Cebes rejoined, such is also the case if that theory is true that you are accustomed to mention frequently, that for us learning is no other than recollection. According to this, we must at some previous time have learned what we now recollect. This is possible only if our soul existed somewhere before it took on this human shape. So according to this theory too, the soul is likely to be something immortal.

Cebes, Simmias interrupted, what are the proofs of this? Remind me, for I do not quite recall them at the moment.

There is one excellent argument, said Cebes, namely that when men are interrogated in the right manner, they always give the right answer of their own

---

7   Endymion was granted eternal sleep by Zeus.

8   Anaxagoras of Clazomenae was born at the beginning of the fifth century B.C. He came to Athens as a young man and spent most of his life there in the study of natural philosophy. He is quoted later in the dialogue (97c ff.) as claiming that the universe is directed by Mind (*Nous*). The reference here is to his statement that in the original state of the world all its elements were thoroughly commingled.

accord, and they could not do this if they did not possess the knowledge and the right explanation inside them. Then if one shows them a diagram or something else of that   b
kind, this will show most clearly that such is the case.[9]

If this does not convince you, Simmias, said Socrates, see whether you agree if we examine it in some such way as this, for do you doubt that what we call learning is recollection?

It is not that I doubt, said Simmias, but I want to experience the very thing we are discussing, recollection, and from what Cebes undertook to say, I am now remembering and am pretty nearly convinced. Nevertheless, I should like to hear now the way you were intending to explain it.

This way, he said. We surely agree that if anyone recollects anything, he must   c
have known it before.

Quite so, he said.

Do we not also agree that when knowledge comes to mind in this way, it is recollection? What way do I mean? Like this: when a man sees or hears or in some other way perceives one thing and not only knows that thing but also thinks of another thing of which the knowledge is not the same but different, are we not right to say that he recollects the second thing that comes into his mind?

How do you mean?   d

Things such as this: to know a man is surely a different knowledge from knowing a lyre.

Of course.

Well, you know what happens to lovers: whenever they see a lyre, a garment or anything else that their beloved is accustomed to use, they know the lyre, and the image of the boy to whom it belongs comes into their mind. This is recollection, just as someone, on seeing Simmias, often recollects Cebes, and there are thousands of other such occurrences.

Thousands indeed, said Simmias.

Is this kind of thing not recollection of a kind? he said, especially so when one   e
experiences it about things that one had forgotten, because one had not seen them for some time?—Quite so.

Further, he said, can a man seeing the picture of a horse or a lyre recollect a man, or seeing a picture of Simmias recollect Cebes?—Certainly.

Or seeing a picture of Simmias, recollect Simmias himself?—He certainly can.

In all these cases the recollection can be occasioned by things that are similar, but   74
it can also be occasioned by things that are dissimilar?—It can.

When the recollection is caused by similar things, must one not of necessity also experience this: to consider whether the similarity to that which one recollects is deficient in any respect or complete?—One must.

[9] Cf. *Meno* 81e ff., where Socrates does precisely that.

Consider, he said, whether this is the case: we say that there is something that is equal. I do not mean a stick equal to a stick or a stone to a stone, or anything of that kind, but something else beyond all these, the Equal itself. Shall we say that this exists or not?

b Indeed we shall, by Zeus, said Simmias, most definitely.

And do we know what this is?—Certainly.

Whence have we acquired the knowledge of it? Is it not from the things we mentioned just now, from seeing sticks or stones or some other things that are equal we come to think of that other which is different from them? Or doesn't it seem to you to be different? Look at it also this way: do not equal stones and sticks sometimes, while remaining the same, appear to one to be equal and to another to be unequal?—Certainly they do.

c But what of the equals themselves? Have they ever appeared unequal to you, or Equality to be Inequality?

Never, Socrates.

These equal things and the Equal itself are therefore not the same?

I do not think they are the same at all, Socrates.

But it is definitely from the equal things, though they are different from that Equal, that you have derived and grasped the knowledge of equality?

Very true, Socrates.

Whether it be like them or unlike them?

Certainly.

It makes no difference. As long as the sight of one thing makes you think of
d another, whether it be similar or dissimilar, this must of necessity be recollection?

Quite so.

Well then, he said, do we experience something like this in the case of equal sticks and the other equal objects we just mentioned? Do they seem to us to be equal in the same sense as what is Equal itself? Is there some deficiency in their being such as the Equal, or is there not?

A considerable deficiency, he said.

Whenever someone, on seeing something, realizes that that which he now sees
e wants to be like some other reality but falls short and cannot be like that other since it is inferior, do we agree that the one who thinks this must have prior knowledge of that to which he says it is like, but deficiently so?

Necessarily.

Well, do we also feel this about the equal objects and the Equal itself, or do we not?

Very definitely.

We must then possess knowledge of the Equal before that time when we first saw
75 the equal objects and realized that all these objects strive to be like the Equal but are deficient in this.

That is so.

Then surely we also agree that this conception of ours derives from seeing or touching or some other sense perception, and cannot come into our mind in any other way, for all these senses, I say, are the same.

They are the same, Socrates, at any rate in respect to that which our argument wishes to make plain.

Our sense perceptions must surely make us realize that all that we perceive   b
through them is striving to reach that which is Equal but falls short of it; or how do we express it?

Like that.

Then before we began to see or hear or otherwise perceive, we must have possessed knowledge of the Equal itself if we were about to refer our sense perceptions of equal objects to it, and realized that all of them were eager to be like it, but were inferior.

That follows from what has been said, Socrates.

But we began to see and hear and otherwise perceive right after birth?

Certainly.

We must then have acquired the knowledge of the Equal before this.   c

Yes.

It seems then that we must have possessed it before birth.

It seems so.

Therefore, if we had this knowledge, we knew before birth and immediately after not only the Equal, but the Greater and the Smaller and all such things, for our present argument is no more about the Equal than about the Beautiful itself, the Good   d
itself, the just, the Pious and, as I say, about all those things which we mark with the seal of "what it is," both when we are putting questions and answering them. So we must have acquired knowledge of them all before we were born.

That is so.

If, having acquired this knowledge in each case, we have not forgotten it, we remain knowing and have knowledge throughout our life, for to know is to acquire knowledge, keep it and not lose it. Do we not call the losing of knowledge forgetting?

Most certainly, Socrates, he said.   e

But, I think, if we acquired this knowledge before birth, then lost it at birth, and then later by the use of our senses in connection with those objects we mentioned, we recovered the knowledge we had before, would not what we call learning be the recovery of our own knowledge, and we are right to call this recollection?

Certainly.

It was seen to be possible for someone to see or hear or otherwise perceive   76
something, and by this to be put in mind of something else which he had forgotten and which is related to it by similarity or difference. One of two things follows, as I say: either we were born with the knowledge of it, and all of us know it throughout life, or those who later, we say, are learning, are only recollecting, and learning would be recollection.

That is certainly the case, Socrates.

Which alternative do you choose, Simmias? That we are born with this   b
knowledge or that we recollect later the things of which we had knowledge previously?

I have no means of choosing at the moment, Socrates.

Well, can you make this choice? What is your opinion about it? A man who has knowledge would be able to give an account of what he knows, or would he not?

He must certainly be able to do so, Socrates, he said.

And do you think everybody can give an account of the things we were mentioning just now?

I wish they could, said Simmias, but I'm afraid it is much more likely that by this time tomorrow there will be no one left who can do so adequately.

c   So you do not think that everybody has knowledge of those things?

No indeed.

So they recollect what they once learned?

They must.

When did our souls acquire the knowledge of them? Certainly not since we were born as men.

Indeed no.

Before that then?

Yes.

So then, Simmias, our souls also existed apart from the body before they took on human form, and they had intelligence.

Unless we acquire the knowledge at the moment of birth, Socrates, for that time is still left to us.

d   Quite so, my friend, but at what other time do we lose it? We just now agreed that we are not born with that knowledge. Do we then lose it at the very time we acquire it, or can you mention any other time?

I cannot, Socrates. I did not realize that I was talking nonsense.

So this is our position, Simmias? he said. If those realities we are always talking about exist, the Beautiful and the Good and all that kind of reality, and we refer all the things we perceive to that reality, discovering that it existed before and is ours,
e   and we compare these things with it, then, just as they exist, so our soul must exist before we are born. If these realities do not exist, then this argument is altogether futile. Is this the position, that there is an equal necessity for those realities to exist, and for our souls to exist before we were born? If the former do not exist, neither do the latter?

I do not think, Socrates, said Simmias, that there is any possible doubt that it is equally necessary for both to exist, and it is opportune that our argument comes to
77   the conclusion that our soul exists before we are born, and equally so that reality of which you are now speaking. Nothing is so evident to me personally as that all such things must certainly exist, the Beautiful, the Good, and all those you mentioned just now. I also think that sufficient proof of this has been given.

Then what about Cebes? said Socrates, for we must persuade Cebes also.

He is sufficiently convinced I think, said Simmias, though he is the most difficult of men to persuade by argument, but I believe him to be fully convinced that our soul
b   existed before we were born. I do not think myself, however, that it has been proved that the soul continues to exist after death; the opinion of the majority which Cebes mentioned still stands, that when a man dies his soul is dispersed and this is the end

of its existence. What is to prevent the soul coming to be and being constituted from some other source, existing before it enters a human body and then, having done so and departed from it, itself dying and being destroyed?

You are right, Simmias, said Cebes. Half of what needed proof has been proved, namely, that our soul existed before we were born, but further proof is needed that it exists no less after we have died, if the proof is to be complete.

It has been proved even now, Simmias and Cebes, said Socrates, if you are ready to combine this argument with the one we agreed on before, that every living thing must come from the dead. If the soul exists before, it must, as it comes to life and birth, come from nowhere else than death and being dead, so how could it avoid existing after death since it must be born again? What you speak of has then even now been proved. However, I think you and Simmias would like to discuss the argument more fully. You seem to have this childish fear that the wind would really dissolve and scatter the soul, as it leaves the body, especially if one happens to die in a high wind and not in calm weather.

Cebes laughed and said: Assuming that we were afraid, Socrates, try to change our minds, or rather do not assume that we are afraid, but perhaps there is a child in us who has these fears; try to persuade him not to fear death like a bogey.

You should, said Socrates, sing a charm over him every day until you have charmed away his fears.

Where shall we find a good charmer for these fears, Socrates, he said, now that you are leaving us?

Greece is a large country, Cebes, he said, and there are good men in it; the tribes of foreigners are also numerous. You should search for such a charmer among them all, sparing neither trouble nor expense, for there is nothing on which you could spend your money to greater advantage. You must also search among yourselves, for you might not easily find people who could do this better than yourselves.

That shall be done, said Cebes, but let us, if it pleases you, go back to the argument where we left it.

Of course it pleases me.

Splendid, he said.

We must then ask ourselves something like this: what kind of thing is likely to be scattered? On behalf of what kind of thing should one fear this, and for what kind of thing should one not fear it? We should then examine to which class the soul belongs, and as a result either fear for the soul or be of good cheer.

What you say is true.

Is not anything that is composite and a compound by nature liable to be split up into its component parts, and only that which is noncomposite, if anything, is not likely to be split up?

I think that is the case, said Cebes.

Are not the things that always remain the same and in the same state most likely not to be composite, whereas those that vary from one time to another and are never the same are composite?

I think that is so.

Let us then return to those same things with which we were dealing earlier, to that
d   reality of whose existence we are giving an account in our questions and answers;
are they ever the same and in the same state, or do they vary from one time to
another; can the Equal itself, the Beautiful itself, each thing in itself, the real, ever
be affected by any change whatever? Or does each of them that really is, being
uniform by itself, remain the same and never in any way tolerate any change
whatever?

It must remain the same, said Cebes, and in the same state, Socrates.

e   What of the many beautiful particulars, be they men, horses, clothes, or other such
things, or the many equal particulars, and all those which bear the same name as those
others? Do they remain the same or, in total contrast to those other realities, one might
say, never in any way remain the same as themselves or in relation to each other?

The latter is the case, they are never in the same state.

79   These latter you could touch and see and perceive with the other senses, but those
that always remain the same can only be grasped by the reasoning power of the
mind? They are not seen but are invisible?

That is altogether true, he said.

Do you then want us to assume two kinds of existences, the visible and the
invisible?

Let us assume this.

And the invisible always remains the same, whereas the visible never does?

Let us assume that too.

b   Now one part of ourselves is the body, another part is the soul?

Quite so.

To which class of existence do we say the body is more alike and akin?

To the visible, as anyone can see.

What about the soul? Is it visible or invisible?

It is not visible to men, Socrates, he said.

Well, we meant visible and invisible to human eyes; or to any others, do
you think?

To human eyes.

Then what do we say about the soul? Is it visible or not visible?

Not visible.

So it is invisible?—Yes.

c   So the soul is more like the invisible than the body, and the body more like the
visible?—Without any doubt, Socrates.

Haven't we also said some time ago that when the soul makes use of the body to
investigate something, be it through hearing or seeing or some other sense—for to
investigate something through the body is to do it through the senses—it is dragged
by the body to the things that are never the same, and the soul itself strays and
is confused and dizzy, as if it were drunk, in so far as it is in contact with that kind
of thing?

Certainly.

But when the soul investigates by itself it passes into the realm of what is pure,   d
ever existing, immortal and unchanging, and being akin to this, it always stays with
it whenever it is by itself and can do so; it ceases to stray and remains in the same
state as it is in touch with things of the same kind, and its experience then is what is
called wisdom?

Altogether well said and very true, Socrates, he said.

Judging from what we have said before and what we are saying now, to which of   e
these two kinds do you think that the soul is more alike and more akin?

I think, Socrates, he said, that on this line of argument any man, even the dullest,
would agree that the soul is altogether more like that which always exists in the same
state rather than like that which does not.

What of the body?

That is like the other.

Look at it also this way: when the soul and the body are together, nature orders   80
the one to be subject and to be ruled, and the other to rule and be master. Then again,
which do you think is like the divine and which like the mortal? Do you not think
that the nature of the divine is to rule and to lead, whereas it is that of the mortal to
be ruled and be subject?

I do.

Which does the soul resemble?

Obviously, Socrates, the soul resembles the divine, and the body resembles
the mortal.

Consider then, Cebes, whether it follows from all that has been said that the soul   b
is most like the divine, deathless, intelligible, uniform, indissoluble, always the same
as itself, whereas the body is most like that which is human, mortal, multiform,
unintelligible, soluble and never consistently the same. Have we anything else to say
to show, my dear Cebes, that this is not the case?

We have not.

Well then, that being so, is it not natural for the body to dissolve easily, and for
the soul to be altogether indissoluble, or nearly so?

Of course.   c

You realize, he said, that when a man dies, the visible part, the body, which exists
in the visible world, and which we call the corpse, whose natural lot it would be to
dissolve, fall apart and be blown away, does not immediately suffer any of these
things but remains for a fair time, in fact, quite a long time if the man dies with his
body in a suitable condition and at a favorable season? If the body is emaciated or
embalmed, as in Egypt, it remains almost whole for a remarkable length of time, and   d
even if the body decays, some parts of it, namely bones and sinews and the like, are
nevertheless, one might say, deathless. Is that not so?—Yes.

Will the soul, the invisible part which makes its way to a region of the same kind,
noble and pure and invisible, to Hades in fact, to the good and wise god whither, god
willing, my soul must soon be going—will the soul, being of this kind and nature, be
scattered and destroyed on leaving the body, as the majority of men say? Far from it,

e   my dear Cebes and Simmias, but what happens is much more like this: if it is pure
when it leaves the body and drags nothing bodily with it, as it had no willing
association with the body in life, but avoided it and gathered itself together by itself
and always practiced this, which is no other than practising philosophy in the right
81   way, in fact, training to die easily. Or is this not training for death?

It surely is.

A soul in this state makes its way to the invisible, which is like itself, the divine
and immortal and wise, and arriving there it can be happy, having rid itself of
confusion, ignorance, fear, violent desires and the other human ills and, as is said of
the initiates, truly spend the rest of time with the gods. Shall we say this, Cebes, or
something different?

This, by Zeus, said Cebes.

b   But I think that if the soul is polluted and impure when it leaves the body, having
always been associated with it and served it, bewitched by physical desires and
pleasures to the point at which nothing seems to exist for it but the physical, which
one can touch and see or eat and drink or make use of for sexual enjoyment, and if
that soul is accustomed to hate and fear and avoid that which is dim and invisible to
the eyes but intelligible and to be grasped by philosophy—do you think such a soul
will escape pure and by itself?

c   Impossible, he said.

It is no doubt permeated by the physical, which constant intercourse and
association with the body, as well as considerable practice, has caused to become
ingrained in it?

Quite so.

We must believe, my friend, that this bodily element is heavy, ponderous, earthy
and visible. Through it, such a soul has become heavy and is dragged back to the
visible region in fear of the unseen and of Hades. It wanders, as we are told, around
d   graves and monuments, where shadowy phantoms, images that such souls produce,
have been seen, souls that have not been freed and purified but share in the visible,
and are therefore seen.

That is likely, Socrates.

It is indeed, Cebes. Moreover, these are not the souls of good but of inferior men,
which are forced to wander there, paying the penalty for their previous bad
e   upbringing. They wander until their longing for that which accompanies them, the
physical, again imprisons them in a body, and they are then, as is likely, bound to
such characters as they have practiced in their life.

What kind of characters do you say these are, Socrates?

Those, for example, who have carelessly practiced gluttony, violence and
drunkenness are likely to join a company of donkeys or of similar animals. Do you
82   not think so?

Very likely.

Those who have esteemed injustice highly, and tyranny and plunder will join the
tribes of wolves and hawks and kites, or where else shall we say that they go?

Certainly to those, said Cebes.

And clearly, the destination of the others will conform to the way in which they have behaved?

Clearly, of course.

The happiest of these, who will also have the best destination, are those who have b practiced popular and social virtue, which they call moderation and justice and which was developed by habit and practice, without philosophy or understanding?

How are they the happiest?

Because it is likely that they will again join a social and gentle group, either of bees or wasps or ants, and then again the same kind of human group, and so be moderate men.

That is likely.

No one may join the company of the gods who has not practiced philosophy and c is not completely pure when he departs from life, no one but the lover of learning. It is for this reason, my friends Simmias and Cebes, that those who practice philosophy in the right way keep away from all bodily passions, master them and do not surrender themselves to them; it is not at all for fear of wasting their substance and of poverty, which the majority and the money-lovers fear, nor for fear of dishonor and ill repute, like the ambitious and lovers of honors, that they keep away from them.

That would not be natural for them, Socrates, said Cebes.

By Zeus, no, he said. Those who care for their own soul and do not live for the d service of their body dismiss all these things. They do not travel the same road as those who do not know where they are going but, believing that nothing should be done contrary to philosophy and their deliverance and purification, they turn to this and follow wherever philosophy leads.

How so, Socrates?

I will tell you, he said. The lovers of learning know that when philosophy gets e hold of their soul, it is imprisoned in and clinging to the body, and that it is forced to examine other things through it as through a cage and not by itself, and that it wallows in every kind of ignorance. Philosophy sees that the worst feature of this imprisonment is that it is due to desires, so that the prisoner himself is contributing to his own incarceration most of all. As I say, the lovers of learning know that 83 philosophy gets hold of their soul when it is in that state, then gently encourages it and tries to free it by showing them that investigation through the eyes is full of deceit, as is that through the ears and the other senses. Philosophy then persuades the soul to withdraw from the senses in so far as it is not compelled to use them and bids the soul to gather itself together by itself, to trust only itself and whatever reality, b existing by itself, the soul by itself understands, and not to consider as true whatever it examines by other means, for this is different in different circumstances and is sensible and visible, whereas what the soul itself sees is intelligible and invisible. The soul of the true philosopher thinks that this deliverance must not be opposed and so keeps away from pleasures and desires and pains as far as he can; he reflects that violent pleasure or pain or passion does not cause merely such evils as one might expect, such as one suffers when one has been sick or extravagant through desire, but c the greatest and most extreme evil, though one does not reflect on this.

What is that, Socrates? asked Cebes.

That the soul of every man, when it feels violent pleasure or pain in connection with some object, inevitably believes at the same time that what causes such feelings must be very clear and very true, which it is not. Such objects are mostly visible, are they not?

Certainly.

d   And doesn't such an experience tie the soul to the body most completely?

How so?

Because every pleasure and every pain provides, as it were, another nail to rivet the soul to the body and to weld them together. It makes the soul corporeal, so that it believes that truth is what the body says it is. As it shares the beliefs and delights of the body, I think it inevitably comes to share its ways and manner of life and is unable ever to reach Hades in a pure state; it is always full of body when it departs, so that it soon falls back into another body and grows with it as if it had been sewn

e   into it. Because of this, it can have no part in the company of the divine, the pure and uniform.

What you say is very true, Socrates, said Cebes.

This is why genuine lovers of learning are moderate and brave, or do you think it is for the reasons the majority says they are?

84   I certainly do not.

Indeed no. This is how the soul of a philosopher would reason: it would not think that while philosophy must free it, it should while being freed surrender itself to pleasures and pains and imprison itself again, thus laboring in vain like Penelope at her web. The soul of the philosopher achieves a calm from such emotions; it follows reason and ever stays with it contemplating the true, the divine, which is not the object of opinion. Nurtured by this, it believes that one should live in this manner as

b   long as one is alive and, after death, arrive at what is akin and of the same kind, and escape from human evils. After such nurture there is no danger, Simmias and Cebes, that one should fear that, on parting from the body, the soul would be scattered and dissipated by the winds and no longer be anything anywhere.

c   When Socrates finished speaking there was a long silence. He appeared to be concentrating on what had been said, and so were most of us. But Cebes and Simmias were whispering to each other. Socrates observed them and questioned them. Come, he said, do you think there is something lacking in my argument? There are still many doubtful points and many objections for anyone who wants a thorough discussion of these matters. If you are discussing some other subject, I have nothing to say, but if you have some difficulty about this one, do not hesitate to speak for yourselves and expound it if you think the argument could be improved, and if you

d   think you will do better, take me along with you in the discussion.

I will tell you the truth, Socrates, said Simmias. Both of us have been in difficulty for some time, and each of us has been urging the other to question you because we wanted to hear what you would say, but we hesitated to bother you, lest it be displeasing to you in your present misfortune.

e   When Socrates heard this he laughed quietly and said: "Really, Simmias, it would be hard for me to persuade other people that I do not consider my present fate a misfortune if I cannot persuade even you, and you are afraid that it is more difficult to deal with me than before. You seem to think me inferior to the swans in prophecy. They sing before too, but when they realize that they must die they sing most and most beautifully, as they rejoice that they are about to depart to join the god whose   85 servants they are. But men, because of their own fear of death, tell lies about the swans and say that they lament their death and sing in sorrow. They do not reflect that no bird sings when it is hungry or cold or suffers in any other way, neither the nightingale nor the swallow nor the hoopoe, though they do say that these sing laments when in pain. Nor do the swans, but I believe that as they belong to Apollo,   b they are prophetic, have knowledge of the future and sing of the blessings of the underworld, sing and rejoice on that day beyond what they did before. As I believe myself to be a fellow servant with the swans and dedicated to the same god, and have received from my master a gift of prophecy not inferior to theirs, I am no more despondent than they on leaving life. Therefore, you must speak and ask whatever you want as long as the authorities allow it."

Well spoken, said Simmias. I will tell you my difficulty, and then Cebes will say   c why he does not accept what was said. I believe, as perhaps you do, that precise knowledge on that subject is impossible or extremely difficult in our present life, but that it surely shows a very poor spirit not to examine thoroughly what is said about it, and to desist before one is exhausted by an all-round investigation. One should achieve one of these things: learn the truth about these things or find it for oneself, or, if that is impossible, adopt the best and most irrefutable of men's theories, and,   d borne upon this, sail through the dangers of life as upon a raft, unless someone should make that journey safer and less risky upon a firmer vessel of some divine doctrine. So even now, since you have said what you did, I will feel no shame at asking questions, and I will not blame myself in the future because I did not say what I think. As I examine what we said, both by myself and with Cebes, it does not seem to be adequate.

Said Socrates: "You may well be right, my friend, but tell me how it is   e inadequate."

In this way, as it seems to me, he said: "One might make the same argument about harmony, lyre and strings, that a harmony is something invisible, without body, beautiful and divine in the attuned lyre, whereas the lyre itself and its strings are   86 physical, bodily, composite, earthy and akin to what is mortal. Then if someone breaks the lyre, cuts or breaks the strings and then insists, using the same argument as you, that the harmony must still exist and is not destroyed because it would be impossible for the lyre and the strings, which are mortal, still to exist when the strings are broken, and for the harmony, which is akin and of the same nature as the divine and immortal, to be destroyed before that which is mortal; he would say that   b the harmony itself still must exist and that the wood and the strings must rot before the harmony can suffer. And indeed Socrates, I think you must have this in mind, that we really do suppose the soul to be something of this kind; as the body is stretched and held together by the hot and the cold, the dry and the moist and other such things, and our soul is a mixture and harmony of those things when they are mixed with each   c other rightly and in due measure. If then the soul is a kind of harmony or attunement, clearly, when our body is relaxed or stretched without due measure by diseases and other evils, the soul must immediately be destroyed, even if it be most divine, as are the other harmonies found in music and all the works of artists, and the remains of each body last for a long time until they rot or are burned. Consider what we shall

d   say in answer to one who deems the soul to be a mixture of bodily elements and to be the first to perish in the process we call death."

Socrates looked at us keenly, as was his habit, smiled and said: "What Simmias says is quite fair. If one of you is more resourceful than I am, why did he not answer him, for he seems to have handled the argument competently. However, I think that

e   before we answer him, we should hear Cebes' objection, in order that we may have time to deliberate on an answer. When we have heard him we should either agree with them, if we think them in tune with us or, if not, defend our own argument. Come then, Cebes. What is troubling you?"

87   I tell you, said Cebes, the argument seems to me to be at the same point as before and open to the same objection. I do not deny that it has been very elegantly and, if it is not offensive to say so, sufficiently proved that our soul existed before it took on this present form, but I do not believe the same applies to its existing somewhere after our death. Not that I agree with Simmias' objection that the soul is not stronger and much more lasting than the body, for I think it is superior in all these respects. "Why then," the argument might say, "are you still unconvinced? Since you see that when the man dies, the weaker part continues to exist, do you not think that the more

b   lasting part must be preserved during that time?" On this point consider whether what I say makes sense.

Like Simmias, I too need an image, for I think this argument is much as if one said at the death of an old weaver that the man had not perished but was safe and

c   sound somewhere, and offered as proof the fact that the cloak the old man had woven himself and was wearing was still sound and had not perished. If one was not convinced, he would be asked whether a man lasts longer than a cloak which is in use and being worn, and if the answer was that a man lasts much longer, this would be taken as proof that the man was definitely safe and sound, since the more temporary thing had not perished. But Simmias, I do not think that is so, for consider what I say. Anybody could see that the man who said this was talking nonsense. That

d   weaver had woven and worn out many such cloaks. He perished after many of them, but before the last. That does not mean that a man is inferior and weaker than a cloak. The image illustrates, I think, the relationship of the soul to the body, and anyone who says the same thing about them would appear to me to be talking sense, that the soul lasts a long time while the body is weaker and more short-lived. He might say that each soul wears out many bodies, especially if it lives many years. If the body

e   were in a state of flux and perished while the man was still alive, and the soul wove afresh the body that is worn out, yet it would be inevitable that whenever the soul perished it would be wearing the last body it wove and perish only before this last. Then when the soul perished, the body would show the weakness of its nature by soon decaying and disappearing. So we cannot trust this argument and be confident

88   that our soul continues to exist somewhere after our death. For, if one were to concede, even more than you do, to a man using that argument, if one were to grant

him not only that the soul exists in the time before we are born, but that there is no
reason why the soul of some should not exist and continue to exist after our death,
and thus frequently be born and die in turn; if one were to grant him that the soul's
nature is so strong that it can survive many bodies, but if, having granted all this, one
does not further agree that the soul is not damaged by its many births and is not, in
the end, altogether destroyed in one of those deaths, he might say that no one knows   b
which death and dissolution of the body brings about the destruction of the soul,
since not one of us can be aware of this. And in that case, any man who faces death
with confidence is foolish, unless he can prove that the soul is altogether immortal.
If he cannot, a man about to die must of necessity always fear for his soul, lest the
present separation of the soul from the body bring about the complete destruction of
the soul.

When we heard what they said we were all depressed, as we told each other   c
afterwards. We had been quite convinced by the previous argument, and they seemed
to confuse us again, and to drive us to doubt not only what had already been said but
also what was going to be said, lest we be worthless as critics or the subject itself
admitted of no certainty.

ECHECRATES: By the gods, Phaedo, you have my sympathy, for as I listen to you   d
now I find myself saying to myself: "What argument shall we trust? That of Socrates,
which was extremely convincing, has now fallen into discredit; the statement that the
soul is some kind of harmony has a remarkable hold on me, now and always, and
when it was mentioned it reminded me that I had myself previously thought so. And
now I am again quite in need, as if from the beginning, of some other argument to
convince me that the soul does not die along with the man. Tell me then, by Zeus, how
Socrates tackled the argument. Was he obviously distressed, as you say you people
were, or was he not, but quietly came to the rescue of his argument, and did he do so   e
satisfactorily or inadequately? Tell us everything as precisely as you can.

PHAEDO: I have certainly often admired Socrates, Echecrates, but never more
than on this occasion. That he had a reply was perhaps not strange. What I wondered   89
at most in him was the pleasant, kind and admiring way he received the young men's
argument, and how sharply he was aware of the effect the discussion had on us, and
then how well he healed our distress and, as it were, recalled us from our flight and
defeat and turned us around to join him in the examination of their argument.

ECHECRATES: How did he do this?

PHAEDO: I will tell you. I happened to be sitting on his right by the couch on a
low stool, so that he was sitting well above me. He stroked my head and pressed the   b
hair on the back of my neck, for he was in the habit of playing with my hair at times.
"Tomorrow, Phaedo," he said, "you will probably cut this beautiful hair."

Likely enough, Socrates, I said.

Not if you take my advice, he said.

Why not? said I.

It is today, he said, that I shall cut my hair and you yours, if our argument dies on
us, and we cannot revive it. If I were you, and the argument escaped me, I would take   c
an oath, as the Argives did, not to let my hair grow before I fought again and defeated
the argument of Simmias and Cebes.

But, I said, they say that not even Heracles could fight two people.

Then call on me as your Iolaus, as long as the daylight lasts.

I shall call on you, but in this case as Iolaus calling on Heracles.

It makes no difference, he said, but first there is a certain experience we must be careful to avoid.

What is that? I asked.

d   That we should not become misologues, as people become misanthropes. There is no greater evil one can suffer than to hate reasonable discourse. Misology and misanthropy arise in the same way. Misanthropy comes when a man without knowledge or skill has placed great trust in someone and believes him to be altogether truthful, sound and trustworthy; then, a short time afterwards he finds him to be wicked and unreliable, and then this happens in another case; when one has frequently had that experience, especially with those whom one believed to be one's

e   closest friends, then, in the end, after many such blows, one comes to hate all men and to believe that no one is sound in any way at all. Have you not seen this happen?

I surely have, I said.

This is a shameful state of affairs, he said, and obviously due to to an attempt to have human relations without any skill in human affairs, for such skill would lead

90   one to believe, what is in fact true, that the very good and the very wicked are both quite rare, and that most men are between those extremes.

How do you mean? said I.

The same as with the very tall and the very short, he said. Do you think anything is rarer than to find an extremely tall man or an extremely short one? Or a dog or any thing else whatever? Or again, one extremely swift or extremely slow, ugly or beautiful, white or black? Are you not aware that in all those cases the most extreme at either end are rare and few, but those in between are many and plentiful?

Certainly, I said.

b   Therefore, he said, if a contest of wickedness were established, there too the winners, you think, would be very few?

That is likely, said I.

Likely indeed, he said, but arguments are not like men in this particular. I was merely following your lead just now. The similarity lies rather in this: it is as when one who lacks skill in arguments puts his trust in an argument as being true, then shortly afterwards believes it to be false—as sometimes it is and sometimes it is not—and so with another argument and then another. You know how those in

c   particular who spend their time studying contradiction in the end believe themselves to have become very wise and that they alone have understood that there is no soundness or reliability in any object or in any argument, but that all that exists simply fluctuates up and down as if it were in the Euripus[10] and does not remain in the same place for any time at all.

What you say, I said, is certainly true.

---

[10] The Euripus is the straits between the island of Euboea and Boeotia on the Greek mainland; its currents were both violent and variable.

It would be pitiable, Phaedo, he said, when there is a true and reliable argument
and one that can be understood, if a man who has dealt with such arguments as
appear at one time true, at another time untrue, should not blame himself or his own   d
lack of skill but, because of his distress, in the end gladly shift the blame away from
himself to the arguments, and spend the rest of his life hating and reviling reasonable
discussion and so be deprived of truth and knowledge of reality.

Yes, by Zeus, I said, that would be pitiable indeed.

This then is the first thing we should guard against, he said. We should not allow   e
into our minds the conviction that argumentation has nothing sound about it; much
rather we should believe that it is we who are not yet sound and that we must take
courage and be eager to attain soundness, you and the others for the sake of your   91
whole life still to come, and I for the sake of death itself. I am in danger at this
moment of not having a philosophical attitude about this, but like those who are quite
uneducated, I am eager to get the better of you in argument, for the uneducated, when
they engage in argument about anything, give no thought to the truth about the
subject of discussion but are only eager that those present will accept the position
they have set forth. I differ from them only to this extent: I shall not be eager to get
the agreement of those present that what I say is true, except incidentally, but I shall
be very eager that I should myself be thoroughly convinced that things are so. For I
am thinking—see in how contentious a spirit—that if what I say is true, it is a fine
thing to be convinced; if, on the other hand, nothing exists after death, at least for   b
this time before I die I shall distress those present less with lamentations and my
folly will not continue to exist along with me—that would be a bad thing—but will
come to an end in a short time. Thus prepared, Simmias and Cebes, he said, I come
to deal with your argument. If you will take my advice, you will give but little
thought to Socrates but much more to the truth. If you think that what I say is true,   c
agree with me; if not, oppose it with every argument and take care that in my
eagerness I do not deceive myself and you and, like a bee, leave my sting in you
when I go.

We must proceed, he said, and first remind me of what you said if I do not appear
to remember it. Simmias, as I believe, is in doubt and fear that the soul, though it is
more divine and beautiful than the body, yet predeceases it, being a kind of harmony.   d
Cebes, I thought, agrees with me that the soul lasts much longer than the body, but
that no one knows whether the soul often wears out many bodies and then, on
leaving its last body, is now itself destroyed. This then is death, the destruction of the
soul, since the body is always being destroyed. Are these the questions, Simmias and
Cebes, which we must investigate?

They both agreed that they were.   e

Do you then, he asked, reject all our previous statements, or some but not others?

Some, they both said, but not others.

What, he said, about the statements we made that learning is recollection and that,
if this was so, our soul must of necessity exist elsewhere before us, before it was   92
imprisoned in the body?

For myself, said Cebes, I was wonderfully convinced by it at the time and I stand
by it now also, more than by any other statement.

That, said Simmias, is also my position, and I should be very surprised if I ever changed my opinion about this.

But you must change your opinion, my Theban friend, said Socrates, if you still believe that a harmony is a composite thing, and that the soul is a kind of harmony of the elements of the body in a state of tension, for surely you will not allow

b   yourself to maintain that a composite harmony existed before those elements from which it had to be composed, or would you?

Never, Socrates, he said.

Do you realize, he said, that this is what you are in fact saying when you state that the soul exists before it takes on the form and body of a man and that it is composed of elements which do not yet exist? A harmony is not like that to which you compare

c   it; the lyre and the strings and the notes, though still unharmonized, exist; the harmony is composed last of all, and is the first to be destroyed. How will you harmonize this statement with your former one?

In no way, said Simmias.

And surely, he said, a statement about harmony should do so more than any other.

It should, said Simmias.

So your statement is inconsistent? Consider which of your statements you prefer, that learning is recollection or that the soul is a harmony?

d   I much prefer the former, Socrates. I adopted the latter without proof, because of a certain probability and plausibility, which is why it appeals to most men. I know that arguments of which the proof is based on probability are pretentious and, if one does not guard against them, they certainly deceive one, in geometry and everything else. The theory of recollection and learning, however, was based on an assumption worthy of acceptance, for our soul was said to exist also before it came into the body,

e   just as the reality does that is of the kind that we qualify by the words "what it is," and I convinced myself that I was quite correct to accept it. Therefore, I cannot accept the theory that the soul is a harmony either from myself or anyone else.

93   What of this, Simmias? Do you think it natural for a harmony, or any other composite, to be in a different state from that of the elements of which it is composed?

Not at all, said Simmias.

Nor, as I think, can it act or be acted upon in a different way than its elements?

He agreed.

One must therefore suppose that a harmony does not direct its components, but is directed by them.

He accepted this.

A harmony is therefore far from making a movement, or uttering a sound, or doing anything else, in a manner contrary to that of its parts.

Far from it indeed, he said.

Does not the nature of each harmony depend on the way it has been harmonized?

I do not understand, he said.

b   Will it not, if it is more and more fully harmonized, be more and more fully a harmony, and if it is less and less fully harmonized, it will be less and less fully a harmony?

Certainly.

Can this be true about the soul, that one soul is more and more fully a soul than another, or is less and less fully a soul, even to the smallest extent?

Not in any way.

Come now, by Zeus, he said. One soul is said to have intelligence and virtue and to be good, another to have folly and wickedness and to be bad. Are those things truly said?   c

They certainly are.

What will someone who holds the theory that the soul is a harmony say that those things are which reside in the soul, that is, virtue and wickedness? Are these some other harmony and disharmony? That the good soul is harmonized and, being a harmony, has within itself another harmony, whereas the evil soul is both itself a lack of harmony and has no other within itself?

I don't know what to say, said Simmias, but one who holds that assumption must obviously say something of that kind.

We have previously agreed, he said, that one soul is not more and not less a soul   d
than another, and this means that one harmony is not more and more fully, or less and less fully, a harmony than another. Is that not so?

Certainly.

Now that which is no more and no less a harmony is not more or less harmonized. Is that so?

It is.

Can that which is neither more nor less harmonized partake more or less of harmony, or does it do so equally?

Equally.

Then if a soul is neither more nor less a soul than another, it has been harmonized   e
to the same extent?

This is so.

If that is so, it would have no greater share of disharmony or of harmony?

It would not.

That being the case, could one soul have more wickedness or virtue than another, if wickedness is disharmony and virtue harmony?

It could not.

But rather, Simmias, according to correct reasoning, no soul, if it is a harmony,   94
will have any share of wickedness, for harmony is surely altogether this very thing, harmony, and would never share in disharmony.

It certainly would not.

Nor would a soul, being altogether this very thing, a soul, share in wickedness?

How could it, in view of what has been said?

So it follows from this argument that all the souls of all living creatures will be equally good, if souls are by nature equally this very thing, souls.

I think so, Socrates.

Does our argument seem right, he said, and does it seem that it should have come   b
to this, if the hypothesis that the soul is a harmony was correct?

Not in any way, he said.

Further, of all the parts of a man, can you mention any other part that rules him than his soul, especially if it is a wise soul?

I cannot.

Does it do so by following the affections of the body or by opposing them? I mean, for example, that when the body is hot and thirsty the soul draws him to the opposite, to not drinking; when the body is hungry, to not eating, and we see a thousand other examples of the soul opposing the affections of the body. Is that not so?

It certainly is.

On the other hand we previously agreed that if the soul were a harmony, it would never be out of tune with the stress and relaxation and the striking of the strings or anything else done to its composing elements, but that it would follow and never direct them?

We did so agree, of course.

Well, does it now appear to do quite the opposite, ruling over all the elements of which one says it is composed, opposing nearly all of them throughout life, directing all their ways, inflicting harsh and painful punishment on them, at times in physical culture and medicine, at other times more gently by threats and exhortations, holding converse with desires and passions and fears as if it were one thing talking to a different one, as Homer wrote somewhere in the *Odyssey* where he says that Odysseus "struck his breast and rebuked his heart saying, 'Endure, my heart, you have endured worse than this.'"[11]

Do you think that when he composed this the poet thought that his soul was a harmony, a thing to be directed by the affections of the body? Did he not rather regard it as ruling over them and mastering them, itself a much more divine thing than a harmony?

Yes, by Zeus, I think so, Socrates.

Therefore, my good friend, it is quite wrong for us to say that the soul is a harmony, and in saying so we would disagree both with the divine poet Homer and with ourselves.

That is so, he said.

Very well, said Socrates. Harmonia of Thebes seems somehow reasonably propitious to us. How and by what argument, my dear Cebes, can we propitiate Cadmus?[12]

I think, Cebes said, that you will find a way. You dealt with the argument about harmony in a manner that was quite astonishing to me. When Simmias was speaking of his difficulties I was very much wondering whether anyone would be able to deal with his argument, and I was quite dumbfounded when right away he could not resist your argument's first onslaught. I should not wonder therefore if that of Cadmus suffered the same fate.

---

[11] *Odyssey* xx. 17–18.

[12] Harmonia was in legend the wife of Cadmus, the founder of Thebes. Socrates' punning joke is simply that, having dealt with Harmonia (harmony), we must now deal with Cadmus (i.e. Cebes, the other Theban).

My good sir, said Socrates, do not boast, lest some malign influence upset the argument we are about to make. However, we leave that to the care of the god, but let us come to grips with it in the Homeric fashion, to see if there is anything in what you say. The sum of your problem is this: you consider that the soul must be proved to be immortal and indestructible before a philosopher on the point of death, who is confident that he will fare much better in the underworld than if he had led any other kind of life, can avoid being foolish and simple-minded in this confidence. To prove that the soul is strong, that it is divine, that it existed before we were born as men, all this, you say, does not show the soul to be immortal but only long-lasting. That it existed for a very long time before, that it knew much and acted much, makes it no more immortal because of that; indeed, its very entering into a human body was the beginning of its destruction, like a disease; it would live that life in distress and would in the end be destroyed in what we call death. You say it makes no difference whether it enters a body once or many times as far as the fear of each of us is concerned, for it is natural for a man who is no fool to be afraid, if he does not know and cannot prove that the soul is immortal. This, I think, is what you maintain, Cebes; I deliberately repeat it often, in order that no point may escape us, and that you may add or subtract something if you wish.

And Cebes said: "There is nothing that I want to add or subtract at the moment. That is what I say."

Socrates paused for a long time, deep in thought. He then said: "This is no unimportant problem that you raise, Cebes, for it requires a thorough investigation of the cause of generation and destruction. I will, if you wish, give you an account of my experience in these matters. Then if something I say seems useful to you, make use of it to persuade us of your position."

I surely do wish that, said Cebes.

Listen then, and I will, Cebes, he said. When I was a young man I was wonderfully keen on that wisdom which they call natural science, for I thought it splendid to know the causes of everything, why it comes to be, why it perishes and why it exists. I was often changing my mind in the investigation, in the first instance, of questions such as these: Are living creatures nurtured when heat and cold produce a kind of putrefaction, as some say? Do we think with our blood, or air, or fire, or none of these, and does the brain provide our senses of hearing and sight and smell, from which come memory and opinion, and from memory and opinion which has become stable, comes knowledge? Then again, as I investigated how these things perish and what happens to things in the sky and on the earth, finally I became convinced that I have no natural aptitude at all for that kind of investigation, and of this I will give you sufficient proof. This investigation made me quite blind even to those things which I and others thought that I clearly knew before, so that I unlearned what I thought I knew before, about many other things and specifically about how men grew. I thought before that it was obvious to anybody that men grew through eating and drinking, for food adds flesh to flesh and bones to bones, and in the same way appropriate parts were added to all other parts of the body, so that the man grew from an earlier small bulk to a large bulk later, and so a small man became big. That is what I thought then. Do you not think it was reasonable?

c

d

e

96

b

c

d

I do, said Cebes.

e   Then further consider this: I thought my opinion was satisfactory, that when a large man stood by a small one he was taller by a head, and so a horse was taller than a horse. Even clearer than this, I thought that ten was more than eight because two had been added, and that a two-cubit length is larger than a cubit because it surpasses it by half its length.

And what do you think now about those things?

That I am far, by Zeus, from believing that I know the cause of any of those things. I will not even allow myself to say that where one is added to one either the

97   one to which it is added or the one that is added becomes two, or that the one added and the one to which it is added become two because of the addition of the one to the other. I wonder that, when each of them is separate from the other, each of them is one, nor are they then two, but that, when they come near to one another, this is the cause of their becoming two, the coming together and being placed closer to one

b   another. Nor can I any longer be persuaded that when one thing is divided, this division is the cause of its becoming two, for just now the cause of becoming two was the opposite. At that time it was their coming close together and one was added to the other, but now it is because one is taken and separated from the other.

I do not any longer persuade myself that I know why a unit or anything else comes to be, or perishes or exists by the old method of investigation, and I do not

c   accept it, but I have a confused method of my own. One day I heard someone reading, as he said, from a book of Anaxagoras, and saying that it is Mind that directs and is the cause of everything. I was delighted with this cause and it seemed to me good, in a way, that Mind should be the cause of all. I thought that if this were so, the directing Mind would direct everything and arrange each thing in the way that

d   was best. If then one wished to know the cause of each thing, why it comes to be or perishes or exists, one had to find what was the best way for it to be, or to be acted upon, or to act. On these premises then it befitted a man to investigate only, about this and other things, what is best. The same man must inevitably also know what is worse, for that is part of the same knowledge. As I reflected on this subject I was glad to think that I had found in Anaxagoras a teacher about the cause of things after my

e   own heart, and that he would tell me, first, whether the earth is flat or round, and then would explain why it is so of necessity, saying which is better, and that it was better to be so. If he said it was in the middle of the universe, he would go on to show that it was better for it to be in the middle, and if he showed me those things I should be

98   prepared never to desire any other kind of cause. I was ready to find out in the same way about the sun and the moon and the other heavenly bodies, about their relative speed, their turnings and whatever else happened to them, how it is best that each should act or be acted upon. I never thought that Anaxagoras, who said that those things were directed by Mind, would bring in any other cause for them than that it was best for them to be as they are. Once he had given the best for each as the cause

b   for each and the general cause of all, I thought he would go on to explain the common good for all, and I would not have exchanged my hopes for a fortune. I eagerly acquired his books and read them as quickly as I could in order to know the best and the worst as soon as possible.

This wonderful hope was dashed as I went on reading and saw that the man made no use of Mind, nor gave it any responsibility for the management of things, but mentioned as causes air and ether and water and many other strange things. That seemed to me much like saying that Socrates' actions are all due to his mind, and then in trying to tell the causes of everything I do, to say that the reason that I am sitting here is because my body consists of bones and sinews, because the bones are hard and are separated by joints, that the sinews are such as to contract and relax, that they surround the bones along with flesh and skin which hold them together, then as the bones are hanging in their sockets, the relaxation and contraction of the sinews enable me to bend my limbs, and that is the cause of my sitting here with my limbs bent.

Again, he would mention other such causes for my talking to you: sounds and air and hearing, and a thousand other such things, but he would neglect to mention the true causes, that, after the Athenians decided it was better to condemn me, for this reason it seemed best to me to sit here and more right to remain and to endure whatever penalty they ordered. For by the dog, I think these sinews and bones could long ago have been in Megara or among the Boeotians, taken there by my belief as to the best course, if I had not thought it more right and honorable to endure whatever penalty the city ordered rather than escape and run away. To call those things causes is too absurd. If someone said that without bones and sinews and all such things, I should not be able to do what I decided, he would be right, but surely to say that they are the cause of what I do, and not that I have chosen the best course, even though I act with my mind, is to speak very lazily and carelessly. Imagine not being able to distinguish the real cause from that without which the cause would not be able to act as a cause. It is what the majority appear to do, like people groping in the dark; they call it a cause, thus giving it a name that does not belong to it. That is why one man surrounds the earth with a vortex to make the heavens keep it in place, another makes the air support it like a wide lid. As for their capacity of being in the best place they could possibly be put, this they do not look for, nor do they believe it to have any divine force, but they believe that they will some time discover a stronger and more immortal Atlas to hold everything together more, and they do not believe that the truly good and "binding" binds and holds them together. I would gladly become the disciple of any man who taught the workings of that kind of cause. However, since I was deprived and could neither discover it myself nor learn it from another, do you wish me to give you an explanation of how, as a second best, I busied myself with the search for the cause, Cebes?

I would wish it above all else, he said.

After this, he said, when I had wearied of investigating things, I thought that I must be careful to avoid the experience of those who watch an eclipse of the sun, for some of them ruin their eyes unless they watch its reflection in water or some such material. A similar thought crossed my mind, and I feared that my soul would be altogether blinded if I looked at things with my eyes and tried to grasp them with each of my senses. So I thought I must take refuge in discussions and investigate the truth of things by means of words. However, perhaps this analogy is inadequate, for I certainly do not admit that one who investigates things by means of words is dealing with images any more than one who looks at facts. However, I started in this manner: taking as my hypothesis in each case the theory that seemed to me the most compelling, I would consider as true, about cause and everything else, whatever agreed with this, and as untrue whatever did not so agree. But I want to put my meaning more clearly for I do not think that you understand me now.

No, by Zeus, said Cebes, not very well.

b   This, he said, is what I mean. It is nothing new, but what I have never stopped talking about, both elsewhere and in the earlier part of our conversation. I am going to try to show you the kind of cause with which I have concerned myself. I turn back to those oft-mentioned things and proceed from them. I assume the existence of a Beautiful, itself by itself, of a Good and a Great and all the rest. If you grant me these and agree that they exist, I hope to show you the cause as a result, and to find the soul to be immortal.

c   Take it that I grant you this, said Cebes, and hasten to your conclusion.

Consider then, he said, whether you share my opinion as to what follows, for I think that, if there is anything beautiful besides the Beautiful itself, it is beautiful for no other reason than that it shares in that Beautiful, and I say so with everything. Do you agree to this sort of cause?—I do.

d   I no longer understand or recognize those other sophisticated causes, and if someone tells me that a thing is beautiful because it has a bright color or shape or any such thing, I ignore these other reasons—for all these confuse me—but I simply, naively and perhaps foolishly cling to this, that nothing else makes it beautiful other than the presence of, or the sharing in, or however you may describe its relationship to that Beautiful we mentioned, for I will not insist on the precise nature of the relationship, but that all beautiful things are beautiful by the Beautiful. That, I think,

e   is the safest answer I can give myself or anyone else. And if I stick to this I think I shall never fall into error. This is the safe answer for me or anyone else to give, namely, that it is through Beauty that beautiful things are made beautiful. Or do you not think so too?—I do.

And that it is through Bigness that big things are big and the bigger are bigger, and that smaller things are made small by Smallness?—Yes.

And you would not accept the statement that one man is taller than another by a

101   head and the shorter man shorter by the same, but you would bear witness that you mean nothing else than that everything that is bigger is made bigger by nothing else than by Bigness, and that is the cause of its being bigger, and the smaller is made smaller only by Smallness and this is why it is smaller. I think you would be afraid that some opposite argument would confront you if you said that someone is bigger or smaller by a head, first, because the bigger is bigger and the smaller smaller by

b   the same, then because the bigger is bigger by a head which is small, and this would be strange, namely, that someone is made bigger by something small. Would you not be afraid of this?

I certainly would, said Cebes, laughing.

Then you would be afraid to say that ten is more than eight by two, and that this is the cause of the excess, and not magnitude and because of magnitude, or that two cubits is bigger than one cubit by half and not by Bigness, for this is the same fear.—Certainly.

Then would you not avoid saying that when one is added to one it is the addition and when it is divided it is the division that is the cause of two? And you would   c loudly exclaim that you do not know how else each thing can come to be except by sharing in the particular reality in which it shares, and in these cases you do not know of any other cause of becoming two except by sharing in Twoness, and that the things that are to be two must share in this, as that which is to be one must share in Oneness, and you would dismiss these additions and divisions and other such subtleties, and leave them to those wiser than yourself to answer. But you, afraid, as they say, of your own shadow and your inexperience, would cling to the safety of your own   d hypothesis and give that answer. If someone then attacked your hypothesis itself, you would ignore him and would not answer until you had examined whether the, consequences that follow from it agree with one another or contradict one another.[13] And when you must give an account of your hypothesis itself you will proceed in the same way: you will assume another hypothesis, the one which seems to you best of the higher ones until you come to something acceptable, but you will not jumble the   e two as the debaters do by discussing the hypothesis and its consequences at the same time, if you wish to discover any truth. This they do not discuss at all nor give any thought to, but their wisdom enables them to mix everything up and yet to be pleased with themselves, but if you are a philosopher I think you will do as I say.   102

What you say is very true, said Simmias and Cebes together.

ECHECRATES: Yes, by Zeus, Phaedo, and they were right, I think he made these things wonderfully clear to anyone of even small intelligence.

PHAEDO: Yes indeed, Echecrates, and all those present thought so too.

ECHECRATES: And so do we who were not present but hear of it now. What was said after that?

PHAEDO: As I recall it, when the above had been accepted, and it was agreed   b that each of the Forms existed, and that other things acquired their name by having a share in them, he followed this up by asking: If you say these things are so, when you then say that Simmias is taller than Socrates but shorter than Phaedo, do you not mean that there is in Simmias both tallness and shortness?—I do.

But, he said, do you agree that the words of the statement 'Simmias is taller than   c Socrates' do not express the truth of the matter? It is not, surely, the nature of Simmias to be taller than Socrates because he is Simmias but because of the tallness he happens to have? Nor is he taller than Socrates because Socrates is Socrates, but because Socrates has smallness compared with the tallness of the other?—True.

---

[13] Alternatively: "If someone should cling to your hypothesis itself, you would dismiss him and would not answer until you had examined whether the consequences that follow from it agree with one another or contradict one another."

Nor is he shorter than Phaedo because Phaedo is Phaedo, but because Phaedo has tallness compared with the shortness of Simmias?—That is so.

d   So then Simmias is called both short and tall, being between the two, presenting his shortness to be overcome by the tallness of one, and his tallness to overcome the shortness of the other. He smilingly added, I seem to be going to talk like a book, but it is as I say. The other agreed.

My purpose is that you may agree with me. Now it seems to me that not only Tallness itself is never willing to be tall and short at the same time, but also that the
e   tallness in us will never admit the short or be overcome, but one of two things happens: either it flees and retreats whenever its opposite, the short, approaches, or it is destroyed by its approach. It is not willing to endure and admit shortness and be other than it was, whereas I admit and endure shortness and still remain the same
103   person and am this short man. But Tallness, being tall, cannot venture to be small. In the same way, the short in us is unwilling to become or to be tall ever, nor does any other of the opposites become or be its opposite while still being what it was; either it goes away or is destroyed when that happens.—I altogether agree, said Cebes.

When he heard this, someone of those present—I have no clear memory of who it was—said: "By the gods, did we not agree earlier in our discussion[14] to the very opposite of what is now being said, namely, that the larger came from the smaller and the smaller from the larger, and that this simply was how opposites came to be, from their opposites, but now I think we are saying that this would never happen?"

On hearing this, Socrates inclined his head towards the speaker and said: "You
b   have bravely reminded us, but you do not understand the difference between what is said now and what was said then, which was that an opposite thing came from an opposite thing; now we say that the opposite itself could never become opposite to itself, neither that in us nor that in nature. Then, my friend, we were talking of things that have opposite qualities and naming these after them, but now we say that these opposites themselves, from the presence of which in them things get their name,
c   never can tolerate the coming to be from one another." At the same time he looked to Cebes and said: "Does anything of what this man says also disturb you?"

Not at the moment, said Cebes, but I do not deny that many things do disturb me.

We are altogether agreed then, he said, that an opposite will never be opposite to itself.—Entirely agreed.

Consider then whether you will agree to this further point. There is something you call hot and something you call cold.—There is.
d   Are they the same as what you call snow and fire?—By Zeus, no.

So the hot is something other than fire, and the cold is something other than snow?—Yes.

You think, I believe, that being snow it will not admit the hot, as we said before, and remain what it was and be both snow and hot, but when the hot approaches it will either retreat before it or be destroyed.—Quite so.

---

[14] The reference is to 70d–71a above.

So fire, as the cold approaches, will either go away or be destroyed; it will never venture to admit coldness and remain what it was, fire and cold.—What you say is true.

It is true then about some of these things that not only the Form itself deserves its own name for all time, but there is something else that is not the Form but has its character whenever it exists. Perhaps I can make my meaning clearer: the Odd must always be given this name we now mention. Is that not so?—Certainly.

Is it the only one of existing things to be called odd?—this is my question —or is there something else than the Odd which one must nevertheless also always call odd, as well as by its own name, because it is such by nature as never to be separated from the Odd? I mean, for example, the number three and many others. Consider three: do you not think that it must always be called both by its own name and by that of the Odd, which is not the same as three? That is the nature of three, and of five, and of half of all the numbers; each of them is odd, but it is not the Odd. Then again, two and four and the whole other column of numbers; each of them, while not being the same as the Even, is always even. Do you not agree?—Of course.

Look now. What I want to make clear is this: not only do those opposites not admit each other, but this is also true of those things which, while not being opposite to each other yet always contain the opposites, and it seems that these do not admit that Form which is opposite to that which is in them; when it approaches them, they either perish or give way. Shall we not say that three will perish or undergo anything before, while remaining three, becoming even?—Certainly, said Cebes.

Yet surely two is not the opposite of three?—Indeed it is not.

It is then not only opposite Forms that do not admit each other's approach, but also some other things that do not admit the onset of opposites.—Very true.

Do you then want us, if we can, to define what these are?—I surely do.

Would they be the things that are compelled by whatever occupies them not only to contain that thing's Form but also always that of some opposite?—How do you mean?

As we were saying just now, you surely know that what the Form of three occupies must not only be three but also odd.—Certainly.

And we say that the opposite Form to the Form that achieves this result could never come to it.—It could not.

Now it is Oddness that has done this?—Yes.

And opposite to this is the Form of the Even?—Yes.

So then the Form of the Even will never come to three?—Never.

Then three has no share in the Even?—Never.

So three is uneven?—Yes.

As for what I said we must define, that is, what kind of things, while not being opposites to something, yet do not admit the opposite, as for example the triad, though it is not the opposite of the Even, yet does not admit it because it always brings along the opposite of the Even, and so the dyad in relation to the Odd, fire to the Cold, and very many other things, see whether you would define it thus: Not only does the opposite not admit its opposite, but that which brings along some opposite into that which it occupies, that which brings this along will not admit the opposite to that which it brings along. Refresh your memory, it is no worse for being heard often. Five does not admit the form of the Even, nor will ten, its double, admit the form of the Odd. The double itself is an opposite of something else, yet it will not admit the form

b   of the Odd. Nor do one-and-a-half and other such fractions admit the form of the Whole, nor will one-third, and so on, if you follow me and agree to this.

I certainly agree, he said, and I follow you.

Tell me again from the beginning, he said, and do not answer in the words of the question, but do as I do. I say that beyond that safe answer, which I spoke of first, I

c   see another safe answer. If you should ask me what, coming into a body, makes it hot, my reply would not be that safe and ignorant one, that it is heat, but our present argument provides a more sophisticated answer, namely, fire, and if you ask me what, on coming into a body, makes it sick, I will not say sickness but fever. Nor, if asked the presence of what in a number makes it odd, I will not say oddness but oneness, and so with other things. See if you now sufficiently understand what I want.—Quite sufficiently.

Answer me then, he said, what is it that, present in a body, makes it living?—A soul.

d   And is that always so?—Of course.

Whatever the soul occupies, it always brings life to it?—It does.

Is there, or is there not, an opposite to life?—There is.

What is it?—Death.

So the soul will never admit the opposite of that which it brings along, as we agree from what has been said?

Most certainly, said Cebes.

Well, and what do we call that which does not admit the form of the even?—The uneven.

What do we call that which will not admit the just and that which will not admit the musical?

e   The unmusical, and the other the unjust.

Very well, what do we call that which does not admit death?

The deathless, he said.

Now the soul does not admit death?—No.

So the soul is deathless?—It is.

Very well, he said. Shall we say that this has been proved, do you think?

Quite adequately proved, Socrates.

Well now, Cebes, he said, if the uneven were of necessity indestructible, surely

106   three would be indestructible?—Of course.

And if the non-hot were of necessity indestructible, then whenever anyone brought heat to snow, the snow would retreat safe and unthawed, for it could not be destroyed, nor again could it stand its ground and admit the heat?—What you say is true.

In the same way, if the non-cold were indestructible, then when some cold attacked the fire, it would neither be quenched nor destroyed, but retreat safely.—Necessarily.

Must then the same not be said of the deathless? If the deathless is also indestructible, it is impossible for the soul to be destroyed when death comes upon   b
it. For it follows from what has been said that it will not admit death or be dead, just as three, we said, will not be even nor will the odd; nor will fire be cold, nor the heat that is in the fire. But, someone might say, what prevents the odd, while not becoming even as has been agreed, from being destroyed, and the even to come to   c
be instead? We could not maintain against the man who said this that it is not destroyed, for the uneven is not indestructible. If we had agreed that it was indestructible we could easily have maintained that at the coming of the even, the odd and the three have gone away and the same would hold for fire and the hot and the other things.—Surely.

And so now, if we are agreed that the deathless is indestructible, the soul, besides   d
being deathless, is indestructible. If not, we need another argument.

—There is no need for one as far as that goes, for hardly anything could resist destruction if the deathless, which lasts forever, would admit destruction.

All would agree, said Socrates, that the god, and the Form of life itself, and anything that is deathless, are never destroyed.—All men would agree, by Zeus, to that, and the gods, I imagine, even more so.

If the deathless is indestructible, then the soul, if it is deathless, would also be   e
indestructible?—Necessarily.

Then when death comes to man, the mortal part of him dies, it seems, but his deathless part goes away safe and indestructible, yielding the place to death.—So it appears.

Therefore the soul, Cebes, he said, is most certainly deathless and indestructible   107
and our souls will really dwell in the underworld.

—I have nothing more to say against that, Socrates, said Cebes, nor can I doubt your arguments. If Simmias here or someone else has something to say, he should not remain silent, for I do not know to what further occasion other than the present he could put it off if he wants to say or to hear anything on these subjects.

Certainly, said Simmias, I myself have no remaining grounds for doubt after what has been said; nevertheless, in view of the importance of our subject and my low   b
opinion of human weakness, I am bound still to have some private misgivings about what we have said.

You are not only right to say this, Simmias, Socrates said, but our first hypotheses require clearer examination, even though we find them convincing. And if you analyze them adequately, you will, I think, follow the argument as far as a man can and if the conclusion is clear, you will look no further.—That is true.

It is right to think then, gentlemen, that if the soul is immortal, it requires our care   c
not only for the time we call our life, but for the sake of all time, and that one is in

terrible danger if one does not give it that care. If death were escape from everything, it would be a great boon to the wicked to get rid of the body and of their wickedness

d together with their soul. But now that the soul appears to be immortal, there is no escape from evil or salvation for it except by becoming as good and wise as possible, for the soul goes to the underworld possessing nothing but its education and upbringing, which are said to bring the greatest benefit or harm to the dead right at the beginning of the journey yonder.

We are told that when each person dies, the guardian spirit who was allotted to

e him in life proceeds to lead him to a certain place, whence those who have been gathered together there must, after being judged, proceed to the underworld with the guide who has been appointed to lead them thither from here. Having there undergone what they must and stayed there the appointed time, they are led back

108 here by another guide after long periods of time. The journey is not as Aeschylus' Telephus[15] describes it. He says that only one single path leads to Hades, but I think it is neither one nor simple, for then there would be no need of guides; one could not make any mistake if there were but one path. As it is, it is likely to have many forks and crossroads; and I base this judgment on the sacred rites and customs here.

The well-ordered and wise soul follows the guide and is not without familiarity with its surroundings, but the soul that is passionately attached to the body, as I said before, hovers around it and the visible world for a long time, struggling and

b suffering much until it is led away by force and with difficulty by its appointed spirit. When the impure soul which has performed some impure deed joins the others after being involved in unjust killings, or committed other crimes which are akin to these and are actions of souls of this kind, everybody shuns it and turns away, unwilling to be its fellow traveller or its guide; such a soul wanders alone completely at a loss

c until a certain time arrives and it is forcibly led to its proper dwelling place. On the other hand, the soul that has led a pure and moderate life finds fellow travellers and gods to guide it, and each of them dwells in a place suited to it.

There are many strange places upon the earth, and the earth itself is not such as those who are used to discourse upon it believe it to be in nature or size, as someone has convinced me.

Simmias said: "What do you mean, Socrates? I have myself heard many things

d said about the earth, but certainly not the things that convince you. I should be glad to hear them."

Indeed, Simmias, I do not think it requires the skill of Glaucus[16] to tell you what they are, but to prove them true requires more than that skill, and I should perhaps not be able to do so. Also, even if I had the knowledge, my remaining time would not be long enough to tell the tale. However, nothing prevents my telling you what I

e am convinced is the shape of the earth and what its regions are.

Even that is sufficient, said Simmias.

---

[15] The *Telephus* of Aeschylus is not extant.
[16] A proverbial expression whose origin is obscure.

Well then, he said, the first thing of which I am convinced is that if the earth is a sphere in the middle of the heavens, it has no need of air or any other force to prevent it from falling. The homogeneous nature of the heavens on all sides and the earth's own equipoise are sufficient to hold it, for an object balanced in the middle of something homogeneous will have no tendency to incline more in any direction than any other but will remain unmoved. This, he said, is the first point of which I am persuaded. 109

And rightly so, said Simmias.

Further, the earth is very large, and we live around the sea in a small portion of it between Phasis and the pillars of Heracles, like ants or frogs around a swamp; many other peoples live in many such parts of it. Everywhere about the earth there are numerous hollows of many kinds and shapes and sizes into which the water and the mist and the air have gathered. The earth itself is pure and lies in the pure sky where the stars are situated, which the majority of those who discourse on these subjects call the ether. The water and mist and air are the sediment of the ether and they always flow into the hollows of the earth. We, who dwell in the hollows of it, are unaware of this and we think that we live above, on the surface of the earth. It is as if someone who lived deep down in the middle of the ocean thought he was living on its surface. Seeing the sun and the other heavenly bodies through the water, he would think the sea to be the sky; because he is slow and weak, he has never reached the surface of the sea or risen with his head above the water or come out of the sea to our region here, nor seen how much purer and more beautiful it is than his own region, nor has he ever heard of it from anyone who has seen it. b c d

Our experience is the same: living in a certain hollow of the earth, we believe that we live upon its surface; the air we call the heavens, as if the stars made their way through it; this too is the same: because of our weakness and slowness we are not able to make our way to the upper limit of the air; if anyone got to this upper limit, if anyone came to it or reached it on wings and his head rose above it, then just as fish on rising from the sea see things in our region, he would see things there and, if his nature could endure to contemplate them, he would know that there is the true heaven, the true light and the true earth, for the earth here, these stones and the whole region, are spoiled and eaten away, just as things in the sea are by the salt water. e 110

Nothing worth mentioning grows in the sea, nothing, one might say, is fully developed; there are caves and sand and endless slime and mud wherever there is earth—not comparable in any way with the beauties of our region. So those things above are in their turn far superior to the things we know. Indeed, if this is the moment to tell a tale, Simmias, it is worth hearing about the nature of things on the surface of the earth under the heavens. b

At any rate, Socrates, said Simmias, we should be glad to hear this story.

Well then, my friend, in the first place it is said that the earth, looked at from above, looks like those spherical balls made up of twelve pieces of leather; it is multi-colored, and of these colors those used by our painters give us an indication; up there the whole earth has these colors, but much brighter and purer than these; one c part is sea-green and of marvelous beauty, another is golden, another is white, whiter than chalk or snow; the earth is composed also of the other colors, more numerous and beautiful than any we have seen. The very hollows of the earth, full of water and air, gleaming among the variety of other colors, present a color of their own so that

d the whole is seen as a continuum of variegated colors. On the surface of the earth the plants grow with corresponding beauty, the trees and the flowers and the fruits, and so with the hills and the stones, more beautiful in their smoothness and transparency and color. Our precious stones here are but fragments, our cornelians, jaspers,

e emeralds and the rest. All stones there are of that kind, and even more beautiful. The reason is that there they are pure, not eaten away or spoiled by decay and brine, or corroded by the water and air which have flowed into the hollows here and bring ugliness and disease upon earth, stones, the other animals and plants. The earth itself

111 is adorned with all these things, and also with gold and silver and other metals. These stand out, being numerous and massive and occurring everywhere, so that the earth is a sight for the blessed. There are many other living creatures upon the earth, and also men, some living inland, others at the edge of the air, as we live on the edge of the sea, others again live on islands surrounded by air close to the mainland. In a word, what water and the sea are to us, the air is to them and the ether is to them what

b the air is to us. The climate is such that they are without disease, and they live much longer than people do here; their eyesight, hearing and intelligence and all such are as superior to ours as air is superior to water and ether to air in purity; they have groves and temples dedicated to the gods, in which the gods really dwell, and they communicate with them by speech and prophecy and by the sight of them; they see

c the sun and moon and stars as they are, and in other ways their happiness is in accord with this.

This then is the nature of the earth as a whole and of its surroundings; around the whole of it there are many regions in the hollows; some are deeper and more open than that in which we live; others are deeper and have a narrower opening than ours, and there are some that have less depth and more width. All these are connected with

d each other below the surface of the earth in many places by narrow and broader channels, and thus have outlets through which much water flows from one to another as into mixing bowls; huge rivers of both hot and cold water thus flow beneath the earth eternally, much fire and large rivers of fire, and many of wet mud, both more pure and more muddy, such as those flowing in advance of the lava and the stream

e of lava itself in Sicily. These streams then fill up every and all regions as the flow reaches each, and all these places move up and down with the oscillating movement of the earth. The natural cause of the oscillation is as follows: one of the hollows of the earth, which is also the biggest, pierces through the whole earth; it is that which

112 Homer mentioned when he said: "Far down where is the deepest pit below the earth . . . ," [17] and which he elsewhere, and many other poets, call Tartarus; into this chasm all the rivers flow together, and again flow out of it, and each river is affected by the nature of the land through which it flows. The reason for their flowing into and out

[17] *Iliad* viii.14; cf. viii.481.

of Tartarus is that this water has no bottom or solid base but it oscillates up and down   b
in waves, and the air and wind about it do the same, for they follow it when it flows
to this or that part of the earth. Just as when people breathe, the flow of air goes in
and out, so here the air oscillates with the water and creates terrible winds as it goes
in and out. Whenever the water retreats to what we call the lower part of the earth,
it flows into those parts and fills them up as if the water were pumped in; when it   c
leaves that part for this, it fills these parts again, and the parts filled flow through the
channels and through the earth and in each case arrive at the places to which
the channels lead and create seas and marshes and rivers and springs. From there the
waters flow under the earth again, some flowing around larger and more numerous
regions, some round smaller and shallower ones, then flow back into Tartarus, some   d
at a point much lower than where they issued forth, others only a little way, but all
of them at a lower point, some of them at the opposite side of the chasm, some on
the same side; some flow in a wide circle round the earth once or many times like
snakes, then go as far down as possible, then go back into the chasm of Tartarus.
From each side it is possible to flow down as far as the center, but not beyond, for
this part that faces the river flow from either side is steep.   e

There are many other large rivers of all kinds, and among these there are four of
note; the biggest which flows on the outside (of the earth) in a circle is called
Oceanus; opposite it and flowing in the opposite direction is the Acheron; it flows
through many other deserted regions and further underground makes its way to the   113
Acherusian lake to which the souls of the majority come after death and, after
remaining there for a certain appointed time, longer for some, shorter for others, they
are sent back to birth as living creatures. The third river issues between the first two,
and close to its source it falls into a region burning with much fire and makes a lake
larger than our sea, boiling with water and mud. From there it goes in a circle, foul   b
and muddy, and winding on its way it comes, among other places, to the edge of the
Acherusian lake but does not mingle with its waters; then, coiling many times
underground it flows lower down into Tartarus; this is called the Pyriphlegethon, and
its lava streams throw off fragments of it in various parts of the earth. Opposite this
the fourth river issues forth, which is called Stygion, and it is said to flow first into   c
a terrible and wild region, all of it blue-gray in color, and the lake that this river
forms by flowing into it is called the Styx. As its waters fall into the lake they acquire
dread powers; then diving below and winding round it flows in the opposite direction
from the Pyriphlegethon and into the opposite side of the Acherusian lake; its waters
do not mingle with any other; it too flows in a circle and into Tartarus opposite the
Pyriphlegethon. The name of that fourth river, the poets tell us, is Cocytus.[18]

Such is the nature of these things. When the dead arrive at the place to which each
has been led by his guardian spirit, they are first judged as to whether they have led   d
a good and pious life. Those who have lived an average life make their way to the
Acheron and embark upon such vessels as there are for them and proceed to the lake.
There they dwell and are purified by penalties for any wrongdoing they may have

[18] For these features of the underworld, see *Odyssey* x.511 ff, xi.157.

e   committed; they are also suitably rewarded for their good deeds as each deserves. Those who are deemed incurable because of the enormity of their crimes, having committed many great sacrileges or wicked and unlawful murders and other such wrongs—their fitting fate is to be hurled into Tartarus never to emerge from it. Those who are deemed to have committed great but curable crimes, such as doing violence to their father or mother in a fit of temper but who have felt remorse for the rest of their lives, or who have killed someone in a similar manner, these must of necessity

114   be thrown into Tartarus, but a year later the current throws them out, those who are guilty of murder by way of Cocytus, and those who have done violence to their parents by way of the Pyriphlegethon. After they have been carried along to the Acherusian lake, they cry out and shout, some for those they have killed, others for those they have maltreated, and calling them they then pray to them and beg them to allow them to step out into the lake and to receive them. If they persuade them, they

b   do step out and their punishment comes to an end; if they do not, they are taken back into Tartarus and from there into the rivers, and this does not stop until they have persuaded those they have wronged, for this is the punishment which the judges imposed on them.

    Those who are deemed to have lived an extremely pious life are freed and

c   released from the regions of the earth as from a prison; they make their way up to a pure dwelling place and live on the surface of the earth. Those who have purified themselves sufficiently by philosophy live in the future altogether without a body; they make their way to even more beautiful dwelling places which it is hard to describe clearly, nor do we now have the time to do so. Because of the things we have enunciated, Simmias, one must make every effort to share in virtue and wisdom in one's life, for the reward is beautiful and the hope is great.

    No sensible man would insist that these things are as I have described them, but

d   I think it is fitting for a man to risk the belief—for the risk is a noble one—that this, or something like this, is true about our souls and their dwelling places, since the soul is evidently immortal, and a man should repeat this to himself as if it were an incantation, which is why I have been prolonging my tale. That is the reason why a man should be of good cheer about his own soul, if during life he has ignored the pleasures of the body and its ornamentation as of no concern to him and doing him

e   more harm than good, but has seriously concerned himself with the pleasures of learning, and adorned his soul not with alien but with its own ornaments, namely, moderation, righteousness, courage, freedom and truth, and in that state awaits his

115   journey to the underworld.

    Now you, Simmias, Cebes and the rest of you, Socrates continued, will each take that journey at some other time but my fated day calls me now, as a tragic character might say, and it is about time for me to have my bath, for I think it better to have it before I drink the poison and save the women the trouble of washing the corpse.

    When Socrates had said this Crito spoke. Very well, Socrates, what are your

b   instructions to me and the others about your children or anything else? What can we do that would please you most?—Nothing new, Crito, said Socrates, but what I am

always saying, that you will please me and mine and yourselves by taking good care
of your own selves in whatever you do, even if you do not agree with me now, but
if you neglect your own selves, and are unwilling to live following the tracks, as it
were, of what we have said now and on previous occasions, you will achieve nothing
even if you strongly agree with me at this moment.

We shall be eager to follow your advice, said Crito, but how shall we bury you?

In any way you like, said Socrates, if you can catch me and I do not escape you.
And laughing quietly, looking at us, he said: I do not convince Crito that I am this
Socrates talking to you here and ordering all I say, but he thinks that I am the thing
which he will soon be looking at as a corpse, and so he asks how he shall bury me.
I have been saying for some time and at some length that after I have drunk the
poison I shall no longer be with you but will leave you to go and enjoy some good
fortunes of the blessed, but it seems that I have said all this to him in vain in an
attempt to reassure you and myself too. Give a pledge to Crito on my behalf, he said,
the opposite pledge to that he gave the jury. He pledged that I would stay, you must
pledge that I will not stay after I die, but that I shall go away, so that Crito will bear
it more easily when he sees my body being burned or buried and will not be angry
on my behalf, as if I were suffering terribly, and so that he should not say at the
funeral that he is laying out, or carrying out, or burying Socrates. For know you well,
my dear Crito, that to express oneself badly is not only faulty as far as the language
goes, but does some harm to the soul. You must be of good cheer, and say you are
burying my body, and bury it in any way you like and think most customary.

After saying this he got up and went to another room to take his bath, and Crito
followed him and he told us to wait for him. So we stayed, talking among ourselves,
questioning what had been said, and then again talking of the great misfortune that
had befallen us. We all felt as if we had lost a father and would be orphaned for the
rest of our lives. When he had washed, his children were brought to him—two of his
sons were small and one was older—and the women of his household came to him.
He spoke to them before Crito and gave them what instructions he wanted. Then he
sent the women and children away, and he himself joined us. It was now close to
sunset, for he had stayed inside for some time. He came and sat down after his bath
and conversed for a short while, when the officer of the Eleven came and stood by
him and said: "I shall not reproach you as I do the others, Socrates. They are angry
with me and curse me when obeying the orders of my superiors, I tell them to drink
the poison. During the time you have been here I have come to know you in other
ways as the noblest, the gentlest and the best man who has ever come here. So now
too I know that you will not make trouble for me; you know who is responsible and
you will direct your anger against them. You know what message I bring. Fare you
well, and try to endure what you must as easily as possible." The officer was weeping
as he turned away and went out. Socrates looked up at him and said: "Fare you well
also, we shall do as you bid us." And turning to us he said: "How pleasant the man
is! During the whole time I have been here he has come in and conversed with me

from time to time, a most agreeable man. And how genuinely he now weeps for me. Come, Crito, let us obey him. Let someone bring the poison if it is ready; if not, let the man prepare it."

e   But Socrates, said Crito, I think the sun still shines upon the hills and has not yet set. I know that others drink the poison quite a long time after they have received the order, eating and drinking quite a bit, and some of them enjoy intimacy with their loved ones. Do not hurry; there is still some time.

It is natural, Crito, for them to do so, said Socrates, for they think they derive
117   some benefit from doing this, but it is not fitting for me. I do not expect any benefit from drinking the poison a little later, except to become ridiculous in my own eyes for clinging to life, and be sparing of it when there is none left. So do as I ask and do not refuse me.

Hearing this, Crito nodded to the slave who was standing near him; the slave went out and after a time came back with the man who was to administer the poison, carrying it made ready in a cup. When Socrates saw him he said: "Well, my good man, you are an expert in this, what must one do?"—"Just drink it and walk around
b   until your legs feel heavy, and then lie down and it will act of itself." And he offered the cup to Socrates who took it quite cheerfully, Echecrates, without a tremor or any change of feature or color, but looking at the man from under his eyebrows as was his wont, asked: "What do you say about pouring a libation from this drink? It is allowed?"—"We only mix as much as we believe will suffice," said the man.

c   I understand, Socrates said, but one is allowed, indeed one must, utter a prayer to the gods that the journey from here to yonder may be fortunate. This is my prayer and may it be so.

And while he was saying this, he was holding the cup, and then drained it calmly and easily. Most of us had been able to hold back our tears reasonably well up till then, but when we saw him drinking it and after he drank it, we could hold them back no longer; my own tears came in floods against my will. So I covered my face. I was weeping for myself, not for him—for my misfortune in being deprived of such a
d   comrade. Even before me, Crito was unable to restrain his tears and got up. Apollodorus had not ceased from weeping before, and at this moment his noisy tears and anger made everybody present break down, except Socrates. "What is this," he said, "you strange fellows. It is mainly for this reason that I sent the women away,
e   to avoid such unseemliness, for I am told one should die in good omened silence. So keep quiet and control yourselves."

His words made us ashamed, and we checked our tears. He walked around, and when he said his legs were heavy he lay on his back as he had been told to do, and the man who had given him the poison touched his body, and after a while tested his feet and legs, pressed hard upon his foot and asked him if he felt this, and Socrates
118   said no. Then he pressed his calves, and made his way up his body and showed us that it was cold and stiff. He felt it himself and said that when the cold reached his
118a   heart he would be gone. As his belly was getting cold Socrates uncovered his head— he had covered it—and said—these were his last words—"Crito, we owe a cock to

Asclepius;[19] make this offering to him and do not forget,"—"It shall be done," said Crito, "tell us if there is anything else." But there was no answer. Shortly afterwards Socrates made a movement; the man uncovered him and his eyes were fixed. Seeing this Crito closed his mouth and his eyes.

Such was the end of our comrade, Echecrates, a man who, we would say, was of all those we have known the best, and also the wisest and the most upright.

---

[19] A cock was sacrificed to Asclepius by the sick people who slept in his temples, hoping for a cure. Socrates apparently means that death is a cure for the ills of life.

3

GORGIAS

Gorgias was a famous teacher of oratory and the author of oratorical display pieces. He had served his native Leontini in Greek Sicily on embassies, including one to Athens in 427 B.C., *when his artistically elaborate prose style made a great and lasting impression. We loosely consider him a 'sophist', like the intellectuals whom Plato gathers together at Callias' house in* Protagoras, *but Plato pointedly reports Gorgias' teaching as restricted to the art of public speaking: he did not offer to instruct young people in 'virtue'—the qualities, whatever they were, that made a good person overall and a good citizen. Nonetheless, as Plato also makes clear, he praised so highly the speaking abilities that his own teaching imparted that one could pardon ambitious young Athenians like Callicles if they thought that, by learning oratory from him, they would know everything a man needs in order to secure for himself the best life possible. And, as we learn from* Meno, *he did have striking things to say about the nature of, and differences between, virtue in men and women, old persons and young, and so on. So in the end not much separates him from the other itinerant teachers that, with him, we classify as 'sophists'.*

Socrates begins by skeptically seeking clarification from the elderly, respected Gorgias about the nature and power of his 'craft'—the skill at persuading people massed in assemblies and juries about what is good and what is right. Gorgias is trapped in a contradiction when he admits that the true, skilled orator must know (and not merely speak persuasively on) his most particular subjects—right and wrong, justice and injustice in the lawcourts. When Gorgias bows out, a fellow rhetorician takes over his side of the argument—the young and rambunctious Polus, a real person. His name means 'colt'—almost too good to be true! Polus is intoxicated with the thought that rhetoric gives the power to do what one pleases, even injustice if that suits the situation. Against him, Socrates insists that in fact it is better to suffer injustice than to do it—and, unable to deny this consistently, Polus in his turn falls to Socrates' dialectic. In the remainder of the dialogue—more than half—Socrates contends with Callicles, apparently also a real person, though we hear nothing about him outside this dialogue. The discussion develops into a contentious and sometimes bitter dispute about which way of life is best—the selfish, domineering, pleasure-seeking one that Callicles associates with his own unbounded admiration for rhetorical skill, or the philosophical life that Socrates champions, committed to the objective existence of justice and the other virtues and devoted to learning about and living in accordance with them. Socrates struggles and struggles to undermine Callicles' views. He tries to bring Callicles to admit that some of his own deepest convictions commit him to agreeing with Socrates: Socrates thinks he knows better than Callicles what Callicles really believes. In giving vent to strongly worded assertions of his own moral commitments, he seems to adopt a conception of 'irrational' desires like that of Republic IV, *incompatible with the views he works with in the other 'Socratic' dialogues. Callicles, though personally well disposed, is equally*

*vehement and contemptuous in rejecting Socrates' outlook—he refuses to succumb to
the toils of Socratic logic. If the methods of argument Socrates employs here produce
at best an uneasy standoff, the different methods of* Republic *II–IX may seem to
Plato to offer a resolution.*

Gorgias *is so long, complex, and intellectually ambitious that it strains the confines of a simple 'Socratic' dialogue—a portrait of Socrates carrying out moral
inquiries by his customary method of questioning others and examining their opinions. Here Socrates is on the verge of becoming the take-charge, independent philosophical theorist that he is in such dialogues as* Phaedo *and* Republic. *Like those two
works,* Gorgias *concludes with an eschatological myth, affirming the soul's survival
after our death and its punishment or reward in the afterlife for a life lived unjustly
or the reverse.*

In Phaedrus *Socrates makes connected but different arguments about the nature
and value of rhetoric. Whereas in* Gorgias *Socrates paints an unrelievedly negative
picture of the practice of rhetoric, in* Phaedrus *he finds legitimate uses for it, so long
as it is kept properly subordinate to philosophy.*

J.M.C.

447   CALLICLES: This, they say, is how you're supposed to do your part in a war or a
battle, Socrates.

SOCRATES: Oh? Did we "arrive when the feast was over," as the saying goes?
Are we late?[1]

CALLICLES: Yes, and a very urbane one it was! Gorgias gave us an admirable,
varied presentation[2] just a short while ago.

SOCRATES: But that's Chaerephon's fault, Callicles. He kept us loitering about
in the marketplace.

b   CHAEREPHON: That's no problem, Socrates. I'll make up for it, too. Gorgias is
a friend of mine, so he'll give us a presentation—now, if you see fit, or else some
other time, if you like.

Translated by Donald J. Zeyl. Text: E. R. Dodds, Oxford (1959).

[1] The setting of the dialogue is not clear. We may suppose that the conversation takes place outside a
    public building in Athens such as the gymnasium (see the reference to persons "inside" at 447c
    and 455c).
        In the exchange that opens the dialogue, Callicles and Socrates are evidently alluding to a Greek
    saying, unknown to us, the equivalent of the English phrase, "first at a feast, last at a fray."
    Cf. Shakespeare, *Henry IV, Part 1*, Act 4, Sc. 2.

[2] Gk. *epideiknusthai*. An *epideixis* was a lecture regularly given by sophists as a public display of their
    oratorical prowess.

CALLICLES: What's this, Chaerephon? Is Socrates eager to hear Gorgias?

CHAEREPHON: Yes. That's the very thing we're here for.

CALLICLES: Well then, come to my house any time you like. Gorgias is staying with me and will give you a presentation there.

SOCRATES: Very good, Callicles. But would he be willing to have a discussion with us? I'd like to find out from the man what his craft can accomplish, and what it   c
is that he both makes claims about and teaches. As for the other thing, the presentation, let him put that on another time, as you suggest.

CALLICLES: There's nothing like asking him, Socrates. This was, in fact, one part of his presentation. Just now he invited those inside to ask him any question they liked, and he said that he'd answer them all.

SOCRATES: An excellent idea. Ask him, Chaerephon.

CHAEREPHON: Ask him what?

SOCRATES: What he is.   d

CHAEREPHON: What do you mean?

SOCRATES: Well, if he were a maker of shoes, he'd answer that he was a cobbler, wouldn't he? Or don't you see what I mean?

CHAEREPHON: I do. I'll ask him. Tell me, Gorgias, is Callicles right in saying that you make claims about answering any question anyone might put to you?

GORGIAS: He is, Chaerephon. In fact I just now made that very claim, and I say   448
that no one has asked me anything new in many a year.

CHAEREPHON: In that case I'm sure you'll answer this one quite easily, Gorgias.

GORGIAS: Here's your chance to try me, Chaerephon.

POLUS: By Zeus, Chaerephon! Try me, if you like! I think Gorgias is quite worn out. He's only just now finished a long discourse.

CHAEREPHON: Really, Polus? Do you think you'd give more admirable answers than Gorgias?

POLUS: What does it matter, as long as they're good enough for you?   b

CHAEREPHON: Nothing at all! You answer us then, since that's what you want.

POLUS: Ask your questions.

CHAEREPHON: I will. Suppose that Gorgias were knowledgeable in his brother Herodicus' craft. What would be the right name for us to call him by then? Isn't it the same one as his brother's?

POLUS: Yes, it is.

CHAEREPHON: So we'd be right in saying that he's a doctor?

POLUS: Yes.

CHAEREPHON: And if he were experienced in the craft of Aristophon the son of Aglaophon or his brother, what would be the correct thing to call him?

POLUS: A painter, obviously.

CHAEREPHON: Now then, since he's knowledgeable in a craft, what is it, and   c
what would be the correct thing to call him?

POLUS: Many among men are the crafts experientially devised by experience, Chaerephon. Yes, it is experience that causes our times to march along the way of craft, whereas inexperience causes them to march along the way of chance. Of these various crafts various men partake in various ways, the best men partaking of the best of them. Our Gorgias is indeed in this group; he partakes of the most admirable of the crafts.

d   SOCRATES: Polus certainly appears to have prepared himself admirably for giving speeches, Gorgias. But he's not doing what he promised Chaerephon.

GORGIAS: How exactly isn't he, Socrates?

SOCRATES: He hardly seems to me to be answering the question.

GORGIAS: Why don't you question him then, if you like?

SOCRATES: No, I won't, not as long as you yourself may want to answer. I'd much rather ask you. It's clear to me, especially from what he has said, that Polus has devoted himself more to what is called oratory than to discussion.

e   POLUS: Why do you say that, Socrates?

SOCRATES: Because, Polus, when Chaerephon asks you what craft Gorgias is knowledgeable in, you sing its praises as though someone were discrediting it. But you haven't answered what it is.

POLUS: Didn't I answer that it was the most admirable one?

SOCRATES: Very much so. No one, however, asked you what Gorgias' craft is
449   like, but what craft it is, and what one ought to call Gorgias. So, just as when Chaerephon put his earlier questions to you and you answered him in such an admirably brief way, tell us now in that way, too, what his craft is, and what we're supposed to call Gorgias. Or rather, Gorgias, why don't you tell us yourself what the craft you're knowledgeable in is, and hence what we're supposed to call you?

GORGIAS: It's oratory, Socrates.

SOCRATES: So we're supposed to call you an orator?

GORGIAS: Yes, and a good one, Socrates, if you really want to call me "what I boast myself to be," as Homer puts it.[3]

SOCRATES: Of course I do.

GORGIAS: Call me that then.

b   S0CRATES: Aren't we to say that you're capable of making others orators too?

GORGIAS: That's exactly the claim I make. Not only here, but elsewhere, too.

SOCRATES: Well now, Gorgias, would you be willing to complete the discussion in the way we're having it right now, that of alternately asking questions and answering them, and to put aside for another time this long style of speechmaking like the one Polus began with? Please don't go back on your promise, but be willing to give a brief answer to what you're asked.

GORGIAS: There are some answers, Socrates, that must be given by way of long
c   speeches. Even so, I'll try to be as brief as possible. This, too, in fact, is one of my claims. There's no one who can say the same things more briefly than I.

SOCRATES: That's what we need, Gorgias! Do give me a presentation of this very thing, the short style of speech, and leave the long style for some other time.

GORGIAS: Very well, I'll do that. You'll say you've never heard anyone make shorter speeches.

---

[3] *Iliad* vi.211.

SOCRATES: Come then. You claim to be knowledgeable in the craft of oratory and to be able to make someone else an orator, too. With which of the things there are   d
is oratory concerned? Weaving, for example, is concerned with the production of clothes, isn't it?

GORGIAS: Yes.

SOCRATES: And so, too, music is concerned with the composition of tunes?

GORGIAS: Yes.

SOCRATES: By Hera, Gorgias, I do like your answers. They couldn't be shorter!

GORGIAS: Yes, Socrates, I daresay I'm doing it quite nicely.

SOCRATES: And so you are. Come and answer me then that way about oratory, too. About which, of the things there are, is *it* knowledge?

GORGIAS: About speeches.   e

SOCRATES: What sort of speeches, Gorgias? Those that explain how sick people should be treated to get well?

GORGIAS: No.

SOCRATES: So oratory isn't concerned with all speeches.

GORGIAS: Oh, no.

SOCRATES: But it does make people capable of speaking.

GORGIAS: Yes.

SOCRATES: And also to be wise in what they're speaking about?

GORGIAS: Of course.

SOCRATES: Now does the medical craft, the one we were talking about just now,   450
make people able both to have wisdom about and to speak about the sick?

GORGIAS: Necessarily.

SOCRATES: This craft, then, is evidently concerned with speeches too.

GORGIAS: Yes.

SOCRATES: Speeches about diseases, that is?

GORGIAS: Exactly.

SOCRATES: Isn't physical training also concerned with speeches, speeches about good and bad physical condition?

GORGIAS: Yes, it is.

SOCRATES: In fact, Gorgias, the same is true of the other crafts, too. Each of them   b
is concerned with those speeches that are about the object of the particular craft.

GORGIAS: Apparently.

SOCRATES: Then why don't you call the other crafts oratory, since you call any craft whatever that's concerned with speeches oratory? They're concerned with speeches, too!

GORGIAS: The reason, Socrates, is that in the case of the other crafts the knowledge consists almost completely in working with your hands and activities of that sort. In the case of oratory, on the other hand, there isn't any such manual work. Its activity and influence depend entirely on speeches. That's the reason I consider the   c
craft of oratory to be concerned with speeches. And I say that I'm right about this.

SOCRATES: Im not sure I understand what sort of craft you want to call it. I'll soon know more clearly. Tell me this. There are crafts for us to practice, aren't there?

GORGIAS: Yes.

SOCRATES: Of all the crafts there are, I take it that there are those that consist for the most part of making things and that call for little speech, and some that call for none at all, ones whose task could be done even silently. Take painting, for instance, or sculpture, or many others. When you say that oratory has nothing to do with other crafts, it's crafts of this sort I think you're referring to. Or aren't you?

d

GORGIAS: Yes, Socrates. You take my meaning very well.

SOCRATES: And then there are other crafts, the ones that perform their whole task by means of speeches and that call for practically no physical work besides, or very little of it. Take arithmetic or computation or geometry, even checkers and many other crafts. Some of these involve speeches to just about the same degree as they do activity, while many involve speeches more. All their activity and influence depend entirely on speeches. I think you mean that oratory is a craft of this sort.

e

GORGIAS: True.

SOCRATES: But you certainly don't want to call any of *these* crafts oratory, do you, even though, as you phrase it, oratory is the craft that exercises its influence through speech. Somebody might take you up, if he wanted to make a fuss in argument, and say, "So you're saying that arithmetic is oratory, are you, Gorgias?" I'm sure, however, that you're not saying that either arithmetic or geometry is oratory.

451

GORGIAS: Yes, you're quite correct, Socrates. You take my meaning rightly.

SOCRATES: Come on, then. Please complete your answer in the terms of my question. Since oratory is one of those crafts which mostly uses speech, and since there are also others of that sort, try to say *what* it is that oratory, which exercises its influence through speeches, is about. Imagine someone asking me about any of the crafts I mentioned just now, "Socrates, what is the craft of arithmetic?" I'd tell him, just as you told me, that it's one of those that exercise their influence by means of speech. And if he continued, "What are they crafts about?" I'd say that they're about even and odd, however many of each there might be. If he then asked, "What is the craft you call computation?" I'd say that this one, too, is one of those that exercise their influence entirely by speech. And if he then continued, "What is it about?" I'd answer in the style of those who draw up motions in the Assembly that in other respects computation is like arithmetic—for it's about the same thing, even and odd—yet it differs from arithmetic insofar as computation examines the quantity of odd and even, both in relation to themselves and in relation to each other. And if someone asked about astronomy and I replied that it, too, exercises its influence by means of speech, then if he asked, "What are the speeches of astronomy about, Socrates?" I'd say that they're about the motions of the stars, the sun and the moon, and their relative velocities.

b

c

GORGIAS: And you'd be quite right to say so, Socrates.

d

SOCRATES: Come, Gorgias, you take your turn. For oratory is in fact one of those crafts that carry out and exercise their influence entirely by speech, isn't it?

GORGIAS: That's right.

SOCRATES: Tell us then: what are they crafts about? Of the things there are, which is the one that these speeches used by oratory are concerned with?

GORGIAS: The greatest of human concerns, Socrates, and the best.

SOCRATES: But that statement, too, is debatable, Gorgias. It isn't at all clear yet, either. I'm sure that you've heard people at drinking parties singing that song in which they count out as they sing that "to enjoy good health is the best thing; second is to have turned out good looking; and third"—so the writer of the song puts it—"is to be honestly rich."

GORGIAS: Yes, I've heard it. Why do you mention it?

SOCRATES: Suppose that the producers of the things the songwriter praised were here with you right now: a doctor, a physical trainer, and a financial expert. Support that first the doctor said, "Socrates, Gorgias is telling you a lie. It isn't his craft that is concerned with the greatest good for humankind, but mine." If I then asked him, "What are you, to say that?" I suppose he'd say that he's a doctor. "What's this you're saying? Is the product of your craft really the greatest good?" "Of course, Socrates," I suppose he'd say, "seeing that its product is health. What greater good for humankind is there than health?" And suppose that next in his turn the trainer said, "I too would be amazed, Socrates, if Gorgias could present you with a greater good derived from his craft than the one I could provide from mine." I'd ask this man, too, "What are you, sir, and what's your product?" "I'm a physical trainer," he'd say, "and my product is making people physically good-looking and strong." And following the trainer the financial expert would say, I'm sure with an air of con- siderable scorn for all, "Do consider, Socrates, whether you know of any good, Gorgias' or anyone else's, that's a greater good than wealth." We'd say to him, "Really? Is that what you produce?" He'd say yes. "As what?" "As a financial expert." "Well," we'll say, "is wealth in your judgment the greatest good for humankind?" "Of course," he'll say. "Ah, but Gorgias here disputes that. He claims that his craft is the source of a good that's greater than yours," we'd say. And it's obvious what question he'd ask next. "And what is this good, please? Let Gorgias answer me that!" So come on, Gorgias. Consider yourself questioned by both these men and myself, and give us your answer. What is this thing that you claim is the greatest good for humankind, a thing you claim to be a producer of?

GORGIAS: The thing that is in actual fact the greatest good, Socrates. It is the source of freedom for humankind itself and at the same time it is for each person the source of rule over others in one's own city.

SOCRATES: And what is this thing you're referring to?

GORGIAS: I'm referring to the ability to persuade by speeches judges in a law court, councillors in a council meeting, and assemblymen in an assembly or in any other political gathering that might take place. In point of fact, with this ability you'll have the doctor for your slave, and the physical trainer, too. As for this financial expert of yours, he'll turn out to be making more money for somebody else instead of himself; for you, in fact, if you've got the ability to speak and to persuade the crowds.

SOCRATES: *Now* I think you've come closest to making clear what craft you take oratory to be, Gorgias. If I follow you at all, you're saying that oratory is a pro- ducer of persuasion. Its whole business comes to that, and that's the long and short of it. Or can you mention anything else oratory can do besides instilling persuasion in the souls of an audience?

GORGIAS: None at all, Socrates. I think you're defining it quite adequately. That is indeed the long and short of it.

b   SOCRATES: Listen then, Gorgias. You should know that I'm convinced I'm one of those people who in a discussion with someone else really want to have knowledge of the subject the discussion's about. And I consider you one of them, too.

GORGIAS: Well, what's the point, Socrates?

SOCRATES: Let me tell you now. You can know for sure that I don't know what this persuasion derived from oratory that you're talking about is, or what subjects it's persuasion about. Even though I do have my suspicions about which persuasion I

c   think you mean and what it's about, I'll still ask you just the same what you say this persuasion produced by oratory is, and what it's about. And why, when I have my suspicions, do I ask you and refrain from expressing them myself? It's not you I'm after, it's our discussion, to have it proceed in such a way as to make the thing we're talking about most clear to us. Consider, then, whether you think I'm being fair in resuming my questions to you. Suppose I were to ask you which of the painters Zeuxis is. If you told me that he's the one who paints pictures, wouldn't it be fair for me to ask, "Of what sort of pictures is he the painter, and where?"

GORGIAS: Yes, it would.

d   SOCRATES: And isn't the reason for this the fact that there are other painters, too, who paint many other pictures?

GORGIAS: Yes.

SOCRATES: But if no one besides Zeuxis were a painter, your answer would have been a good one?

GORGIAS: Of course.

SOCRATES: Come then, and tell me about oratory. Do you think that oratory alone instills persuasion, or do other crafts do so too? This is the sort of thing I mean: Does a person who teaches some subject or other persuade people about what he's teaching, or not?

GORGIAS: He certainly does, Socrates. He persuades most of all.

e   SOCRATES: Let's talk once more about the same crafts we were talking about just now. Doesn't arithmetic or the arithmetician teach us everything that pertains to number?

GORGIAS: Yes, he does.

SOCRATES: And he also persuades?

GORGIAS: Yes.

SOCRATES: So arithmetic is also a producer of persuasion.

GORGIAS: Apparently.

SOCRATES: Now if someone asks us what sort of persuasion it produces and what it's persuasion about, I suppose we'd answer him that it's the persuasion through teaching about the extent of even and odd. And we'll be able to show that all

454   the other crafts we were just now talking about are producers of persuasion, as well as what the persuasion is and what it's about. Isn't that right?

GORGIAS: Yes.

SOCRATES: So oratory isn't the only producer of persuasion.

GORGIAS: That's true.

SOCRATES: In that case, since it's not the only one to produce this product but other crafts do it too, we'd do right to repeat to our speaker the question we put next in the case of the painter: "Of what sort of persuasion is oratory a craft, and what is its persuasion about?" Or don't you think it's right to repeat that question?   b

GORGIAS: Yes, I do.

SOCRATES: Well then, Gorgias, since you think so too, please answer.

GORGIAS: The persuasion I mean, Socrates, is the kind that takes place in law courts and in those other large gatherings, as I was saying a moment ago. And it's concerned with those matters that are just and unjust.

SOCRATES: Yes, Gorgias, I suspected that this was the persuasion you meant, and that these are the matters it's persuasion about. But so you won't be surprised if in a moment I ask you again another question like this, about what seems to be clear, and yet I go on with my questioning—as I say, I'm asking questions so that we can   c conduct an orderly discussion. It's not you I'm after; it's to prevent our getting in the habit of second-guessing and snatching each other's statements away ahead of time. It's to allow you to work out your assumption in any way you want to.

GORGIAS: Yes, I think that you're quite right to do this, Socrates.

SOCRATES: Come then, and let's examine this point. Is there something you call "to have learned"?

GORGIAS: There is.

SOCRATES: Very well. And also something you call "to be convinced"?   d

GORGIAS: Yes, there is.

SOCRATES: Now, do you think that to have learned, and learning, are the same as to be convinced and conviction, or different?

GORGIAS: I certainly suppose that they're different, Socrates.

SOCRATES: You suppose rightly. This is how you can tell: If someone asked you, "Is there such a thing as true and false conviction, Gorgias?" you'd say yes, I'm sure.

GORGIAS: Yes.

SOCRATES: Well now, is there such a thing as true and false knowledge?

GORGIAS: Not at all.

SOCRATES: So it's clear that they're not the same.

GORGIAS: That's true.

SOCRATES: But surely both those who have learned and those who are con-   e vinced have come to be persuaded?

GORGIAS: That's right.

SOCRATES: Would you like us then to posit two types of persuasion, one providing conviction without knowledge, the other providing knowledge?

GORGIAS: Yes, I would.

SOCRATES: Now which type of persuasion does oratory produce in law courts and other gatherings concerning things that are just and unjust? The one that results in being convinced without knowing or the one that results in knowing?

GORGIAS: It's obvious, surely, that it's the one that results in conviction.

SOCRATES: So evidently oratory produces the persuasion that comes from being
455   convinced, and not the persuasion that comes from teaching, concerning what's just
and unjust.

GORGIAS: Yes.

SOCRATES: And so an orator is not a teacher of law courts and other gatherings
about things that are just and unjust, either, but merely a persuader, for I don't suppose
that he could teach such a large gathering about matters so important in a short time.

GORGIAS: No, he certainly couldn't.

b   SOCRATES: Well now, let's see what we're really saying about oratory. For,
mind you, even I myself can't get clear yet about what I'm saying. When the city
holds a meeting to appoint doctors or shipbuilders or some other variety of craftsmen, that's surely not the time when the orator will give advice, is it? For obviously
it's the most accomplished craftsman who should be appointed in each case. Nor will
the orator be the one to give advice at a meeting that concerns the building of walls
or the equipping of harbors or dockyards, but the master builders will be the ones.
And when there is a deliberation about the appointment of generals or an
c   arrangement of troops against the enemy or an occupation of territory, it's not the
orators but the generals who'll give advice then. What do you say about such cases,
Gorgias? Since you yourself claim both to be an orator and to make others orators,
we'll do well to find out from you the characteristics of your craft. You must think of
me now as eager to serve your interests, too. Perhaps there's actually someone inside
who wants to become your pupil. I notice some, in fact a good many, and they may
well be embarrassed to question you. So, while you're being questioned by me, con-
d   sider yourself being questioned by them as well: "What will we get if we associate
with you, Gorgias? What will we be able to advise the city on? Only about what's
just and unjust or also about the things Socrates was mentioning just now?" Try to
answer them.

GORGIAS: Well, Socrates, I'll try to reveal to you clearly everything oratory can
accomplish. You yourself led the way nicely, for you do know, don't you, that these
e   dockyards and walls of the Athenians and the equipping of the harbor came about
through the advice of Themistocles and in some cases through that of Pericles, but
not through that of the craftsmen?[4]

SOCRATES: That's what they say about Themistocles, Gorgias. I myself heard
Pericles when he advised us on the middle wall.

456   GORGIAS: And whenever those craftsmen you were just now speaking of are
appointed, Socrates, you see that the orators are the ones who give advice and whose
views on these matters prevail.

SOCRATES: Yes, Gorgias, my amazement at that led me long ago to ask what it
is that oratory can accomplish. For as I look at it, it seems to me to be something
supernatural in scope.

GORGIAS: Oh yes, Socrates, if only you knew all of it, that it encompasses and
b   subordinates to itself just about everything that can be accomplished. And I'll give
you ample proof. Many a time I've gone with my brother or with other doctors to call

---

4 Themistocles and Pericles were Athenian statesmen of the fifth century B.C.

on some sick person who refuses to take his medicine or allow the doctor to perform surgery or cauterization on him. And when the doctor failed to persuade him, I succeeded, by means of no other craft than oratory. And I maintain too that if an orator and a doctor came to any city anywhere you like and had to compete in speaking in the assembly or some other gathering over which of them should be appointed doctor, the doctor wouldn't make any showing at all, but the one who had the ability to   c
speak would be appointed, if he so wished. And if he were to compete with any other craftsman whatever, the orator more than anyone else would persuade them that they should appoint him, for there isn't anything that the orator couldn't speak more persuasively about to a gathering than could any other craftsman whatever. That's how great the accomplishment of this craft is, and the sort of accomplishment it is! One should, however, use oratory like any other competitive skill, Socrates. In other cases, too, one ought not to use a competitive skill against any and everybody, just   d
because he has learned boxing, or boxing and wrestling combined, or fighting in armor, so as to make himself be superior to his friends as well as to his enemies. That's no reason to strike, stab, or kill one's own friends! Imagine someone who after attending wrestling school, getting his body into good shape and becoming a boxer, went on to strike his father and mother or any other family member or friend. By Zeus, that's no reason to hate physical trainers and people who teach fighting in   e
armor, and to exile them from their cities! For while these people imparted their skills to be used justly against enemies and wrongdoers, and in defense, not aggression, their pupils pervert their strength and skill and misuse them. So it's not their   457
teachers who are wicked, nor does that make the craft guilty or wicked; those who misuse it, surely, are the wicked ones. And the same is true for oratory as well. The orator has the ability to speak against everyone on every subject, so as in gatherings to be more persuasive, in short, about anything he likes, but the fact that he has the   b
ability to rob doctors or other craftsmen of their reputations doesn't give him any more of a reason to do it. He should use oratory justly, as he would any competitive skill. And I suppose that if a person who has become an orator goes on with this ability and this craft to commit wrongdoing, we shouldn't hate his teacher and exile him from our cities. For while the teacher imparted it to be used justly, the pupil is making the opposite use of it. So it's the misuser whom it's just to hate and exile or put to   c
death, not the teacher.

SOCRATES: Gorgias, I take it that you, like me, have experienced many discussions and that you've observed this sort of thing about them: it's not easy for the participants to define jointly what they're undertaking to discuss, and so, having learned   d
from and taught each other, to conclude their session. Instead, if they're disputing some point and one maintains that the other isn't right or isn't clear, they get irritated, each thinking the other is speaking out of spite. They become eager to win instead of investigating the subject under discussion. In fact, in the end some have a most shameful parting of the ways, abuse heaped upon them, having given and gotten to hear such things that make even the bystanders upset with themselves for having thought it worthwhile to come to listen to such people. What's my point in saying   e
this? It's that I think you're now saying things that aren't very consistent or compatible with what you were first saying about oratory. So, I'm afraid to pursue my

examination of you, for fear that you should take me to be speaking with eagerness
458   to win against you, rather than to have our subject become clear. For my part, I'd be
pleased to continue questioning you if you're the same kind of man I am, otherwise I
would drop it. And what kind of man am I? One of those who would be pleased to be
refuted if I say anything untrue, and who would be pleased to refute anyone who says
anything untrue; one who, however, wouldn't be any less pleased to be refuted than
to refute. For I count being refuted a greater good, insofar as it is a greater good for
oneself to be delivered from the worst thing there is than to deliver someone else
from it. I don't suppose there's anything quite so bad for a person as having false
b   belief about the things we're discussing right now. So if you say you're this kind of
man, too, let's continue the discussion; but if you think we should drop it, let's be
done with it and break it off.

GORGIAS: Oh yes, Socrates, I say that I myself, too, am the sort of person you
describe. Still, perhaps we should keep in mind the people who are present here, too.
For quite a while ago now, even before you came, I gave them a long presentation,
c   and perhaps we'll stretch things out too long if we continue the discussion. We
should think about them, too, so as not to keep any of them who want to do something else.

CHAEREPHON: You yourselves hear the commotion these men are making,
Gorgias and Socrates. They want to hear anything you have to say. And as for
myself, I hope I'll never be so busy that I'd forego discussions such as this, conducted in the way this one is, because I find it more practical to do something else.

d   CALLICLES: By the gods, Chaerephon, as a matter of fact I, too, though I've
been present at many a discussion before now, don't know if I've ever been so
pleased as I am at the moment. So if you're willing to discuss, even if it's all day
long, you'll be gratifying me.

SOCRATES: For my part there's nothing stopping me, Callicles, as long as
Gorgias is willing.

GORGIAS: It'll be to my shame ever after, Socrates, if I weren't willing, when I
myself have made the claim that anyone may ask me anything he wants. All right, if
e   it suits these people, carry on with the discussion, and ask what you want.

SOCRATES: Well then, Gorgias, let me tell you what surprises me in the things
you've said. It may be that what you said was correct and that I'm not taking your
meaning correctly. Do you say that you're able to make an orator out of anyone who
wants to study with you?

GORGIAS: Yes.

SOCRATES: So that he'll be persuasive in a gathering about all subjects, not by
teaching but by persuading?

459   GORGIAS: Yes, that's right.

SOCRATES: You were saying just now, mind you, that the orator will be more
persuasive even about health than a doctor is.

GORGIAS: Yes I was, more persuasive in a gathering, anyhow.

SOCRATES: And doesn't "in a gathering" just mean "among those who don't
have knowledge"? For, among those who do have it, I don't suppose that he'll be
more persuasive than the doctor.

GORGIAS: That's true.

SOCRATES: Now if he'll be more persuasive than a doctor, doesn't he prove to be more persuasive than the one who has knowledge?

GORGIAS: Yes, that's right.

SOCRATES: Even though he's not a doctor, right? b

GORGIAS: Yes.

SOCRATES: And a non-doctor, I take it, isn't knowledgeable in the thing in which a doctor is knowledgeable.

GORGIAS: That's obvious.

SOCRATES: So when an orator is more persuasive than a doctor, a non-knower will be more persuasive than a knower among non-knowers. Isn't this exactly what follows?

GORGIAS: Yes it is, at least in this case.

SOCRATES: The same is true about the orator and oratory relative to the other crafts, too, then. Oratory doesn't need to have any knowledge of the state of their c subject matters; it only needs to have discovered some device to produce persuasion in order to make itself appear to those who don't have knowledge that it knows more than those who actually do have it.

GORGIAS: Well, Socrates, aren't things made very easy when you come off no worse than the craftsmen even though you haven't learned any other craft but this one?

SOCRATES: Whether the orator does or does not come off worse than the others because of this being so, we'll examine in a moment if it has any bearing on our d argument. For now, let's consider this point first. Is it the case that the orator is in the same position with respect to what's just and unjust, what's shameful and admirable, what's good and bad, as he is about what's healthy and about the subjects of the other crafts? Does he lack knowledge, that is, of what these are, of what is good or what is bad, of what is admirable or what is shameful, or just or unjust? Does he employ devices to produce persuasion about them, so that—even though he doesn't know— he seems, among those who don't know either, to know more than someone who e actually does know? Or is it necessary for him to know, and must the prospective stu- dent of oratory already be knowledgeable in these things before coming to you? And if he doesn't, will you, the oratory teacher, not teach him any of these things when he comes to you—for that's not your job—and will you make him seem among most people to have knowledge of such things when in fact he doesn't have it, and to seem good when in fact he isn't? Or won't you be able to teach him oratory at all, unless he knows the truth about these things to begin with? How do matters such as these 460 stand, Gorgias? Yes, by Zeus, do give us your revelation and tell us what oratory can accomplish, just as you just now said you would.

GORGIAS: Well, Socrates, I suppose that if he really doesn't have this knowl- edge, he'll learn these things from me as well.

SOCRATES: Hold it there. You're right to say so. If you make someone an orator, it's necessary for him to know what's just and what's unjust, either beforehand, or by learning it from you afterwards.

GORGIAS: Yes, it is.

b   SOCRATES: Well? A man who has learned carpentry is a carpenter, isn't he?
         GORGIAS: Yes.
         SOCRATES: And isn't a man who has learned music a musician?
         GORGIAS: Yes.
         SOCRATES: And a man who has learned medicine a doctor? And isn't this so too,
         by the same reasoning, with the other crafts? Isn't a man who has learned a particu-
         lar subject the sort of man his knowledge makes him?
         GORGIAS: Yes, he is.
         SOCRATES: And, by this line of reasoning, isn't a man who has learned what's
         just a just man too?
         GORGIAS: Yes, absolutely.
         SOCRATES: And a just man does just things, I take it?
         GORGIAS: Yes.
         SOCRATES: Now isn't an orator necessarily just, and doesn't a just man
c   necessarily want to do just things?
         GORGIAS: Apparently so.
         SOCRATES: Therefore an orator will never want to do what's unjust.
         GORGIAS: No, apparently not.
         SOCRATES: Do you remember saying a little earlier that we shouldn't complain
d   against physical trainers or exile them from our cities if the boxer uses his boxing
         skill to do what's unjust, and that, similarly, if an orator uses his oratorical skill
         unjustly we shouldn't complain against his teacher or banish him from the city, but
         do so to the one who does what's unjust, the one who doesn't use his oratorical skill
         properly? Was that said or not?
         GORGIAS: Yes, it was.
e   SOCRATES: But now it appears that this very man, the orator, would never have
         done what's unjust, doesn't it?
         GORGIAS: Yes, it does.
         SOCRATES: And at the beginning of our discussion, Gorgias, it was said that ora-
         tory would be concerned with speeches, not those about even and odd, but those
         about what's just and unjust. Right?
         GORGIAS: Yes.
         SOCRATES: Well, at the time you said that, I took it that oratory would never be
         an unjust thing, since it always makes its speeches about justice. But when a little
461   later you were saying that the orator could also use oratory unjustly, I was surprised
         and thought that your statements weren't consistent, and so I made that speech in
         which I said that if you, like me, think that being refuted is a profitable thing, it
         would be worthwhile to continue the discussion, but if you don't, to let it drop. But
         now, as we subsequently examine the question, you see for yourself too that it's
         agreed that, quite to the contrary, the orator is incapable of using oratory unjustly and
b   of being willing to do what's unjust. By the Dog, Gorgias, it'll take more than a short
         session to go through an adequate examination of how these matters stand!
         POLUS: Really, Socrates? Is what you're now saying about oratory what you
         actually think of it? Or do you really think, just because Gorgias was too ashamed
         not to concede your further claim that the orator also knows what's just, what's

admirable, and what's good, and that if he came to him without already having this knowledge to begin with, he said that he would teach him himself, and then from this admission maybe some inconsistency crept into his statements—just the thing that gives you delight, you're the one who leads him on to face such questions—who do you think would deny that he himself knows what's just and would teach others? To lead your arguments to such an outcome is a sign of great rudeness.

SOCRATES: Most admirable Polus, it's not for nothing that we get ourselves companions and sons. It's so that, when we ourselves have grown older and stumble, you younger men might be on hand to straighten our lives up again, both in what we do and what we say. And if Gorgias and I are stumbling now in what we say—well, you're on hand, straighten us up again. That's only right. And if you think we were wrong to agree on it, I'm certainly willing to retract any of our agreements you like, provided that you're careful about just one thing.

POLUS: What do you mean?

SOCRATES: That you curb your long style of speech, Polus, the style you tried using at first.

POLUS: Really? Won't I be free to say as much as I like?

SOCRATES: You'd certainly be in a terrible way, my good friend, if upon coming to Athens, where there's more freedom of speech than anywhere else in Greece, you alone should miss out on it here. But look at it the other way. If you spoke at length and were unwilling to answer what you're asked, wouldn't I be in a terrible way if I'm not to have the freedom to stop listening to you and leave? But if you care at all about the discussion we've had and want to straighten it up, please retract whatever you think best, as I was saying just now. Take your turn in asking and being asked questions the way Gorgias and I did, and subject me and yourself to refutation. You say, I take it, that you know the same craft that Gorgias knows? Or don't you?

POLUS: Yes, I do.

SOCRATES: And don't you also invite people to ask you each time whatever they like, because you believe you'll answer as one who has knowledge?

POLUS: Certainly.

SOCRATES: So now please do whichever of these you like: either ask questions or answer them.

POLUS: Very well, I shall. Tell me, Socrates, since you think Gorgias is confused about oratory, what do you say it is?

SOCRATES: Are you asking me what *craft* I say it is?

POLUS: Yes, I am.

SOCRATES: To tell you the truth, Polus, I don't think it's a craft at all.

POLUS: Well then, what do you think oratory is?

SOCRATES: In the treatise that I read recently, it's the thing that you say has produced craft.[5]

POLUS: What do you mean?

SOCRATES: I mean a knack.[6]

---

[5] Alternatively, " . . . it's something of which you claim to have made a craft."
[6] Gk. *empeiria*, translated "experience" at 448c.

POLUS: So you think oratory's a knack?

SOCRATES: Yes, I do, unless you say it's something else.

POLUS: A knack for what?

SOCRATES: For producing a certain gratification and pleasure.

POLUS: Don't you think that oratory's an admirable thing, then, to be able to give gratification to people?

SOCRATES: Really, Polus! Have you already discovered from me what I say it
d   is, so that you go on to ask me next whether I don't think it's admirable?

POLUS: Haven't I discovered that you say it's a knack?

SOCRATES: Since you value gratification, would you like to gratify me on a small matter?

POLUS: Certainly.

SOCRATES: Ask me now what craft I think pastry baking is.

POLUS: All right, I will. What craft is pastry baking?

SOCRATES: It isn't one at all, Polus. Now say, "What is it then?"

POLUS: All right.

SOCRATES: It's a knack. Say, "A knack for what?"

POLUS: All right.
e   SOCRATES: For producing gratification and pleasure, Polus.

POLUS: So oratory is the same thing as pastry baking?

SOCRATES: Oh no, not at all, although it *is* a part of the same practice.

POLUS: What practice do you mean?

SOCRATES: I'm afraid it may be rather crude to speak the truth. I hesitate to do so for Gorgias' sake, for fear that he may think I'm satirizing what he practices. I don't know whether this is the kind of oratory that Gorgias practices—in fact in our
463 discussion a while ago we didn't get at all clear on just what he thinks it is. But what *I* call oratory is a part of some business that isn't admirable at all.

GORGIAS: Which one's that, Socrates? Say it, and don't spare my feelings.

SOCRATES: Well then, Gorgias, I think there's a practice that's not craftlike, but one that a mind given to making hunches takes to, a mind that's bold and naturally
b   clever at dealing with people. I call it flattery, basically. I think that this practice has many other parts as well, and pastry baking, too, is one of them. This part *seems* to be a craft, but in my account of it it isn't a craft but a knack and a routine. I call oratory a part of this, too, along with cosmetics and sophistry. These are four parts, and
c   they're directed to four objects. So if Polus wants to discover them, let him do so. He hasn't discovered yet what sort of part of flattery I say oratory is. Instead, it's escaped him that I haven't answered that question yet, and so he goes on to ask whether I don't consider it to be admirable. And I won't answer him whether I think it's admirable or shameful until I first tell what it is. That wouldn't be right, Polus. If, however, you do want to discover this, ask me what sort of part of flattery I say oratory is.

POLUS: I shall. Tell me what sort of part it is.
d   SOCRATES: Would you understand my answer? By my reasoning, oratory is an image of a part of politics.

POLUS: Well? Are you saying that it's something admirable or shameful?

SOCRATES: I'm saying that it's a shameful thing—I call bad things shameful—since I must answer you as though you already know what I mean.

GORGIAS: By Zeus, Socrates, I myself don't understand what you mean, either!

SOCRATES: Reasonably enough, Gorgias. I'm not saying anything clear yet.   e
This colt here is youthful and impulsive.

GORGIAS: Never mind him. Please tell me what you mean by saying that oratory is an image of a part of politics.

SOCRATES: All right, I'll try to describe my view of oratory. If this isn't what it   464
actually is, Polus here will refute me. There is, I take it, something you call *body* and something you call *soul*?

GORGIAS: Yes, of course.

SOCRATES: And do you also think that there's a state of fitness for each of these?

GORGIAS: Yes, I do.

SOCRATES: All right. Is there also an apparent state of fitness, one that isn't real? The sort of thing I mean is this. There are many people who *appear* to be physically fit, and unless one is a doctor or one of the fitness experts, one wouldn't readily notice that they're not fit.

GORGIAS: That's true.

SOCRATES: I'm saying that this sort of thing exists in the case of both the body and the soul, a thing that makes the body and the soul seem fit when in fact they   b
aren't any the more so.

GORGIAS: That's so.

SOCRATES: Come then, and I'll show you more clearly what I'm saying, if I can. I'm saying that of this pair of subjects there are two crafts. The one for the soul I call politics; the one for the body, though it is one, I can't give you a name for offhand, but while the care of the body is a single craft, I'm saying it has two parts: gymnastics and medicine. And in politics, the counterpart of gymnastics is legislation, and the part that corresponds to medicine is justice. Each member of these pairs has features in common with the other, medicine with gymnastics and justice with legisla-   c
tion, because they're concerned with the same thing. They do, however, differ in some way from each other. These, then, are the four parts, and they always provide care, in the one case for the body, in the other for the soul, with a view to what's best. Now flattery takes notice of them, and—I won't say by *knowing*, but only by *guessing*—divides itself into four, masks itself with each of the parts, and then pretends to   d
be the characters of the masks. It takes no thought at all of whatever is best; with the lure of what's most pleasant at the moment, it sniffs out folly and hoodwinks it, so that it gives the impression of being most deserving. Pastry baking has put on the mask of medicine, and pretends to know the foods that are best for the body, so that if a pastry baker and a doctor had to compete in front of children, or in front of men just as foolish as children, to determine which of the two, the doctor or the pastry baker, had expert knowledge of good food and bad, the doctor would die of starva-tion. I call this flattery, and I say that such a thing is shameful, Polus—it's you I'm   465
saying this to—because it guesses at what's pleasant with no consideration for what's best. And I say that it isn't a craft, but a knack, because it has no account of

the nature of whatever things it applies by which it applies them,[7] so that it's unable
to state the cause of each thing. And I refuse to call anything that lacks such an
account a craft. If you have any quarrel with these claims, I'm willing to submit them
for discussion.

So pastry baking, as I say, is the flattery that wears the mask of medicine.
b   Cosmetics is the one that wears that of gymnastics in the same way; a mischievous,
deceptive, disgraceful and ill-bred thing, one that perpetrates deception by means of
shaping and coloring, smoothing out and dressing up, so as to make people assume
an alien beauty and neglect their own, which comes through gymnastics. So that I
won't make a long-style speech, I'm willing to put it to you the way the geometers
c   do—for perhaps you follow me now—that what cosmetics is to gymnastics, pastry
baking is to medicine; or rather, like this: what cosmetics is to gymnastics, sophistry
is to legislation, and what pastry baking is to medicine, oratory is to justice.
However, as I was saying, although these activities are naturally distinct in this way,
yet because they are so close, sophists and orators tend to be mixed together as people who work in the same area and concern themselves with the same things. They
don't know what to do with themselves, and other people don't know what to do with
them. In fact, if the soul didn't govern the body but the body governed itself, and if
d   pastry baking and medicine weren't kept under observation and distinguished by the
soul, but the body itself made judgments about them, making its estimates by reference to the gratification it receives, then the world according to Anaxagoras would
prevail, Polus my friend—you're familiar with these views—all things would be
mixed together in the same place, and there would be no distinction between matters
of medicine and health, and matters of pastry baking.[8]

You've now heard what I say oratory is. It's the counterpart in the soul to pastry
e   baking, its counterpart in the body. Perhaps I've done an absurd thing: I wouldn't let
you make long speeches, and here I've just composed a lengthy one myself. I
deserve to be forgiven, though, for when I made my statements short you didn't
understand and didn't know how to deal with the answers I gave you, but you needed
a narration. So if I don't know how to deal with your answers either, you must spin
466   out a speech, too. But if I do, just let me deal with them. That's only fair. And if you
now know how to deal with my answer, please deal with it.

POLUS: What is it you're saying, then? You think oratory is flattery?

SOCRATES: I said that it was a *part* of flattery. Don't you remember, Polus,
young as you are? What's to become of you?

POLUS: So you think that good orators are held in low regard in their cities, as
flatterers?

b   SOCRATES: Is this a question you're asking, or some speech you're beginning?

POLUS: I'm asking a question.

SOCRATES: I don't think they're held in any regard at all.

---

[7] The translation here follows the mss, rejecting Dodds' emendation.
[8] Anaxagoras' book began with the words "All things were together," describing the primordial state of
the universe.

POLUS: What do you mean, they're not held in any regard? Don't they have the greatest power in their cities?

SOCRATES: No, if by "having power" you mean something that's good for the one who has the power.

POLUS: That's just what I do mean.

SOCRATES: In that case I think that orators have the least power of any in the city.

POLUS: Really? Don't they, like tyrants, put to death anyone they want, and con- c fiscate the property and banish from their cities anyone they see fit?

SOCRATES: By the Dog, Polus! I can't make out one way or the other with each thing you're saying whether you're saying these things for yourself and revealing your own view, or whether you're questioning me.

POLUS: I'm questioning you.

SOCRATES: Very well, my friend. In that case, are you asking me two questions at once?

POLUS: What do you mean, two?

SOCRATES: Weren't you just now saying something like "Don't orators, like d tyrants, put to death anyone they want, don't they confiscate the property of anyone they see fit, and don't they banish them from their cities?"

POLUS: Yes, I was.

SOCRATES: In that case I say that these are two questions, and I'll answer you both of them. I say, Polus, that both orators and tyrants have the least power in their e cities, as I was saying just now. For they do just about nothing they want to, though they certainly do whatever they see most fit to do.

POLUS: Well, isn't this having great power?

SOCRATES: No; at least Polus says it isn't.

POLUS: I say it isn't? I certainly say it is!

SOCRATES: By . . . , you certainly don't! since you say that having great power is good for the one who has it.

POLUS: Yes, I do say that.

SOCRATES: Do you think it's good, then, if a person does whatever he sees most fit to do when he lacks intelligence? Do you call this "having great power" too?

POLUS: No, I do not.

SOCRATES: Will you refute me, then, and prove that orators do have intelligence, and that oratory is a craft, and not flattery? If you leave me unrefuted, 467 then the orators who do what they see fit in their cities, and the tyrants, too, won't have gained any good by this. Power is a good thing, you say, but you agree with me that doing what one sees fit without intelligence is bad. Or don't you?

POLUS: Yes, I do.

SOCRATES: How then could it be that orators or tyrants have great power in their cities, so long as Socrates is not refuted by Polus to show that they do what they want? POLUS: This fellow— b

SOCRATES: —denies that they do what they want. Go ahead and refute me.

POLUS: Didn't you just now agree that they do what they see fit?

SOCRATES: Yes, and I still do.

POLUS: Don't they do what they want, then?

SOCRATES: I say they don't.

POLUS: Even though they do what they see fit?

SOCRATES: That's what I say.

POLUS: What an outrageous thing to say, Socrates! Perfectly monstrous!

SOCRATES: Don't attack me, my peerless Polus, to address you in your own
c   style. Instead, question me if you can, and prove that I'm wrong. Otherwise you must
answer me.

POLUS: All right, I'm willing to answer, to get some idea of what you're saying.

SOCRATES: Do you think that when people do something, they want the thing
they're doing at the time, or the thing for the sake of which they do what they're
doing? Do you think that people who take medicines prescribed by their doctors, for
instance, want what they're doing, the act of taking the medicine, with all its discom-
fort, or do they want to be healthy, the thing for the sake of which they're taking it?

POLUS: Obviously they want their being healthy.

d   SOCRATES: With seafarers, too, and those who make money in other ways, the
thing they're doing at the time is not the thing they want—for who wants to make
dangerous and troublesome sea voyages? What they want is their being wealthy, the
thing for the sake of which, I suppose, they make their voyages. It's for the sake of
wealth that they make them.

POLUS: Yes, that's right.

SOCRATES: Isn't it just the same in all cases, in fact? If a person does anything
for the sake of something, he doesn't want this thing that he's doing, but the thing for
e   the sake of which he's doing it?

POLUS: Yes.

SOCRATES: Now is there any thing that isn't either *good,* or *bad,* or, what is
between these, *neither good nor bad*?

POLUS: There can't be, Socrates.

SOCRATES: Do you say that wisdom, health, wealth and the like are good, and
their opposites bad?

POLUS: Yes, I do.

SOCRATES: And by things which are neither good nor bad you mean things
which sometimes partake of what's good, sometimes of what's bad, and sometimes
468   of neither, such as sitting or walking, running or making sea voyages, or stones and
sticks and the like? Aren't these the ones you mean? Or are there any others that you
call things neither good nor bad?

POLUS: No, these are the ones.

SOCRATES: Now whenever people do things, do they do these intermediate
things for the sake of good ones, or the good things for the sake of the intermediate ones?

b   POLUS: The intermediate things for the sake of the good ones, surely.

SOCRATES: So it's because we pursue what's good that we walk whenever we
walk; we suppose that it's better to walk. And conversely, whenever we stand still,
we stand still for the sake of the same thing, what's good. Isn't that so?

POLUS: Yes.

SOCRATES: And don't we also put a person to death, if we do, or banish him and confiscate his property because we suppose that doing these things is better for us than not doing them?

POLUS: That's right.

SOCRATES: Hence, it's for the sake of what's good that those who do all these things do them.

POLUS: I agree.

SOCRATES: Now didn't we agree that we want, not those things that we do for   c
the sake of something, but that thing for the sake of which we do them?

POLUS: Yes, very much so.

SOCRATES: Hence, we don't simply want to slaughter people, or exile them from their cities and confiscate their property as such; we want to do these things if they are beneficial, but if they're harmful we don't. For we want the things that are good, as you agree, and we don't want those that are neither good nor bad, nor those that are bad. Right? Do you think that what I'm saying is true, Polus, or don't you? Why don't you answer?

POLUS: I think it's true.

SOCRATES: Since we're in agreement about that then, if a person who's a tyrant   d
or an orator puts somebody to death or exiles him or confiscates his property because he supposes that doing so is better for himself when actually it's worse, this person, I take it, is doing what he sees fit, isn't he?

POLUS: Yes.

SOCRATES: And is he also doing what he wants, if these things are actually bad? Why don't you answer?

POLUS: All right, I don't think he's doing what he wants.

SOCRATES: Can such a man possibly have great power in that city, if in fact hav-   e
ing great power is, as you agree, something good?

POLUS: He cannot.

SOCRATES: So, what I was saying is true, when I said that it is possible for a man who does in his city what he sees fit not to have great power, nor to be doing what he wants.

POLUS: Really, Socrates! As if *you* wouldn't welcome being in a position to do what you see fit in the city, rather than not! As if *you* wouldn't be envious whenever you'd see anyone putting to death some person he saw fit, or confiscating his property or tying him up!

SOCRATES: Justly, you mean, or unjustly?

POLUS: Whichever way he does it, isn't he to be envied either way?   469

SOCRATES: Hush, Polus.

POLUS: What for?

SOCRATES: Because you're not supposed to envy the unenviable or the miser-able. You're supposed to pity them.

POLUS: Really? Is this how you think it is with the people I'm talking about?

SOCRATES: Of course.

POLUS: So, you think that a person who puts to death anyone he sees fit, and does so justly, is miserable and to be pitied?

SOCRATES: No, I don't, but I don't think he's to be envied either.

POLUS: Weren't you just now saying that he's miserable?

b   SOCRATES: Yes, the one who puts someone to death unjustly is, my friend, and he's to be pitied besides. But the one who does so justly isn't to be envied.

POLUS: Surely the one who's put to death unjustly is the one who's both to be pitied and miserable.

SOCRATES: Less so than the one putting him to death, Polus, and less than the one who's justly put to death.

POLUS: How can that be, Socrates?

SOCRATES: It's because doing what's unjust is actually the worst thing there is.

POLUS: Really? Is *that* the worst? Isn't suffering what's unjust still worse?

SOCRATES: No, not in the least.

POLUS: So you'd rather want to suffer what's unjust than do it?

c   SOCRATES: For my part, I wouldn't want either, but if it had to be one or the other, I would choose suffering over doing what's unjust.

POLUS: You wouldn't welcome being a tyrant, then?

SOCRATES: No, if by being a tyrant you mean what I do.

POLUS: I mean just what I said a while ago, to be in a position to do whatever you see fit in the city, whether it's putting people to death or exiling them, or doing any and everything just as you see fit.

d   SOCRATES: Well, my wonderful fellow! I'll put you a case, and you criticize it. Imagine me in a crowded marketplace, with a dagger up my sleeve, saying to you, "Polus, I've just got myself some marvelous tyrannical power. So, if I see fit to have any one of these people you see here put to death right on the spot, to death he'll be put. And if I see fit to have one of them have his head bashed in, bashed in it will be, right away. If I see fit to have his coat ripped apart, ripped it will be. That's how great

e   my power in this city is!" Suppose you didn't believe me and I showed you the dagger. On seeing it, you'd be likely to say, "But Socrates, *everybody* could have great power that way. For this way any house you see fit might be burned down, and so might the dockyards and triremes of the Athenians, and all their ships, both public and private." But then *that's* not what having great power is, doing what one sees fit. Or do you think it is?

POLUS: No, at least not like that.

470   SOCRATES: Can you then tell me what your reason is for objecting to this sort of power?

POLUS: Yes, I can.

SOCRATES: What is it? Tell me.

POLUS: It's that the person who acts this way is necessarily punished.

SOCRATES: And isn't being punished a bad thing?

POLUS: Yes, it really is.

SOCRATES: Well then, my surprising fellow, here again you take the view that as long as acting as one sees fit coincides with acting beneficially, it is good, and this,

b   evidently, is having great power. Otherwise it is a bad thing, and is having little power. Let's consider this point, too. Do we agree that sometimes it's better to do those things we were just now talking about, putting people to death and banishing them and confiscating their property, and at other times it isn't?

POLUS: Yes, we do.

SOCRATES: This point is evidently agreed upon by you and me both?

POLUS: Yes.

SOCRATES: When do you say that it's better to do these things then? Tell me where you draw the line.

POLUS: Why don't you answer that question yourself, Socrates.

SOCRATES: Well then, Polus, if you find it more pleasing to listen to me, I say   c
that when one does these things justly, it's better, but when one does them unjustly, it's worse.

POLUS: How hard it is to refute you, Socrates! Why, even a child could refute you and show that what you're saying isn't true!

SOCRATES: In that case, I'll be very grateful to the child, and just as grateful to you if you refute me and rid me of this nonsense. Please don't falter now in doing a friend a good turn. Refute me.

POLUS: Surely, Socrates, we don't need to refer to ancient history to refute you.   d
Why, current events quite suffice to do that, and to prove that many people who behave unjustly are happy.

SOCRATES: What sorts of events are these?

POLUS: You can picture this man Archelaus, the son of Perdiccas, ruling Macedonia, I take it?

SOCRATES: Well, if I can't picture him, I do hear things about him.

POLUS: Do you think he's happy or miserable?

SOCRATES: I don't know, Polus. I haven't met the man yet.

POLUS: Really? You'd know this if you had met him, but without that you don't   e
know straight off that he's happy?

SOCRATES: No, I certainly don't, by Zeus!

POLUS: It's obvious, Socrates, that you won't even claim to know that the Great King[9] is happy.

SOCRATES: Yes, and that would be true, for I don't know how he stands in regard to education and justice.

POLUS: Really? Is happiness determined entirely by that?

SOCRATES: Yes, Polus, so I say anyway. I say that the admirable and good person, man or woman, is happy, but that the one who's unjust and wicked is miserable.

POLUS: So on your reasoning this man Archelaus is miserable?   471

SOCRATES: Yes, my friend, if he is in fact unjust.

POLUS: Why of course he's unjust! The sovereignty which he now holds doesn't belong to him at all, given the fact that his mother was a slave of Alcetas, Perdiccas' brother. By rights he was a slave of Alcetas, and if he wanted to do what's just, he'd still be a slave to Alcetas, and on your reasoning would be happy. As it is, how mar-

---

[9] The King of Persia, whose riches and imperial power embodied the popular idea of supreme happiness.

velously "miserable" he's turned out to be, now that he's committed the most heinous crimes. First he sends for this man, his very own master and uncle, on the
b   pretext of restoring to him the sovereignty that Perdiccas had taken from him. He entertains him, gets him drunk, both him and his son Alexander, his own cousin and a boy about his own age. He then throws them into a wagon, drives it away at night, and slaughters and disposes of them both. And although he's committed these crimes, he remains unaware of how "miserable" he's become, and feels no remorse either. He refuses to become "happy" by justly bringing up his brother and conferring the sovereignty upon him, the legitimate son of Perdiccas, a boy of about seven
c   to whom the sovereignty was by rights due to come. Instead, not long afterward, he throws him into a well and drowns him, telling the boy's mother Cleopatra that he fell into the well chasing a goose and lost his life. For this very reason now, because he's committed the most terrible of crimes of any in Macedonia, he's the most "miserable" of all Macedonians instead of the happiest, and no doubt there are some in Athens, beginning with yourself, who'd prefer being any other Macedonian at all to
d   being Archelaus.

SOCRATES: Already at the start of our discussions, Polus, I praised you because I thought you were well educated in oratory. But I also thought that you had neglected the practice of discussion. And now is *this* all there is to the argument by which even a child could refute me, and do you suppose that when I say that a person who acts unjustly is not happy, I now stand refuted by you by means of *this* argument? Where did you get that idea, my good man? As a matter of fact, I disagree with every single thing you say!

e   POLUS: You're just unwilling to admit it. You really do think it's the way I say it is.

SOCRATES: My wonderful man, you're trying to refute me in oratorical style, the way people in law courts do when they think they're refuting some claim. There, too, one side thinks it's refuting the other when it produces many reputable witnesses on behalf of the arguments it presents, while the person who asserts the opposite produces only one witness, or none at all. This "refutation" is worthless, as far as truth is
472 concerned, for it might happen sometimes that an individual is brought down by the false testimony of many reputable people. Now too, nearly every Athenian and alien will take your side on the things you're saying, if it's witnesses you want to produce against me to show that what I say isn't true. Nicias the son of Niceratus will testify for you, if you like, and his brothers along with him, the ones whose tripods are
b   standing in a row in the precinct of Dionysus. Aristocrates the son of Scellias will too, if you like, the one to whom that handsome votive offering in the precinct of Pythian Apollo belongs. And so will the whole house of Pericles, if you like, or any other local family you care to choose. Nevertheless, though I'm only one person, I don't agree with you. You don't compel me; instead you produce many false witnesses against me and try to banish me from my property, the truth. For my part, if I don't produce you as a single witness to agree with what I'm saying, then I suppose
c   I've achieved nothing worth mentioning concerning the things we've been discussing. And I suppose you haven't either, if I don't testify on your side, though I'm just one person, and you disregard all these other people.

There is, then, this style of refutation, the one you and many others accept. There's also another, one that I accept. Let's compare the one with the other and see if they'll differ in any way. It's true, after all, that the matters in dispute between us are not at all insignificant ones, but pretty nearly those it's most admirable to have knowledge about, and most shameful not to. For the heart of the matter is that of recognizing or failing to recognize who is happy and who is not. To take first the immediate question our present discussion's about: you believe that it's possible for a man who behaves unjustly and who is unjust to be happy, since you believe Archaelaus to be both unjust and happy. Are we to understand that this is precisely your view?

POLUS: That's right.

SOCRATES: And I say that that's impossible. This is one point in dispute between us. Fair enough. Although he acts unjustly, he'll be happy—that is, if he gets his due punishment?

POLUS: Oh no, certainly not! That's how he'd be the most miserable!

SOCRATES: But if a man who acts unjustly doesn't get his due, then, on your reasoning, he'll be happy?

POLUS: That's what I say.

SOCRATES: On my view of it, Polus, a man who acts unjustly, a man who is unjust, is thoroughly miserable, the more so if he doesn't get his due punishment for the wrongdoing he commits, the less so if he pays and receives what is due at the hands of both gods and men.

POLUS: What an absurd position you're trying to maintain, Socrates!

SOCRATES: Yes, and I'll try to get you to take the same position too, my good man, for I consider you a friend. For now, these are the points we differ on. Please look at them with me. I said earlier, didn't I, that doing what's unjust is worse than suffering it?

POLUS: Yes, you did.

SOCRATES: And you said that suffering it is worse.

POLUS: Yes.

SOCRATES: And I said that those who do what's unjust are miserable, and was "refuted" by you.

POLUS: You certainly were, by Zeus!

SOCRATES: So you think, Polus.

POLUS: So I *truly* think.

SOCRATES: Perhaps. And again, you think that those who do what's unjust are happy, so long as they don't pay what is due.

POLUS: I certainly do.

SOCRATES: Whereas I say that they're the most miserable, while those who pay their due are less so. Would you like to refute this too?

POLUS: Why, that's even more "difficult" to refute than the other claim, Socrates!

SOCRATES: Not difficult, surely, Polus. it's impossible. What's true is never refuted.

POLUS: What do you mean? Take a man who's caught doing something unjust, say, plotting to set himself up as tyrant. Suppose that he's caught, put on the rack, castrated, and has his eyes burned out. Suppose that he's subjected to a host of other abuses of all sorts, and then made to witness his wife and children undergo the same. In the end he's impaled or tarred. Will he be happier than if he hadn't got caught, had set himself up as tyrant, and lived out his life ruling in his city and doing whatever he liked, a person envied and counted happy by fellow citizens and aliens alike? Is *this* what you say is impossible to refute?

d

SOCRATES: This time you're spooking me, Polus, instead of refuting me. Just before, you were arguing by testimony. Still, refresh my memory on a small point: if the man plots to set himself up as tyrant *unjustly,* you said?

POLUS: Yes, I did.

SOCRATES: In that case neither of them will ever be the happier one, neither the one who gains tyrannical power unjustly, nor the one who pays what is due, for of two miserable people one could not be happier than the other. But the one who avoids getting caught and becomes a tyrant is the more miserable one. What's this, Polus? You're laughing? Is this now some further style of refutation, to laugh when somebody makes a point, instead of refuting him?

e

POLUS: Don't you think you've been refuted already, Socrates, when you're saying things the likes of which no human being would maintain? Just ask any one of these people.

SOCRATES: Polus, I'm not one of the politicians. Last year I was elected to the Council by lot, and when our tribe was presiding and I had to call for a vote, I came in for a laugh. I didn't know how to do it. So please don't tell me to call for a vote from the people present here. If you have no better "refutations" than these to offer, do as I suggested just now: let me have my turn, and you try the kind of refutation I think is called for. For I do know how to produce one witness to whatever I'm saying, and that's the man I'm having a discussion with. The majority I disregard. And I do know how to call for a vote from one man, but I don't even discuss things with the majority. See if you'll be willing to give me a refutation, then, by answering the questions you're asked. For I do believe that you and I and everybody else consider doing what's unjust worse than suffering it, and not paying what is due worse than paying it.

474

b

POLUS: And I do believe that I don't, and that no other person does, either. So you'd take suffering what's unjust over doing it, would you?

SOCRATES: Yes, and so would you and everyone else.

POLUS: Far from it! I wouldn't, you wouldn't, and nobody else would, either.

c

SOCRATES: Won't you answer, then?

POLUS: I certainly will. I'm eager to know what you'll say, in fact.

SOCRATES: So that you'll know, answer me as though this were my first question to you. Which do you think is worse, Polus, doing what's unjust or suffering it?

POLUS: I think suffering it is.

SOCRATES: You do? Which do you think is more shameful, doing what's unjust or suffering it? Tell me.

POLUS: Doing it.

SOCRATES: Now if doing it is in fact more shameful, isn't it also worse?

POLUS: No, not in the least.

SOCRATES: I see. Evidently you don't believe that *admirable* and *good* are the   d
same, or that *bad* and *shameful* are.

POLUS: No, I certainly don't.

SOCRATES: Well, what about this? When you call all admirable things
admirable, bodies, for example, or colors, shapes and sounds, or practices, is it with
nothing in view that you do so each time? Take admirable bodies first. Don't you call
them admirable either in virtue of their usefulness, relative to whatever it is that each
is useful for, or else in virtue of some pleasure, if it makes the people who look at
them get enjoyment from looking at them? In the case of the admirability of a body,
can you mention anything other than these?

POLUS: No, I can't.   e

SOCRATES: Doesn't the same hold for all the other things? Don't you call shapes
and colors admirable on account of either some pleasure or benefit or both?

POLUS: Yes, I do.

SOCRATES: Doesn't this also hold for sounds and all things musical?

POLUS: Yes.

SOCRATES: And certainly things that pertain to laws and practices—the
admirable ones, that is—don't fall outside the limits of being either pleasant or beneficial, or both, I take it.

POLUS: No, I don't think they do.   475

SOCRATES: Doesn't the same hold for the admirability of the fields of learning, too?

POLUS: Yes indeed. Yes, Socrates, your present definition of the admirable in
terms of pleasure and good is an admirable one.

SOCRATES: And so is my definition of the shameful in terms of the opposite,
pain and bad, isn't it?

POLUS: Necessarily so.

SOCRATES: Therefore, whenever one of two admirable things is more admirable
than the other, it is so because it surpasses the other either in one of these, pleasure or
benefit, or in both.

POLUS: Yes, that's right.

SOCRATES: And whenever one of two shameful things is more shameful than
the other, it will be so because it surpasses the other either in pain or in badness. Isn't   b
that necessarily so?

POLUS: Yes.

SOCRATES: Well now, what were we saying a moment ago about doing what's
unjust and suffering it? Weren't you saying that suffering it is worse, but doing it
more shameful?

POLUS: I was.

SOCRATES: Now if doing what's unjust is in fact more shameful than suffering
it, wouldn't it be so either because it is more painful and surpasses the other in pain,
or because it surpasses it in badness, or both? Isn't that necessarily so, too?

POLUS: Of course it is.

SOCRATES: Let's look at this first: does doing what's unjust surpass suffering it   c
in pain, and do people who do it hurt more than people who suffer it?

POLUS: No, Socrates, that's not the case at all!

SOCRATES: So it doesn't surpass it in pain, anyhow.

POLUS: Certainly not.

SOCRATES: So, if it doesn't surpass it in pain, it couldn't at this point surpass it in both.

POLUS: Apparently not.

SOCRATES: This leaves it surpassing it only in the other thing.

POLUS: Yes.

SOCRATES: In badness.

POLUS: Evidently.

SOCRATES: So, because it surpasses it in badness, doing what's unjust would be worse than suffering it.

POLUS: That's clear.

d SOCRATES: Now didn't the majority of mankind, and you earlier, agree with us that doing what's unjust is more shameful than suffering it?

POLUS: Yes.

SOCRATES: And now, at least, it's turned out to be worse.

POLUS: Evidently.

SOCRATES: Would you then welcome what's worse and what's more shameful over what is less so? Don't shrink back from answering, Polus. You won't get hurt in any way. Submit yourself nobly to the argument, as you would to a doctor, and answer me. Say yes or no to what I ask you.

e POLUS: No, I wouldn't, Socrates.

SOCRATES: And would any other person?

POLUS: No, I don't think so, not on this reasoning, anyhow.

SOCRATES: I was right, then, when I said that neither you nor I nor any other person would take doing what's unjust over suffering it, for it really is something worse.

POLUS: So it appears.

SOCRATES: So you see, Polus, that when the one refutation is compared with the
476 other, there is no resemblance at all. Whereas everyone but me agrees with you, you are all I need, although you're just a party of one, for your agreement and testimony. It's you alone whom I call on for a vote; the others I disregard. Let this be our verdict on this matter, then. Let's next consider the second point in dispute between us, that is whether a wrongdoer's paying what is due is the worst thing there is, as you were supposing, or whether his not paying it is even worse, as I was.

Let's look at it this way. Are you saying that paying what is due and being justly disciplined for wrongdoing are the same thing?

b POLUS: Yes, I do.

SOCRATES: Can you say, then, that all just things aren't admirable, insofar as they are just? Think carefully and tell me.

POLUS: Yes, I think they are.

SOCRATES: Consider this point, too. If somebody acts upon something, there also has to be something that has something done to it by the one acting upon it?

POLUS: Yes, I think so.

SOCRATES: And that it has done to it what the thing acting upon it does, and in the sort of way the thing acting upon it does it? I mean, for example, that if somebody hits, there has to be something that's being hit?

POLUS: There has to be.

SOCRATES: And if the hitter hits hard or quickly, the thing being hit is hit that   c
way, too?

POLUS: Yes.

SOCRATES: So the thing being hit gets acted upon in whatever way the hitting thing acts upon it?

POLUS: Yes, that's right.

SOCRATES: So, too, if somebody performs surgical burning, then there has to be something that's being burned?

POLUS: Of course.

SOCRATES: And if he burns severely or painfully, the thing that's being burned is burned in whatever way the burning thing burns it?

POLUS: That's right.

SOCRATES: Doesn't the same account also hold if a person makes a surgical cut? For something is being cut.

POLUS: Yes.

SOCRATES: And if the cut is large or deep or painful, the thing being cut is cut in   d
whatever way the cutting thing cuts it?

POLUS: So it appears.

SOCRATES: Summing it up, see if you agree with what I was saying just now, that in all cases, in whatever way the thing acting upon something acts upon it, the thing acted upon is acted upon in just that way.

POLUS: Yes, I do agree.

SOCRATES: Taking this as agreed, is paying what is due a case of being acted upon or of acting upon something?

POLUS: It must be a case of being acted upon, Socrates.

SOCRATES: By someone who acts?

POLUS: Of course. By the one administering discipline.

SOCRATES: Now one who disciplines correctly disciplines justly?   e
POLUS: Yes.

SOCRATES: Thereby acting justly, or not?

POLUS: Yes, justly.

SOCRATES: So the one being disciplined is being acted upon justly when he pays what is due?

POLUS: Apparently.

SOCRATES: And it was agreed, I take it, that just things are admirable?

POLUS: That's right.

SOCRATES: So one of these men does admirable things, and the other, the one being disciplined, has admirable things done to him.

POLUS: Yes.

SOCRATES: If they're admirable, then, aren't they good? For they're either pleasant or beneficial.

POLUS: Necessarily so.

SOCRATES: Hence, the one paying what is due has good things being done to him?

POLUS: Evidently.

SOCRATES: Hence, he's being benefited?

POLUS: Yes.

SOCRATES: Is his benefit the one I take it to be? Does his soul undergo improvement if he's justly disciplined?

POLUS: Yes, that's likely.

SOCRATES: Hence, one who pays what is due gets rid of something bad in his soul?

POLUS: Yes.

SOCRATES: Now, is the bad thing he gets rid of the most serious one? Consider it this way: in the matter of a person's financial condition, do you detect any bad thing other than poverty?

POLUS: No, just poverty.

SOCRATES: What about that of a person's physical condition? Would you say that what is bad here consists of weakness, disease, ugliness, and the like?

POLUS: Yes, I would.

SOCRATES: Do you believe that there's also some corrupt condition of the soul?

POLUS: Of course.

SOCRATES: And don't you call this condition injustice, ignorance, cowardice, and the like?

POLUS: Yes, certainly.

SOCRATES: Of these three things, one's finances, one's body, and one's soul, you said there are three states of corruption, namely poverty, disease, and injustice?

POLUS: Yes.

SOCRATES: Which of these states of corruption is the most shameful? Isn't it injustice, and corruption of one's soul in general?

POLUS: Very much so.

SOCRATES: And if it's the most shameful, it's also the worst?

POLUS: What do you mean, Socrates?

SOCRATES: I mean this: What we agreed on earlier implies that what's most shameful is so always because it's the source either of the greatest pain, or of harm, or of both.

POLUS: Very much so.

SOCRATES: And now we've agreed that injustice, and corruption of soul as a whole, is the most shameful thing.

POLUS: So we have.

SOCRATES: So either it's most painful and is most shameful because it surpasses the others in pain, or else in harm, or in both?

POLUS: Necessarily so.

SOCRATES: Now is being unjust, undisciplined, cowardly, and ignorant more painful than being poor or sick?

POLUS: No, I don't think so, Socrates, given what we've said, anyhow.

SOCRATES: So the reason that corruption of one's soul is the most shameful of them all is that it surpasses the others by some monstrously great harm and astounding badness, since it doesn't surpass them in pain, according to your reasoning. e

POLUS: So it appears.

SOCRATES: But what is surpassing in greatest harm would, I take it, certainly be the worst thing there is.

POLUS: Yes.

SOCRATES: Injustice, then, lack of discipline and all other forms of corruption of soul are the worst thing there is.

POLUS: Apparently so.

SOCRATES: Now, what is the craft that gets rid of poverty? Isn't it that of financial management?

POLUS: Yes.

SOCRATES: What's the one that gets rid of disease? Isn't it that of medicine? 478

POLUS: Necessarily.

SOCRATES: What's the one that gets rid of corruption and injustice? If you're stuck, look at it this way: where and to whom do we take people who are physically sick?

POLUS: To doctors, Socrates.

SOCRATES: Where do we take people who behave unjustly and without discipline?

POLUS: To judges, you mean?

SOCRATES: Isn't it so they'll pay what's due?

POLUS: Yes I agree.

SOCRATES: Now don't those who administer discipline correctly employ a kind of justice in doing so?

POLUS: That's clear.

SOCRATES: It's financial management, then, that gets rid of poverty, medicine that gets rid of disease, and justice that gets rid of injustice and indiscipline. b

POLUS: Apparently.

SOCRATES: Which of these, now, is the most admirable?

POLUS: Of which, do you mean?

SOCRATES: Of financial management, medicine, and justice.

POLUS: Justice is by far, Socrates.

SOCRATES: Doesn't it in that case provide either the most pleasure, or benefit, or both, if it really is the most admirable?

POLUS: Yes.

SOCRATES: Now, is getting medical treatment something pleasant? Do people who get it enjoy getting it?

POLUS: No, I don't think so.

SOCRATES: But it *is* beneficial, isn't it?

POLUS: Yes.

SOCRATES: Because they're getting rid of something very bad, so that it's worth their while to endure the pain and so get well. c

POLUS: Of course.

SOCRATES: Now, would a man be happiest, as far as his body goes, if he's under treatment, or if he weren't even sick to begin with?

POLUS: If he weren't even sick, obviously.

SOCRATES: Because happiness evidently isn't a matter of getting rid of something bad; it's rather a matter of not even contracting it to begin with.

POLUS: That's so.

d   SOCRATES: Very well. Of two people, each of whom has something bad in either body or soul, which is the more miserable one, the one who is treated and gets rid of the bad thing or the one who doesn't but keeps it?

POLUS: The one who isn't treated, it seems to me.

SOCRATES: Now, wasn't paying what's due getting rid of the worst thing there is, corruption?

POLUS: It was.

SOCRATES: Yes, because such justice makes people self-controlled, I take it, and more just. It proves to be a treatment against corruption.

POLUS: Yes.

SOCRATES: The happiest man, then, is the one who doesn't have any badness in his soul, now that this has been shown to be the most serious kind of badness.

POLUS: That's clear.

e   SOCRATES: And second, I suppose, is the man who gets rid of it.

POLUS: Evidently.

SOCRATES: This is the man who gets lectured and lashed, the one who pays what is due.

POLUS: Yes.

SOCRATES: The man who keeps it, then, and who doesn't get rid of it, is the one whose life is the worst.

POLUS: Apparently.

SOCRATES: Isn't this actually the man who, although he commits the most
479   serious crimes and uses methods that are most unjust, succeeds in avoiding being lectured and disciplined and paying his due, as Archelaus according to you, and the other tyrants, orators, and potentates have put themselves in a position to do?

POLUS: Evidently.

SOCRATES: Yes, my good man, I take it that these people have managed to accomplish pretty much the same thing as a person who has contracted very serious illnesses, but, by avoiding treatment manages to avoid paying what's due to the doc-
b   tors for his bodily faults, fearing, as would a child, cauterization or surgery because they're painful. Don't you think so, too?

POLUS: Yes, I do.

SOCRATES: It's because he evidently doesn't know what health and bodily excellence are like. For on the basis of what we're now agreed on, it looks as though those who avoid paying what is due also do the same sort of thing, Polus. They focus on its painfulness, but are blind to its benefit and are ignorant of how much more
c   miserable it is to live with an unhealthy soul than with an unhealthy body, a soul that's rotten with injustice and impiety. This is also the reason they go to any length

to avoid paying what is due and getting rid of the worst thing there is. They find themselves funds and friends, and ways to speak as persuasively as possible. Now if what we're agreed on is true, Polus, are you aware of what things follow from our argument? Or would you like us to set them out?

POLUS: Yes, if you think we should anyhow.

SOCRATES: Does it follow that injustice, and doing what is unjust, is the worst thing there is?

POLUS: Yes, apparently.   d

SOCRATES: And it has indeed been shown that paying what is due is what gets rid of this bad thing?

POLUS: So it seems.

SOCRATES: And that if it isn't paid, the bad thing is retained?

POLUS: Yes.

SOCRATES: So, doing what's unjust is the second worst thing. Not paying what's due when one has done what's unjust is by its nature the first worst thing, the very worst of all.

POLUS: Evidently.

SOCRATES: Now wasn't this the point in dispute between us, my friend? You   e
considered Archelaus happy, a man who committed the gravest crimes without paying what was due, whereas I took the opposite view, that whoever avoids paying his due for his wrongdoing, whether he's Archelaus or any other man, is and deserves to be miserable beyond all other men, and that one who does what's unjust is always more miserable than the one who suffers it, and the one who avoids paying what's due always more miserable than the one who does pay it. Weren't these the things I said?

POLUS: Yes.

SOCRATES: Hasn't it been proved that what was said is true?

POLUS: Apparently.

SOCRATES: Fair enough. If these things are true then, Polus, what is the great   480
use of oratory? For on the basis of what we're agreed on now, what a man should guard himself against most of all is doing what's unjust, knowing that he will have trouble enough if he does. Isn't that so?

POLUS: Yes, that's right.

SOCRATES: And if he or anyone else he cares about acts unjustly, he should voluntarily go to the place where he'll pay his due as soon as possible; he should go to the judge as though he were going to a doctor, anxious that the disease of injustice   b
shouldn't be protracted and cause his soul to fester incurably. What else can we say, Polus, if our previous agreements really stand? Aren't these statements necessarily consistent with our earlier ones in only this way?

POLUS: Well yes, Socrates. What else are we to say?

SOCRATES: So, if oratory is used to defend injustice, Polus, one's own or that of one's relatives, companions, or children, or that of one's country when it acts unjustly, it is of no use to us at all, unless one takes it to be useful for the opposite   c
purpose: that he should accuse himself first and foremost, and then too his family and anyone else dear to him who happens to behave unjustly at any time; and that he should not keep his wrongdoing hidden but bring it out into the open, so that he may

pay his due and get well; and compel himself and the others not to play the coward, but to grit his teeth and present himself with grace and courage as to a doctor for cauterization and surgery, pursuing what's good and admirable without taking any account of the pain. And if his unjust behavior merits flogging, he should present

d   himself to be whipped; if it merits imprisonment, to be imprisoned; if a fine, to pay it; if exile, to be exiled; and if execution, to be executed. He should be his own chief accuser, and the accuser of other members of his family, and use his oratory for the purpose of getting rid of the worst thing there is, injustice, as the unjust acts are being exposed. Are we to affirm or deny this, Polus?

e   POLUS: I think these statements are absurd, Socrates, though no doubt you think they agree with those expressed earlier.

SOCRATES: Then either we should abandon those, or else these necessarily follow?

POLUS: Yes, that's how it is.

SOCRATES: And, on the other hand, to reverse the case, suppose a man had to harm someone, an enemy or anybody at all, provided that he didn't suffer anything unjust from this enemy himself—for this is something to be on guard against—if the

481   enemy did something unjust against another person, then our man should see to it in every way, both in what he does and what he says, that his enemy does not go to the judge and pay his due. And if he does go, he should scheme to get his enemy off without paying what's due. If he's stolen a lot of gold, he should scheme to get him not to return it but to keep it and spend it in an unjust and godless way both on himself and his people. And if his crimes merit the death penalty, he should scheme to keep him from being executed, preferably never to die at all but to live forever in corruption, but

b   failing that, to have him live as long as possible in that condition. Yes, this is the sort of thing I think oratory is useful for, Polus, since for the person who has no intention of behaving unjustly it doesn't seem to me to have much use—if in fact it has any use at all—since its usefulness hasn't in any way become apparent so far.

CALLICLES: Tell me, Chaerephon, is Socrates in earnest about this or is he joking?

CHAEREPHON: I think he's in dead earnest about this, Callicles. There's nothing like asking him, though.

c   CALLICLES: By the gods! Just the thing I'm eager to do. Tell me, Socrates, are we to take you as being in earnest now, or joking? For if you *are* in earnest, and these things you're saying are really true, won't this human life of ours be turned upside down, and won't everything we do evidently be the opposite of what we should do?

SOCRATES: Well, Callicles, if human beings didn't share common experiences,

d   some sharing one, others sharing another, but one of us had some unique experience not shared by others, it wouldn't be easy for him to communicate what he experienced to the other. I say this because I realize that you and I are both now actually sharing a common experience: each of the two of us is a lover of two objects, I of Alcibiades, Clinias' son,[10] and of philosophy, and you of the *demos* [people] of Athens, and the Demos who's the son of Pyrilampes. I notice that in each case you're

[10] See *Symposium* 215a–219d.

unable to contradict your beloved, clever though you are, no matter what he says or   e
what he claims is so. You keep shifting back and forth. If you say anything in the
Assembly and the Athenian *demos* denies it, you shift your ground and say what it
wants to hear. Other things like this happen to you when you're with that good-looking young man, the son of Pyrilampes. You're unable to oppose what your beloveds
say or propose, so that if somebody heard you say what you do on their account and
was amazed at how absurd that is, you'd probably say—if you were minded to tell
him the truth—that unless somebody stops your beloveds from saying what they say,   482
you'll never stop saying these things either. In that case you must believe that you're
bound to hear me say things like that, too, and instead of being surprised at my saying them, you must stop my beloved, philosophy, from saying them. For she always
says what you now hear me say, my dear friend, and she's by far less fickle than my
other beloved. As for that son of Clinias, what he says differs from one time to the
next, but what philosophy says always stays the same, and she's saying things that
now astound you, although you were present when they were said. So, either refute   b
her and show that doing what's unjust without paying what is due for it is not the ultimate of all bad things, as I just now was saying it is, or else, if you leave this unrefuted, then by the Dog, the god of the Egyptians, Callicles will not agree with you,
Callicles, but will be dissonant with you all your life long. And yet for my part, my
good man, I think it's better to have my lyre or a chorus that I might lead out of tune
and dissonant, and have the vast majority of men disagree with me and contradict
me, than to be out of harmony with myself, to contradict myself, though I'm only   c
one person.

  CALLICLES: Socrates, I think you're grandstanding in these speeches, acting
like a true crowd pleaser. Here you are, playing to the crowd now that Polus has had
the same thing happen to him that he accused Gorgias of letting you do to him. For
he said, didn't he, that when Gorgias was asked by you whether he would teach anyone who came to him wanting to learn oratory but without expertise in what's just,   d
Gorgias was ashamed and, out of deference to human custom, since people would
take it ill if a person refused, said that he'd teach him. And because Gorgias agreed
on this point, he said, he was forced to contradict himself, just the thing you like. He
ridiculed you at the time, and rightly so, as I think anyhow. And now the very same
thing has happened to him. And for this same reason *I* don't approve of Polus: he
agreed with you that doing what's unjust is more shameful than suffering it. As a
result of this admission he was bound and gagged by you in the discussion, too   e
ashamed to say what he thought. Although you claim to be pursuing the truth, you're
in fact bringing the discussion around to the sort of crowd-pleasing vulgarities that
are admirable only by law and not by nature. And these, nature and law, are for the
most part opposed to each other, so if a person is ashamed and doesn't dare to say   483
what he thinks, he's forced to contradict himself. This is in fact the clever trick
you've thought of, with which you work mischief in your discussions: if a person
makes a statement in terms of law, you slyly question him in terms of nature; if he
makes it in terms of nature, you question him in terms of law. That's just what happened here, on the question of doing what's unjust versus suffering it. While Polus
meant that doing it is more shameful by law, you pursued the argument as though he

meant by nature. For by nature all that is worse is also more shameful, like suffering what's unjust, whereas by law doing it is more shameful. No, no man would put up
b   with suffering what's unjust; only a slave would do so, one who is better dead than alive, who when he's treated unjustly and abused can't protect himself or anyone else he cares about. I believe that the people who institute our laws are the weak and the many. So they institute laws and assign praise and blame with themselves and their
c   own advantage in mind. As a way of frightening the more powerful among men, the ones who are capable of having a greater share, out of getting a greater share than they, they say that getting more than one's share is "shameful" and "unjust," and that doing what's unjust is nothing but trying to get more than one's share. I think they like getting an equal share, since they are inferior.

      These are the reasons why trying to get a greater share than most is said to be
d   unjust and shameful by law and why they call it doing what's unjust. But I believe that nature itself reveals that it's a just thing for the better man and the more capable man to have a greater share than the worse man and the less capable man. Nature shows that this is so in many places; both among the other animals and in whole cities and races of men, it shows that this is what justice has been decided to be: that the superior rule the inferior and have a greater share than they. For what sort of jus-
e   tice did Xerxes go by when he campaigned against Greece, or his father when he campaigned against Scythia? Countless other such examples could be mentioned. I believe that these men do these things in accordance with the nature of what's just— yes, by Zeus, in accordance with the law of nature, and presumably not with the one we institute. We mold the best and the most powerful among us, taking them while
484   they're still young, like lion cubs, and with charms and incantations we subdue them into slavery, telling them that one is supposed to get no more than his fair share, and that that's what's admirable and just. But surely, if a man whose nature is equal to it arises, he will shake off, tear apart, and escape all this, he will trample underfoot our documents, our tricks and charms, and all our laws that violate nature. He, the slave,
b   will rise up and be revealed as our master, and here the justice of nature will shine forth. I think Pindar, too, refers to what I'm saying in that song in which he says that

>   *Law, the king of all,*
>   *Of mortals and the immortal gods*

—this, he says,

>   *Brings on and renders just what is most violent*
>   *With towering hand. I take as proof of this*
>   *The deeds of Heracles. For he . . . unbought . . .*

His words are something like that—I don't know the song well—he says that
c   Heracles drove off Geryon's cattle, even though he hadn't paid for them and Geryon hadn't given them to him, on the ground that this is what's just by nature, and that cattle and all the other possessions of those who are worse and inferior belong to the one who's better and superior.

This is the truth of the matter, as you will acknowledge if you abandon philosophy and move on to more important things. Philosophy is no doubt a delightful thing, Socrates, as long as one is exposed to it in moderation at the appropriate time of life. But if one spends more time with it than he should, it's a man's undoing. For even if one is naturally well favored but engages in philosophy far beyond that appropriate time of life, he can't help but turn out to be inexperienced in everything a man who's to be admirable and good and well thought of is supposed to be experienced in. Such   d
people turn out to be inexperienced in the laws of their city or in the kind of speech one must use to deal with people on matters of business, whether in public or private, inexperienced also in human pleasures and appetites and, in short, inexperienced in the ways of human beings altogether. So, when they venture into some private or political activity, they become a laughingstock, as I suppose men in politics do when   e
they venture into your pursuits and your kind of speech. What results is Euripides' saying, where he says that "each man shines" in this and "presses on to this,

> *allotting the greatest part of the day to this,*
> *where he finds himself at his best."*

And whatever a man's inferior in, he avoids and rails against, while he praises the   485
other thing, thinking well of himself and supposing that in this way he's praising himself. I believe, however, that it's most appropriate to have a share of both. To partake of as much philosophy as your education requires is an admirable thing, and it's not shameful to practice philosophy while you're a boy, but when you still do it after you've grown older and become a man, the thing gets to be ridiculous, Socrates! My own reaction to men who philosophize is very much like that to men who speak halt-   b
ingly and play like children. When I see a child, for whom it's still quite proper to make conversation this way, halting in its speech and playing like a child, I'm delighted. I find it a delightful thing, a sign of good breeding, and appropriate for the child's age. And when I hear a small child speaking clearly, I think it's a harsh thing; it hurts my ears. I think it is something fit for a slave. But when one hears a man speaking haltingly or sees him playing like a child, it strikes me as ridiculous and   c
unmanly, deserving of a flogging. Now, I react in the same way to men who engage in philosophy, too. When I see philosophy in a young boy, I approve of it; I think it's appropriate and consider such a person well-bred, whereas I consider one who does-n't engage in philosophy ill-bred, one who'll never count himself deserving of any admirable or noble thing. But when I see an older man still engaging in philosophy   d
and not giving it up, I think such a man by this time needs a flogging. For, as I was just now saying, it's typical that such a man, even if he's naturally very well favored, becomes unmanly and avoids the centers of his city and the marketplaces—in which, according to the poet,[11] men attain "preeminence"—and, instead, lives the rest of his   e
life in hiding, whispering in a corner with three or four boys, never uttering anything well-bred, important, or apt.

---

[11] Homer, *Iliad* ix.441.

Socrates, I do have a rather warm regard for you. I find myself feeling what Zethus, whose words I recalled just now, felt toward Amphion in Euripides' play. In fact, the sorts of things he said to his brother come to my mind to say to you. "You're neglecting the things you should devote yourself to, Socrates, and though your spirit's nature is so noble, you show yourself to the world in the shape of a boy. You

486   couldn't put a speech together correctly before councils of justice or utter any plausible or persuasive sound. Nor could you make any bold proposal on behalf of anyone else." And so then, my dear Socrates—please don't be upset with me, for it's with good will toward you that I'll say this—don't you think it's shameful to be the way I take you to be, and others who ever press on too far in philosophy? As it is, if someone got hold of you or of anyone else like you and took you off to prison on the charge that you're doing something unjust when in fact you aren't, be assured that you wouldn't have any use for yourself. You'd get dizzy, your mouth would hang

b   open and you wouldn't know what to say. You'd come up for trial and face some no good wretch of an accuser and be put to death, if death is what he'd want to condemn you to. And yet, Socrates, "how can this be a wise thing, the craft which took a well-favored man and made him worse," able neither to protect himself nor to rescue himself or anyone else from the gravest dangers, to be robbed of all of his property by his

c   enemies, and to live a life with absolutely no rights in his city? Such a man one could knock on the jaw without paying what's due for it, to put it rather crudely. Listen to me, my good man, and stop this refuting. "Practice the sweet music of an active life and do it where you'll get a reputation for being intelligent. Leave these subtleties to others"—whether we should call them just silly or outright nonsense—"which will cause you to live in empty houses,"[12] and envy not those men who refute such trivia,

d   but those who have life and renown, and many other good things as well.

    SOCRATES: If I actually had a soul made of gold, Callicles, don't you think I'd be pleased to find one of those stones on which they test gold? And if this stone to which I intended to take my soul were the best stone and it agreed that my soul had been well cared for, don't you think I could know well at that point that I'm in good shape and need no further test?

e   CALLICLES: What's the point of your question, Socrates?

    SOCRATES: I'll tell you. I believe that by running into you, I've run into just such a piece of luck.

    CALLICLES: Why do you say that?

487   SOCRATES: I know well that if you concur with what my soul believes, then that is the very truth. I realize that a person who is going to put a soul to an adequate test to see whether it lives rightly or not must have three qualities, all of which you have: knowledge, good will, and frankness. I run into many people who aren't able to test me because they're not wise like you. Others are wise, but they're not willing to tell me the truth, because they don't care for me the way you do. As for these two visi-

b   tors, Gorgias and Polus, they're both wise and fond of me, but rather more lacking in frankness, and more ashamed than they should be. No wonder! They've come to such a depth of shame that, because they are ashamed, each of them dares to

---

[12] Here and just above Callicles again quotes or adapts Euripides' *Antiope*.

contradict himself, face to face with many people, and on topics of the greatest importance. You have all these qualities, which the others don't. You're well-enough educated, as many of the Athenians would attest, and you have good will toward me. What's my proof of this? I'll tell you. I know, Callicles, that there are four of you   c
who've become partners in wisdom, you, Teisander of Aphidnae, Andron the son of Androtion, and Nausicydes of Cholarges. Once I overheard you deliberating on how far one should cultivate wisdom, and I know that some such opinion as this was winning out among you: you called on each other not to enthusiastically pursue philosophizing to the point of pedantry but to be careful not to become wiser than necessary   d
and so inadvertently bring yourselves to ruin. So, now that I hear you giving me the same advice you gave your closest companions, I have sufficient proof that you really do have good will toward me. And as to my claim that you're able to speak frankly without being ashamed, you yourself say so and the speech you gave a moment ago bears you out. It's clear, then, that this is how these matters stand at the moment. If there's any point in our discussions on which you agree with me, then   e
that point will have been adequately put to the test by you and me, and it will not be necessary to put it to any further test, for you'd never have conceded the point through lack of wisdom or excess of shame, and you wouldn't do so by lying to me, either. You are my friend, as you yourself say, too. So, our mutual agreement will really lay hold of truth in the end. Most admirable of all, Callicles, is the examination of those issues about which you took me to task, that of what a man is supposed to be like, and of what he's supposed to devote himself to and how far, when he's older and when he's young. For my part, if I engage in anything that's improper in my own life,   488
please know well that I do not make this mistake intentionally but out of my ignorance. So don't leave off lecturing me the way you began, but show me clearly what it is I'm to devote myself to, and in what way I might come by it; if you catch me agreeing with you now but at a later time not doing the very things I've agreed upon, then take me for a very stupid fellow and don't bother ever afterward with lecturing me, on the ground that I'm a worthless fellow.   b

Please restate your position for me from the beginning. What is it that you and Pindar hold to be true of what's just by nature? That the superior should take by force what belongs to the inferior, that the better should rule the worse and the more worthy have a greater share than the less worthy? You're not saying anything else, are you? I do remember correctly?

CALLICLES: Yes, that's what I was saying then, and I still say so now, too.

SOCRATES: Is it the same man you call both "better" and "superior"? I wasn't   c
able then, either, to figure out what you meant. Is it the stronger ones you call superior, and should those who are weaker take orders from the one who's stronger? That's what I think you were trying to show then also, when you said that large cities attack small ones according to what's just by nature, because they're superior and stronger, assuming that *superior, stronger* and *better* are the same. Or is it possible for one to be better and also inferior and weaker, or greater but more wretched? Or   d
do "better" and "superior" have the same definition? Please define this for me clearly. Are *superior, better* and *stronger* the same or are they different?

CALLICLES: Very well, I'm telling you clearly that they're the same.

SOCRATES: Now aren't the many superior by nature to the one? They're the ones who in fact impose the laws upon the one, as you were saying yourself a moment ago.

CALLICLES: Of course.

SOCRATES: So the rules of the many are the rules of the superior.

CALLICLES: Yes, they are.

e SOCRATES: Aren't they the rules of the better? For by your reasoning, I take it, the superior are the better.

CALLICLES: Yes.

SOCRATES: And aren't the rules of these people admirable by nature, seeing that they're the superior ones?

CALLICLES: That's my view.

SOCRATES: Now, isn't it a rule of the many that it's just to have an equal share
489 and that doing what's unjust is more shameful than suffering it, as you yourself were saying just now? Is this so or not? Be careful that you in your turn don't get caught being ashamed now. Do the many observe or do they not observe the rule that it's just to have an equal and not a greater share, and that doing what's unjust is more shameful than suffering it? Don't grudge me your answer to this, Callicles, so that if you agree with me I may have my confirmation from you, seeing that it's the agreement of a man competent to pass judgment.

CALLICLES: All right, the many do have that rule.

b SOCRATES: It's not only by law, then, that doing what's unjust is more shameful than suffering it, or just to have an equal share, but it's so by nature, too. So it looks as though you weren't saying what's true earlier and weren't right to accuse me when you said that nature and law were opposed to each other and that I, well aware of this, am making mischief in my statements, taking any statement someone makes meant in terms of nature, in terms of law, and any statement meant in terms of law, in terms of nature.

CALLICLES: This man will not stop talking nonsense! Tell me, Socrates, aren't
c you ashamed, at your age, of trying to catch people's words and of making hay out of someone's tripping on a phrase? Do you take me to mean by people being *superior* anything else than their being *better?* Haven't I been telling you all along that by "better" and "superior" I mean the same thing? Or do you suppose that I'm saying that if a rubbish heap of slaves and motley men, worthless except perhaps in physical strength, gets together and makes any statements, then these are the rules?

SOCRATES: Fair enough, wisest Callicles. Is this what you're saying?

CALLICLES: It certainly is.

d SOCRATES: Well, my marvelous friend, I guessed some time ago that it's some such thing you mean by "superior," and I'm questioning you because I'm intent upon knowing clearly what you mean. I don't really suppose that you think two are better than one or that your slaves are better than you just because they're stronger than you. Tell me once more from the beginning, what *do* you mean by the *better,* seeing that it's not the stronger? And, my wonderful man, go easier on me in your teaching, so that I won't quit your school.

CALLICLES: You're being ironic, Socrates.   e

SOCRATES: No I'm not, Callicles, by Zethus—the character you were invoking in being ironic with me so often just now! But come and tell me: whom do you mean by *the better?*

CALLICLES: I mean the worthier.

SOCRATES: So do you see that you yourself are uttering words, without making anything clear? Won't you say whether by *the better* and *the superior* you mean *the more intelligent,* or some others?

CALLICLES: Yes, by Zeus, they're very much the ones I mean.

SOCRATES: So on your reasoning it will often be the case that a single intelligent   490
person is superior to countless unintelligent ones, that this person should rule and they be ruled, and that the one ruling should have a greater share than the ones being ruled. This is the meaning I think you intend—and I'm not trying to catch you with a phrase—if the one is superior to these countless others.

CALLICLES: Yes, that's what I do mean. This is what I take the just by nature to be: that the better one, the more intelligent one, that is, both rules over and has a greater share than his inferiors.

SOCRATES: Hold it right there! What can your meaning be this time? Suppose   b
we were assembled together in great numbers in the same place, as we are now, and we held in common a great supply of food and drink, and suppose we were a motley group, some strong and some weak, but one of us, being a doctor, was more intelligent about these things. He would, very likely, be stronger than some and weaker than others. Now this man, being more intelligent than we are, will certainly be better and superior in these matters?

CALLICLES: Yes, he will.

SOCRATES: So should he have a share of this food greater than ours because he's   c
better? Or should he be the one to distribute everything because he's in charge, but not to get a greater share to consume and use up on his own body if he's to escape being punished for it? Shouldn't he, instead, have a greater share than some and a lesser one than others, and if he should happen to be the weakest of all, shouldn't the best man have the least share of all, Callicles? Isn't this so, my good man?

CALLICLES: You keep talking of food and drink and doctors and such nonsense.   d
That's not what I mean!

SOCRATES: Don't you mean that the more intelligent one is the better one? Say yes or no.

CALLICLES: Yes, I do.

SOCRATES: But not that the better should have a greater share?

CALLICLES: Not of food or drink, anyhow.

SOCRATES: I see. Of clothes, perhaps? Should the weaver have the biggest garment and go about wearing the greatest number and the most beautiful clothes?

CALLICLES: What do you mean, clothes?

SOCRATES: But when it comes to shoes, obviously the most intelligent, the best   e
man in that area should have the greater share. Perhaps the cobbler should walk around with the largest and greatest number of shoes on.

CALLICLES: What do you mean, shoes? You keep on with this nonsense!

SOCRATES: Well, if that's not the sort of thing you mean, perhaps it's this. Take a farmer, a man intelligent and admirable and good about land. Perhaps he should have the greater share of seed and use the largest possible quantity of it on his own land.

CALLICLES: How you keep on saying the same things, Socrates!

SOCRATES: Yes, Callicles, not only the same things, but also about the same subjects.

491   CALLICLES: By the gods! You simply don't let up on your continual talk of shoemakers and cleaners, cooks and doctors, as if our discussion were about them!

SOCRATES: Won't you say whom it's about, then? What does the superior, the more intelligent man have a greater share of, and have it justly? Will you neither bear with my promptings nor tell me yourself?

CALLICLES: I've been saying it all along. First of all, by the ones who are the superior I don't mean cobblers or cooks, but those who are intelligent about the affairs of the city, about the way it's to be well managed. And not only intelligent, but also brave, competent to accomplish whatever they have in mind, without slackening off because of softness of spirit.

SOCRATES: Do you see, my good Callicles, that you and I are not accusing each other of the same thing? You claim that I'm always saying the same things, and you criticize me for it, whereas I, just the opposite of you, claim that you never say the same things about the same subjects. At one time you were defining the better and the superior as the stronger, then again as the more intelligent, and now you've come up with something else again: the superior and the better are now said by you to be the braver. But tell me, my good fellow, once and for all, whom you mean by the better and the superior, and what they're better and superior in.

CALLICLES: But I've already said that I mean those who are intelligent in the affairs of the city, and brave, too. It's fitting that they should be the ones who rule their cities, and what's just is that they, as the rulers, should have a greater share than the others, the ruled.

SOCRATES: But what of themselves, my friend?

CALLICLES: What of *what*?

SOCRATES: Ruling or being ruled?

CALLICLES: What do you mean?

SOCRATES: I mean each individual ruling himself. Or is there no need at all for him to rule himself, but only to rule others?

CALLICLES: What do you mean, rule himself?

SOCRATES: Nothing very subtle. Just what the many mean: being self-controlled and master of oneself, ruling the pleasures and appetites within oneself.

CALLICLES: How delightful you are! By the self-controlled you mean the stupid ones!

SOCRATES: How so? There's no one who'd fail to recognize that I mean no such thing.

CALLICLES: Yes you do, Socrates, very much so. How could a man prove to be happy if hes enslaved to anyone at all? Rather, this is what's admirable and just by nature—and I'll say it to you now with all frankness—that the man who'll live

correctly ought to allow his own appetites to get as large as possible and not restrain them. And when they are as large as possible, he ought to be competent to devote   492
himself to them by virtue of his bravery and intelligence, and to fill them with whatever he may have an appetite for at the time. But this isn't possible for the many, I believe; hence, they become detractors of people like this because of the shame they feel, while they conceal their own impotence. And they say that lack of discipline is shameful, as I was saying earlier, and so they enslave men who are better by nature, and while they themselves lack the ability to provide for themselves fulfillment for their pleasures, their own lack of courage leads them to praise self-control and jus-   b
tice. As for all those who were either sons of kings to begin with or else naturally competent to secure some position of rule for themselves as tyrants or potentates, what in truth could be more shameful and worse than self-control and justice for these people who, although they are free to enjoy good things without any interference, should bring as master upon themselves the law of the many, their talk, and their criticism? Or how could they exist without becoming miserable under that "admirable" regime of justice and self-control, allotting no greater share to their   c
friends than to their enemies, and in this way "rule" in their cities? Rather, the truth of it, Socrates—the thing you claim to pursue—is like this: wantonness, lack of discipline, and freedom, if available in good supply, are excellence and happiness; as for these other things, these fancy phrases, these contracts of men that go against nature, they're worthless nonsense!

SOCRATES: The way you pursue your argument, speaking frankly as you do,   d
certainly does you credit, Callicles. For you are now saying clearly what others are thinking but are unwilling to say. I beg you, then, not to relax in any way, so that it may really become clear how we're to live. Tell me: are you saying that if a person is to be the kind of person he should be, he shouldn't restrain his appetites but let them become as large as possible and then should procure their fulfillment from some source or other, and that this is excellence?   e

CALLICLES: Yes, that's what I'm saying.

SOCRATES: So then those who have no need of anything are wrongly said to be happy?

CALLICLES: Yes, for in that case stones and corpses would be happiest.

SOCRATES: But then the life of those people you call happiest is a strange one, too. I shouldn't be surprised that Euripides' lines are true when he says:

> But who knows whether being alive is being dead
> And being dead is being alive?

Perhaps in reality we're dead. Once I even heard one of the wise men say that we are   493
now dead and that our bodies are our tombs, and that the part of our souls in which our appetites reside is actually the sort of thing to be open to persuasion and to shift back and forth. And hence some clever man, a teller of stories, a Sicilian, perhaps, or an Italian, named this part a jar [*pithos*], on account of its being a persuadable [*pithanon*] and suggestible thing, thus slightly changing the name. And fools [*anoē*   b
toi] he named uninitiated [*amuētoi*], suggesting that that part of the souls of fools

where their appetites are located is their undisciplined part, one not tightly closed, a leaking jar, as it were. He based the image on its insatiability. Now this man, Callicles, quite to the contrary of your view, shows that of the people in Hades— meaning the unseen [aïdes]—these, the uninitiated ones, would be the most miserable. They would carry water into the leaking jar using another leaky thing, a sieve.

c   That's why by the sieve he means the soul (as the man who talked with me claimed). And because they leak, he likened the souls of fools to sieves; for their untrustworthiness and forgetfulness makes them unable to retain anything. This account is on the whole a bit strange; but now that I've shown it to you, it does make clear what I want to persuade you to change your mind about if I can: to choose the orderly life, the life that is adequate to and satisfied with its circumstances at any given time

d   instead of the insatiable, undisciplined life. Do I persuade you at all, and are you changing your mind to believe that those who are orderly are happier than those who are undisciplined, or, even if I tell you many other such stories, will you change it none the more for that?

CALLICLES: The latter thing you said is the truer, Socrates.

SOCRATES: Come then, and let me give you another image, one from the same school as this one. Consider whether what you're saying about each life, the life of the self-controlled man and that of the undisciplined one, is like this: Suppose there are two men, each of whom has many jars. The jars belonging to one of them are

e   sound and full, one with wine, another with honey, a third with milk, and many others with lots of other things. And suppose that the sources of each of these things are scarce and difficult to come by, procurable only with much toil and trouble. Now the one man, having filled up his jars, doesn't pour anything more into them and gives them no further thought. He can relax over them. As for the other one, he too has resources that can be procured, though with difficulty, but his containers are

494 leaky and rotten. He's forced to keep on filling them, day and night, or else he suffers extreme pain. Now since each life is the way I describe it, are you saying that the life of the undisciplined man is happier than that of the orderly man? When I say this, do I at all persuade you to concede that the orderly life is better than the undisciplined one, or do I not?

CALLICLES: You do not, Socrates. The man who has filled himself up has no pleasure any more, and when he's been filled up and experiences neither joy nor

b   pain, that's living like a stone, as I was saying just now. Rather, living pleasantly consists in this: having as much as possible flow in.

SOCRATES: Isn't it necessary, then, that if there's a lot flowing in, there should also be a lot going out and that there should be big holes for what's passed out?

CALLICLES: Certainly.

SOCRATES: Now you're talking about the life of a stonecurlew[13] instead of that of a corpse or a stone. Tell me, do you say that there is such a thing as hunger, and eating when one is hungry?

CALLICLES: Yes, there is.

c   SOCRATES: And thirst, and drinking when one is thirsty?

---

[13] Dodds: "A bird of messy habits and uncertain identity."

CALLICLES: Yes, and also having all other appetites and being able to fill them and enjoy it, and so live happily.

SOCRATES: Very good, my good man! Do carry on the way you've begun, and take care not to be ashamed. And I evidently shouldn't shrink from being ashamed, either. Tell me now first whether a man who has an itch and scratches it and can scratch to his heart's content, scratch his whole life long, can also live happily.

CALLICLES: What nonsense, Socrates. You're a regular crowd pleaser.   d

SOCRATES: That's just how I shocked Polus and Gorgias and made them be ashamed. You certainly won't be shocked, however, or be ashamed, for you're a brave man. Just answer me, please.

CALLICLES: I say that even the man who scratches would have a pleasant life.

SOCRATES: And if a pleasant one, a happy one, too?

CALLICLES: Yes indeed.

SOCRATES: What if he scratches only his head—or what am I to ask you fur-   e
ther? See what you'll answer if somebody asked you one after the other every question that comes next. And isn't the climax of this sort of thing, the life of a catamite,[14] a frightfully shameful and miserable one? Or will you have the nerve to say that they are happy as long as they have what they need to their hearts' content?

CALLICLES: Aren't you ashamed, Socrates, to bring our discussion to such matters?

SOCRATES: Is it I who bring them there, my splendid fellow, or is it the man who claims, just like that, that those who enjoy themselves, however they may be doing it,   495
are happy, and doesn't discriminate between good kinds of pleasures and bad? Tell me now too whether you say that the pleasant and the good are the same or whether there is some pleasure that isn't good.

CALLICLES: Well, to keep my argument from being inconsistent if I say that they're different, I say they're the same.

SOCRATES: You're wrecking your earlier statements, Callicles, and you'd no longer be adequately inquiring into the truth of the matter with me if you speak contrary to what you think.

CALLICLES: And you're wrecking yours, too, Socrates.   b

SOCRATES: In that case, it isn't right for me to do it, if it's what I do, or for you either. But consider, my marvelous friend, surely the good isn't just unrestricted enjoyment. For both those many shameful things hinted at just now obviously follow if this is the case, and many others as well.

CALLICLES: That's your opinion, Socrates.

SOCRATES: Do you really assert these things, Callicles?

CALLICLES: Yes, I do.

SOCRATES: So we're to undertake the discussion on the assumption that you're   c
in earnest?

CALLICLES: Most certainly.

---

[14] Catamite: passive partner (esp. boy) in homosexual practices (*Oxford Dictionary of Current English*).

SOCRATES: All right, since that's what you think, distinguish the following things for me: There is something you call knowledge, I take it?

CALLICLES: Yes.

SOCRATES: Weren't you also saying just now that there is such a thing as bravery with knowledge?

CALLICLES: Yes, I was.

SOCRATES: Was it just on the assumption that bravery is distinct from knowledge that you were speaking of them as two?

CALLICLES: Yes, very much so.

SOCRATES: Well now, do you say that pleasure and knowledge are the same or different?

d   CALLICLES: Different of course, you wisest of men.

SOCRATES: And surely that bravery is different from pleasure, too?

CALLICLES: Of course.

SOCRATES: All right, let's put this on the record: Callicles from Acharnae says that *pleasant* and *good* are the same, and that *knowledge* and *bravery* are different both from each other and from what's good.

CALLICLES: And Socrates from Alopece doesn't agree with us about this. Or does he?

e   SOCRATES: He does not. And I believe that Callicles doesn't either when he comes to see himself rightly. Tell me: don't you think that those who do well have the opposite experience of those who do badly?

CALLICLES: Yes, I do.

SOCRATES: Now since these experiences are the opposites of each other, isn't it necessary that it's just the same with them as it is with health and disease? For a man isn't both healthy and sick at the same time, I take it, nor does he get rid of both health and disease at the same time.

CALLICLES: What do you mean?

496   SOCRATES: Take any part of the body you like, for example, and think about it. A man can have a disease of the eyes, can't he, to which we give the name "eye disease"?

CALLICLES: Of course.

SOCRATES: But then surely his eyes aren't also healthy at the same time?

CALLICLES: No, not in any way.

SOCRATES: What if he gets rid of his eye disease? Does he then also get rid of his eyes' health and so in the end he's rid of both at the same time?

CALLICLES: No, not in the least.

SOCRATES: For that, I suppose, is an amazing and unintelligible thing to
b   happen, isn't it?

CALLICLES: Yes, it very much is.

SOCRATES: But he acquires and loses each of them successively, I suppose.

CALLICLES: Yes, I agree.

SOCRATES: Isn't it like this with strength and weakness, too?

CALLICLES: Yes.

SOCRATES: And with speed and slowness?

CALLICLES: Yes, that's right.

SOCRATES: Now, does he acquire and get rid of good things and happiness, and their opposites, bad things and misery, successively too?

CALLICLES: No doubt he does.

SOCRATES: So if we find things that a man both gets rid of and keeps at the same   c
time, it's clear that these things wouldn't be what's good and what's bad. Are we agreed on that? Think very carefully about it and tell me.

CALLICLES: Yes, I agree most emphatically.

SOCRATES: Go back, now, to what we've agreed on previously. You mentioned hunger—as a pleasant or a painful thing? I mean the hunger itself.

CALLICLES: As a painful thing. But for a hungry man to eat is pleasant.

SOCRATES: I agree. I understand. But the hunger itself is painful, isn't it?   d

CALLICLES: So I say.

SOCRATES: And thirst is, too?

CALLICLES: Very much so.

SOCRATES: Am I to ask any further, or do you agree that every deficiency and appetite is painful?

CALLICLES: I do. No need to ask.

SOCRATES: Fair enough. Wouldn't you say that, for a thirsty person, to drink is something pleasant?

CALLICLES: Yes, I would.

SOCRATES: And in the case you speak of, "a thirsty person" means "a person who's in pain," I take it?

CALLICLES: Yes.   e

SOCRATES: And drinking is a filling of the deficiency, and is a pleasure?

CALLICLES: Yes.

SOCRATES: Now, don't you mean that insofar as a person is drinking, he's feeling enjoyment?

CALLICLES: Very much so.

SOCRATES: Even though he's thirsty?

CALLICLES: Yes, I agree.

SOCRATES: Even though he's in pain?

CALLICLES: Yes.

SOCRATES: Do you observe the result, that when you say that a thirsty person drinks, you're saying that a person who's in pain simultaneously feels enjoyment? Or doesn't this happen simultaneously in the same place, in the soul or in the body as you like? I don't suppose it makes any difference which. Is this so or not?

CALLICLES: It is.

SOCRATES: But you do say that it's impossible for a person who's doing well to   497
be doing badly at the same time.

CALLICLES: Yes, I do.

SOCRATES: Yet you did agree that it's possible for a person in pain to feel enjoyment.

CALLICLES: Apparently.

SOCRATES: So, feeling enjoyment isn't the same as doing well, and being in pain isn't the same as doing badly, and the result is that what's pleasant turns out to be different from what's good.

CALLICLES: I don't know what your clever remarks amount to, Socrates.

SOCRATES: You do know. You're just pretending you don't, Callicles. Go just a bit further ahead.

CALLICLES: Why do you keep up this nonsense?

b   SOCRATES: So you'll know how wise you are in scolding me. Doesn't each of us stop being thirsty and stop feeling pleasure at the same time as a result of drinking?

CALLICLES: I don't know what you mean.

GORGIAS: Not at all, Callicles! Answer him for our benefit too, so that the discussion may be carried through.

CALLICLES: But Socrates is always like this, Gorgias. He keeps questioning people on matters that are trivial, hardly worthwhile, and refutes them!

GORGIAS: What difference does that make to you? It's none of your business to appraise them, Callicles. You promised Socrates that he could try to refute you in any way he liked.

c   CALLICLES: Go ahead, then, and ask these trivial, petty questions, since that's what pleases Gorgias.

SOCRATES: You're a happy man, Callicles, in that you've been initiated into the greater mysteries before the lesser. I didn't think it was permitted. So answer where you left off, and tell me whether each of us stops feeling pleasure at the same time as he stops being thirsty.

CALLICLES: That's my view.

SOCRATES: And doesn't he also stop having pleasures at the same time as he stops being hungry or stops having the other appetites?

CALLICLES: That's so.

d   SOCRATES: Doesn't he then also stop having pains and pleasures at the same time?

CALLICLES: Yes.

SOCRATES: But, he certainly doesn't stop having good things and bad things at the same time, as you agree. Don't you still agree?

CALLICLES: Yes I do. Why?

SOCRATES: Because it turns out that good things are not the same as pleasant ones, and bad things not the same as painful ones. For pleasant and painful things come to a stop simultaneously, whereas good things and bad ones do not, because they are in fact different things. How then could pleasant things be the same as good ones and painful things the same as bad ones?

Look at it this way, too, if you like, for I don't suppose that you agree with that
e   argument, either. Consider this. Don't you call men good because of the presence of good things in them, just as you call them good-looking because of the presence of good looks?

CALLICLES: Yes, I do.

SOCRATES: Well then, do you call foolish and cowardly men good? You didn't a while ago; you were then calling brave and intelligent ones good. Or don't you call these men good?

CALLICLES: Oh yes, I do.

SOCRATES: Well then, have you ever seen a foolish child feel enjoyment?

CALLICLES: Yes, I have.

SOCRATES: But you've never yet seen a foolish man feel enjoyment?

CALLICLES: Yes, I suppose I have. What's the point?

SOCRATES: Nothing. Just answer me.   498

CALLICLES: Yes, I've seen it.

SOCRATES: Well now, have you ever seen an intelligent man feel pain or enjoyment?

CALLICLES: Yes, I daresay I have.

SOCRATES: Now who feels pain or enjoyment more, intelligent men or foolish ones?

CALLIGLES: I don't suppose there's a lot of difference.

SOCRATES: Good enough. Have you ever seen a cowardly man in combat?

CALLICLES: Of course I have.

SOCRATES: Well then, when the enemy retreated, who do you think felt enjoyment more, the cowards or the brave men?

CALLICLES: Both felt it, I think; maybe the cowards felt it more. But if not, they   b
felt it to pretty much the same degree.

SOCRATES: It makes no difference. So cowards feel enjoyment too?

CALLICLES: Oh yes, very much so.

SOCRATES: Fools do too, evidently.

CALLICLES: Yes.

SOCRATES: Now when the enemy advances, are the cowards the only ones to feel pain, or do the brave men do so too?

CALLICLES: They both do.

SOCRATES: To the same degree?

CALLICLES: Maybe the cowards feel it more.

SOCRATES: And when the enemy retreats, don't they feel enjoyment more?

CALLICLES: Maybe.

SOCRATES: So don't foolish men and intelligent ones, and cowardly men and   c
brave ones feel enjoyment and pain to pretty much the same degree, as you say, or cowardly men feel them more than brave ones?

CALLICLES: That's my view.

SOCRATES: But surely the intelligent and brave men are good and the cowardly and foolish are bad?

CALLICLES: Yes.

SOCRATES: Hence the degree of enjoyment and pain that good and bad men feel is pretty much the same.

CALLICLES: I agree.

SOCRATES: Now are good and bad men pretty much equally both good and bad, or are the bad ones even better?

d   CALLICLES: By Zeus! I don't know what you mean.

SOCRATES: Don't you know that you say that the good men are good and the bad men bad because of the presence of good or bad things in them, and that the good things are pleasures and the bad ones pains?

CALLICLES: Yes, I do.

SOCRATES: Aren't good things, pleasures, present in men who feel enjoyment, if in fact they do feel it?

CALLICLES: Of course.

SOCRATES: Now aren't men who feel enjoyment good men, because good things are present in them?

CALLICLES: Yes.

SOCRATES: Well then, aren't bad things, pains, present in men who feel pain?

CALLICLES: They are.

e   SOCRATES: And you do say that it's because of the presence of bad things that bad men are bad. Or don't you say this any more?

CALLICLES: Yes, I do.

SOCRATES: So all those who feel enjoyment are good, and all those who feel pain are bad.

CALLICLES: Yes, that's right.

SOCRATES: And those feeling them more are more so, those feeling them less are less so, and those feeling them to pretty much the same degree are good or bad to pretty much the same degree.

CALLICLES: Yes.

SOCRATES: Now aren't you saying that intelligent men and foolish ones, and cowardly and courageous ones, experience pretty much the same degree of enjoyment and pain, or even that cowardly ones experience more of it?

CALLICLES: Yes, I am.

SOCRATES: Join me, then, in adding up what follows for us from our agree-
499   ments. They say it's an admirable thing to speak of and examine what's admirable "twice and even thrice." We say that the intelligent and

brave man is good, don't we?

CALLICLES: Yes.

SOCRATES: And that the foolish and cowardly man is bad?

CALLICLES: Yes, that's right.

SOCRATES: And again, that the man who feels enjoyment is good?

CALLICLES: Yes.

SOCRATES: And the one experiencing pain is bad?

CALLICLES: Necessarily.

SOCRATES: And that the good and the bad man feel pain and enjoyment to the same degree, and that perhaps the bad man feels them even more?

CALLICLES: Yes.

SOCRATES: Doesn't it then turn out that the bad man is both good and bad to the same degree as the good man, or even that he's better? Isn't this what follows, along with those earlier statements, if one holds that pleasant things are the same as good things? Isn't this necessarily the case, Callicles?

CALLICLES: I've been listening to you for quite some time now, Socrates, and agreeing with you, while thinking that even if a person grants some point to you in jest, you gladly fasten on it, the way boys do. As though you really think that I or anybody else at all don't believe that some pleasures are better and others worse.

SOCRATES: Oh, Callicles! What a rascal you are. You treat me like a child. At one time you say that things are one way and at another that the same things are another way, and so you deceive me. And yet I didn't suppose at the beginning that I'd be deceived intentionally by you, because I assumed you were a friend. Now, however, I've been misled, and evidently have no choice but to "make the best with what I have," as the ancient proverb has it, and to accept what I'm given by you. The thing you're saying now, evidently, is that some pleasures are good while others are bad. Is that right?

CALLICLES: Yes.

SOCRATES: Are the good ones the beneficial ones, and the bad ones the harmful ones?

CALLICLES: Yes, that's right.

SOCRATES: And the beneficial ones are the ones that produce something good while the bad ones are those that produce something bad?

CALLICLES: That's my view.

SOCRATES: Now, do you mean pleasures like the ones we were just now mentioning in connection with the body, those of eating and drinking? Do some of these produce health in the body, or strength, or some other bodily excellence, and are these pleasures good, while those that produce the opposites of these things are bad?

CALLICLES: That's right.

SOCRATES: And similarly, aren't some pains good and others bad, too?

CALLICLES: Of course.

SOCRATES: Now, shouldn't we both choose and act to have the good pleasures and pains?

CALLICLES: Yes, we should.

SOCRATES: But not the bad ones?

CALLICLES: Obviously.

SOCRATES: No, for Polus and I both thought, if you recall, that we should, surely, do all things for the sake of what's good.[15] Do you also think as we do that the end of all action is what's good, and that we should do all other things for its sake, but not it for their sake? Are you voting on our side to make it three?

CALLICLES: Yes, I am.

SOCRATES: So we should do the other things, including pleasant things, for the sake of good things, and not good things for the sake of pleasant things.

[15] At 468b.

CALLICLES: That's right.

SOCRATES: Now, is it for every man to pick out which kinds of pleasures are good ones and which are bad ones, or does this require a craftsman in each case?

CALLICLES: It requires a craftsman.

b   SOCRATES: Let's recall what I was actually saying to Polus and Gorgias.[16] I was saying, if you remember, that there are some practices that concern themselves with nothing further than pleasure and procure only pleasure, practices that are ignorant about what's better and worse, while there are other practices that do know what's good and what's bad. And I placed the "knack" (not the craft) of pastry baking among those that are concerned with pleasure, and the medical craft among those concerned with what's good. And by Zeus, the god of friendship, Callicles, please don't think that you should jest with me either, or answer anything that comes to mind, contrary to what you really think, and please don't accept what you get from

c   me as though I'm jesting! For you see, don't you, that our discussion's about this (and what would even a man of little intelligence take more seriously than this?), about the way we're supposed to live. Is it the way you urge me toward, to engage in these manly activities, to make speeches among the people, to practice oratory, and to be active in the sort of politics you people engage in these days? Or is it the life spent in philosophy? And in what way does this latter way of life differ from the for-

d   mer? Perhaps it's best to distinguish them, as I just tried to do; having done that and having agreed that these are two distinct lives, it's best to examine how they differ from each other, and which of them is the one we should live. Now perhaps you don't yet know what I'm talking about.

CALLICLES: No, I certainly don't.

SOCRATES: Well, I'll tell you more clearly. Given that we're agreed, you and I, that there is such a thing as good and such a thing as *pleasant* and that the pleasant is different from the good, and that there's a practice of each of them and a procedure for obtaining it, the quest for the pleasant on the one hand and that for the good on

e   the other—give me first your assent to this point or withhold it. Do you assent to it?

CALLICLES: Yes, I do.

SOCRATES: Come then, and agree further with me about what I was saying to them too, if you think that what I said then was true. I was saying, wasn't I, that I didn't think that pastry baking is a craft, but a knack, whereas medicine is a craft. I

501   said that the one, medicine, has investigated both the nature of the object it serves and the cause of the things it does, and is able to give an account of each of these. The other, the one concerned with pleasure, to which the whole of its service is entirely devoted, proceeds toward its object in a quite uncraftlike way, without having at all considered either the nature of pleasure or its cause. It does so completely irrationally, with virtually no discrimination. Through routine and knack it merely

b   preserves the memory of what customarily happens, and that's how it also supplies its pleasures. So, consider first of all whether you think that this account is an adequate one and whether you think that there are also other, similar preoccupations in the case of the soul. Do you think that some of the latter are of the order of crafts and

16 At 464b–465a.

possess forethought about what's best for the soul, while others slight this and have investigated only, as in the other case, the soul's way of getting its pleasure, without considering which of the pleasures is better or worse, and without having any concerns about anything but mere gratification, whether for the better or for the worse? For my part, Callicles, I think there are such preoccupations, and I say that this sort of thing is flattery, both in the case of the body and that of the soul and in any other case in which a person may wait upon a pleasure without any consideration of what's better or worse. As for you, do you join us in subscribing to the same opinion on these matters or do you dissent from it?   c

CALLICLES: No, I won't dissent. I'm going along with you, both to expedite your argument and to gratify Gorgias here.

SOCRATES: Now is this the case with one soul only, and not with two or many?   d

CALLICLES: No, it's also the case with two or many.

SOCRATES: Isn't it also possible to gratify a group of souls collectively at one and the same time, without any consideration for what's best?

CALLICLES: Yes, I suppose so.

SOCRATES: Can you tell me which ones are the practices that do this? Better yet, if you like I'll ask you and you say yes for any which you think falls in this group,   e and no for any which you think doesn't. Let's look at fluteplaying first. Don't you think that it's one of this kind, Callicles? That it merely aims at giving us pleasure without giving thought to anything else?

CALLICLES: Yes, I think so.

SOCRATES: Don't all such practices do that, too? Lyreplaying at competitions, for example?

CALLICLES: Yes.

SOCRATES: What about training choruses and composing dithyrambs? Doesn't that strike you as being something of the same sort? Do you think that Cinesias the son of Meles gives any thought to saying anything of a sort that might lead to the improvement of his audience, or to what is likely to gratify the crowd of spectators?   502

CALLICLES: Clearly the latter, Socrates, at least in Cinesias' case.

SOCRATES: What about his father Meles? Do you think he sang to the lyre with a regard for what's best? Or did he fail to regard even what's most pleasant? For he inflicted pain upon his spectators with his singing. But consider whether you don't think that all singing to the lyre and composing of dithyrambs has been invented for the sake of pleasure.

CALLICLES: Yes, I do think so.

SOCRATES: And what about that majestic, awe-inspiring practice, the composi-   b tion of tragedy? What is it after? Is the project, the intent of tragic composition merely the gratification of spectators, as you think, or does it also strive valiantly not to say anything that is corrupt, though it may be pleasant and gratifying to them, and to utter in both speech and song anything that might be unpleasant but beneficial, whether the spectators enjoy it or not? In which of these ways do you think tragedy is being composed?

CALLICLES: This much is obvious, Socrates, that it's more bent upon giving   c pleasure and upon gratifying the spectators.

SOCRATES: And weren't we saying just now that this sort of thing is flattery?

CALLICLES: Yes, we were.

SOCRATES: Well then, if one stripped away from the whole composition both melody, rhythm, and meter, does it turn out that what's left is only speeches?

CALLICLES: Necessarily.

SOCRATES: Aren't these speeches given to a large gathering of people?

CALLICLES: I agree.

SOCRATES: So poetry is a kind of popular harangue.[17]

d   CALLICLES: Apparently.

SOCRATES: And such popular harangue would be oratory, then. Or don't you think that poets practice oratory in the theatres?

CALLICLES: Yes, I do.

SOCRATES: So now we've discovered a popular oratory of a kind that's addressed to men, women, and children, slave and free alike. We don't much like it; we say that it's a flattering sort.

CALLICLES: Yes, that's right.

SOCRATES: Very well. What about the oratory addressed to the Athenian people
e   and to those in other cities composed of free men? What is our view of this kind? Do you think that orators always speak with regard to what's best? Do they always set their sights on making the citizens as good as possible through their speeches? Or are they also bent upon the gratification of the citizens and do they slight the common good for the sake of their own private good, and so keep company with the people trying solely to gratify them, without any thought at all for whether this will make
503   them be better or worse?

CALLICLES: This issue you're asking about isn't just a simple one, for there are those who say what they do because they do care for the citizens, and there are also those like the ones you're talking about.

SOCRATES: That's good enough. For if this matter really has two parts to it, then one part of it would be flattery, I suppose, and shameful public harangue, while the other—that of getting the souls of the citizens to be as good as possible and of striving valiantly to say what is best, whether the audience will find it more pleasant or more unpleasant—is something admirable. But you've never seen this type of ora-
b   tory—or, if you can mention any orator of this sort, why haven't you let me also know who he is?

CALLICLES: No, by Zeus! I certainly can't mention any of our contemporary orators to you.

SOCRATES: Well then, can you mention anyone from former times through whom the Athenians are reputed to have become better after he began his public addresses, when previously they had been worse? I certainly don't know who this could be.

---

[17] Gk. *dēmēgoria*. A cognate noun, *dēmēgoros*, was translated "crowd pleaser" at 482c, where the cognate verb *dēmēgorein* was translated "playing to the crowd."

CALLICLES: What? Don't they tell you that Themistocles proved to be a good   c
man, and so did Cimon, Miltiades and Pericles who died just recently, and whom
you've heard speak, too?

SOCRATES: Yes, Callicles, if the excellence you were speaking of earlier, the
filling up of appetites, both one's own and those of others, is the true kind. But if this
is not, and if what we were compelled to agree on in our subsequent discussion is the
true kind instead—that a man should satisfy those of his appetites that, when they are
filled up, make him better, and not those that make him worse, and that this is a   d
matter of craft—I don't see how I can say that any of these men has proved to be
such a man.

CALLICLES: But if you'll look carefully, you'll find that they were.[18]

SOCRATES: Let's examine the matter calmly and see whether any of these men
has proved to be like that. Well then, won't the good man, the man who speaks with   e
regard to what's best, say whatever he says not randomly but with a view to something, just like the other craftsmen, each of whom keeps his own product in view and
so does not select and apply randomly what he applies, but so that he may give his
product some shape? Take a look at painters for instance, if you would, or house-
builders or shipwrights or any of the other craftsmen you like, and see how each one
places what he does into a certain organization, and compels one thing to be suited   504
for another and to fit to it until the entire object is put together in an organized and
orderly way. The other craftsmen, too, including the ones we were mentioning just
lately, the ones concerned with the body, physical trainers and doctors, no doubt give
order and organization to the body. Do we agree that this is so or not?

CALLICLES: Let's take it that way.

SOCRATES: So if a house gets to be organized and orderly it would be a good
one, and if it gets to be disorganized it would be a terrible one?

CALLICLES: I agree.

SOCRATES: This holds true for a boat, too?

CALLICLES: Yes.   b

SOCRATES: And we surely take it to hold true for our bodies, too?

CALLICLES: Yes, we do.

SOCRATES: What about the soul? Will it be a good one if it gets to be disorganized, or if it gets to have a certain organization and order?

CALLICLES: Given what we said before, we must agree that this is so, too.

SOCRATES: What name do we give to what comes into being in the body as a
result of organization and order?

CALLICLES: You mean health and strength, presumably.

---

[18] There are variances in the mss in the text of the last two lines of Socrates' previous speech and this
response. The translation follows one ms, while the other mss, with a conjectural addition of Dodds',
would yield this: "SOCRATES: . . . and not those that make him worse—and this seemed to us to be a
matter of craft—can you say that any of these men has proved to be such a man? CALLICLES: For my
part, I don't know what I would say. SOCRATES: But if you look carefully you'll find out. Let's examine the matter calmly, then, and . . ."

c   SOCRATES: Yes, I do. And which one do we give to what comes into being in the soul as a result of organization and order? Try to find and tell me its name, as in the case of the body.

CALLICLES: Why don't you say it yourself, Socrates?

SOCRATES: All right, if that pleases you more, I'll do so. And if you think I'm right, give your assent. If not, refute me and don't give way. I think that the name for the states of organization of the body is "healthy," as a result of which health and the rest of bodily excellence comes into being in it. Is this so or isn't it?

CALLICLES: It is.

d   SOCRATES: And the name for the states of organization and order of the soul is "lawful" and "law," which lead people to become law-abiding and orderly, and these are justice and self-control. Do you assent to this or not?

CALLICLES: Let it be so.

SOCRATES: So this is what that skilled and good orator will look to when he applies to people's souls whatever speeches he makes as well as all of his actions, and any gift he makes or any confiscation he carries out. He will always give his

e   attention to how justice may come to exist in the souls of his fellow citizens and injustice be gotten rid of, how self-control may come to exist there and lack of discipline be gotten rid of, and how the rest of excellence may come into being there and badness may depart. Do you agree or not?

CALLICLES: I do.

SOCRATES: Yes, for what benefit is there, Callicles, in giving a body that's sick and in wretched shape lots of very pleasant food or drink or anything else when it won't do the man a bit more good, or, quite to the contrary, when by a fair reckoning it'll do him less good? Is that so?

505   CALLICLES: Let it be so.

SOCRATES: Yes, for I don't suppose that it profits a man to be alive with his body in a terrible condition, for this way his life, too, would be necessarily a wretched one. Or wouldn't it be?

CALLICLES: Yes.

SOCRATES: Now, isn't it also true that doctors generally allow a person to fill up his appetites, to eat when he's hungry, for example, or drink when he's thirsty as much as he wants to when he's in good health, but when he's sick they practically never allow him to fill himself with what he has an appetite for? Do you also go along with this point, at least?

CALLICLES: Yes, I do.

b   SOCRATES: And isn't it just the same way with the soul, my excellent friend? As long as it's corrupt, in that it's foolish, undisciplined, unjust and impious, it should be kept away from its appetites and not be permitted to do anything other than what will make it better. Do you agree or not?

CALLICLES: I agree.

SOCRATES: For this is no doubt better for the soul itself?

CALLICLES: Yes, it is.

SOCRATES: Now isn't keeping it away from what it has an appetite for, disciplining it?

CALLICLES: Yes.

SOCRATES: So to be disciplined is better for the soul than lack of discipline, which is what you yourself were thinking just now.

CALLICLES: I don't know what in the world you mean, Socrates. Ask somebody else.

SOCRATES: This fellow won't put up with being benefited and with his undergoing the very thing the discussion's about, with being disciplined.

CALLICLES: And I couldn't care less about anything you say, either. I gave you these answers just for Gorgias' sake.

SOCRATES: Very well. What'll we do now? Are we breaking off in the midst of the discussion?

CALLICLES: That's for you to decide.

SOCRATES: They say that it isn't permitted to give up in the middle of telling stories, either. A head must be put on it, so that it won't go about headless. Please answer the remaining questions, too, so that our discussion may get its head.

CALLICLES: How unrelenting you are, Socrates! If you'll listen to me, you'll drop this discussion or carry it through with someone else.

SOCRATES: Who else is willing? Surely we mustn't leave the discussion incomplete.

CALLICLES: Couldn't you go through the discussion by yourself, either by speaking in your own person or by answering your own questions?

SOCRATES: In that case Epicharmus' saying applies to me: I prove to be sufficient, being "one man, for what two men were saying before."[19] But it looks as though I have no choice at all. Let's by all means do it that way then. I suppose that all of us ought to be contentiously eager to know what's true and what's false about the things we're talking about. That it should become clear is a good common to all. I'll go through the discussion, then, and say how I think it is, and if any of you thinks that what I agree to with myself isn't so, you must object and refute me. For the things I say I certainly don't say with any knowledge at all; no, I'm searching together with you so that if my opponent clearly has a point, I'll be the first to concede it. I'm saying this, however, in case you think the discussion ought to be carried through to the end. If you don't want it to be, then let's drop it now and leave.

GORGIAS: No, Socrates, I don't think we should leave yet. You must finish the discussion. It seems to me that the others think so, too. I myself certainly want to hear you go through the rest of it by yourself.

SOCRATES: All right, Gorgias. I myself would have been glad to continue my discussion with Callicles here, until I returned him Amphion's speech for that of Zethus. Well, Callicles, since you're not willing to join me in carrying the discussion through to the end, please do listen to me and interrupt if you think I'm saying anything wrong. And if you refute me, I shan't be upset with you as you were with me; instead you'll go on record as my greatest benefactor.

CALLICLES: Speak on, my good friend, and finish it up by yourself.

---

[19] Epicharmus was a comic poet; the source of the line is not known.

SOCRATES: Listen, then, as I pick up the discussion from the beginning. Is the pleasant the same as the good?—It isn't, as Callicles and I have agreed.—Is the pleasant to be done for the sake of the good, or the good for the sake of the pleasant?—The pleasant for the sake of the good.—And *pleasant* is that by which, when

d   it's come to be present in us, we feel pleasure, and good that by which, when it's present in us, we are good?—That's right.—But surely we are good, both we and everything else that's good, when some excellence has come to be present in us?— Yes, I do think that that's necessarily so, Callicles.—But the best way in which the excellence of each thing comes to be present in it, whether it's that of an artifact or of a body or a soul as well, or of any animal, is not just any old way, but is due to what- ever organization, correctness, and craftsmanship is bestowed on each of them. Is

e   that right?—Yes, I agree.—So it's due to organization that the excellence of each thing is something which is organized and has order?—Yes, I'd say so.—So it's when a certain order, the proper one for each thing, comes to be present in it that it makes each of the things there are, good?—Yes, I think so.—So also a soul which has its own order is better than a disordered one?—Necessarily so.—But surely one that has order is an orderly one?—Of course it is.—And an orderly soul is a self-

507 controlled one?—Absolutely.—So a self-controlled soul is a good one. I for one can't say anything else beyond that, Callicles my friend; if you can, please teach me.

CALLICLES: Say on, my good man.

SOCRATES: I say that if the self-controlled soul is a good one, then a soul that's been affected the opposite way of the self-controlled one is a bad one. And this, it's turned out, is the foolish and undisciplined one.—That's right.—And surely a self- controlled person would do what's appropriate with respect to both gods and human beings. For if he does what's inappropriate, he wouldn't be self-controlled.—That's

b   necessarily how it is.—And of course if he did what's appropriate with respect to human beings, he would be doing what's just, and with respect to gods he would be doing what's pious, and one who does what's just and pious must necessarily be just and pious.—That's so.—Yes, and he would also necessarily be brave, for it's not like a self-controlled man to either pursue or avoid what isn't appropriate, but to avoid and pursue what he should, whether these are things to do, or people, or pleasures and pains, and to stand fast and endure them where he should. So, it's necessarily

c   very much the case, Callicles, that the self-controlled man, because he's just and brave and pious, as we've recounted, is a completely good man, that the good man does well and admirably whatever he does, and that the man who does well is blessed and happy, while the corrupt man, the one who does badly, is miserable. And this would be the one who's in the condition opposite to that of the self-controlled one, the undisciplined one whom you were praising.

So this is how I set down the matter, and I say that this is true. And if it is true, then a person who wants to be happy must evidently pursue and practice self-control.

d   Each of us must flee away from lack of discipline as quickly as his feet will carry him, and must above all make sure that he has no need of being disciplined, but if he does have that need, either he himself or anyone in his house, either a private citizen or a whole city, he must pay his due and must be disciplined, if he's to be happy. This is the target which I think one should look to in living, and in his actions he should

direct all of his own affairs and those of his city to the end that justice and self-   e
control will be present in one who is to be blessed. He should not allow his appetites
to be undisciplined or undertake to fill them up—that's interminably bad—and live
the life of a marauder. Such a man could not be dear to another man or to a god, for
he cannot be a partner, and where there's no partnership there's no friendship. Yes,
Callicles, wise men claim that partnership and friendship, orderliness, self-control,   508
and justice hold together heaven and earth, and gods and men, and that is why they
call this universe a *world order,* my friend, and not an undisciplined world-disorder.
I believe that you don't pay attention to these facts, even though you're a wise man
in these matters. You've failed to notice that proportionate equality has great power
among both gods and men, and you suppose that you ought to practice getting the
greater share. That's because you neglect geometry.

Very well. We must either refute this argument and show that it's not the posses-   b
sion of justice and self-control that makes happy people happy and the possession of
badness that makes miserable people miserable, or else, if this is true, we must consider what the consequences are. These consequences are all those previous things,
Callicles, the ones about which you asked me whether I was speaking in earnest
when I said that a man should be his own accuser, or his son's or his friend's, if he's
done anything unjust, and should use oratory for that purpose. Also what you thought
Polus was ashamed to concede is true after all, that doing what's unjust is as much   c
worse than suffering it as it is more shameful, and that a person who is to be an orator the right way should be just and be knowledgeable in what is just, the point Polus
in his turn claimed Gorgias to have agreed to out of shame.

That being so, let's examine what it is you're taking me to task for, and whether
it's right or not. You say that I'm unable to protect either myself or any of my friends
or relatives or rescue them from the gravest dangers, and that I'm at the mercy of the
first comer, just as people without rights are, whether he wants to knock me on the   d
jaw, to use that forceful expression of yours, or confiscate my property, or exile me
from the city, or ultimately put me to death. To be in that position is, by your reasoning, the most shameful thing of all. As for what my own reasoning is, that's been told
many times by now, but there's nothing to stop its being told once again. I deny,
Callicles, that being knocked on the jaw unjustly is the most shameful thing, or that   e
having my body or my purse cut is, and I affirm that to knock or cut me or my possessions unjustly is both more shameful and worse, and at the same time that to rob
or enslave me or to break into my house or, to sum up, to commit any unjust act at all
against me and my possessions is both worse and more shameful for the one who
does these unjust acts than it is for me, the one who suffers them. These conclusions,
at which we arrived earlier in our previous discussions are, I'd say, held down and
bound by arguments of iron and adamant, even if it's rather rude to say so. So it
would seem, anyhow. And if you or someone more forceful than you won't undo   509
them, then anyone who says anything other than what I'm now saying cannot be
speaking well. And yet for my part, my account is ever the same: I don't know how
these things are, but no one I've ever met, as in this case, can say anything else without being ridiculous. So once more I set it down that these things are so. And if they
are—if injustice is the worst thing there is for the person committing it and if that   b

person's failure to pay what's due is something even worse, if possible, than this one that's the greatest—what is the protection which would make a man who's unable to provide it for himself truly ridiculous? Isn't it the One that will turn away what harms us most? Yes, it's necessarily very much the case that this is the most shameful kind of protection not to be able to provide, either for oneself or for one's friends or relatives. And the second kind's the one that turns away the second worst thing,

c   the third kind the one against the third worst, and so on. The greater by its nature each bad thing is, the more admirable it is to be able to provide protection against it, too, and the more shameful not to be able to. Is this the way it is, Callicles, or is it some other way?

CALLICLES: No, it's not any other way.

SOCRATES: Of these two things, then, of doing what's unjust and suffering it, we say that doing it is worse and suffering it is less bad. With what, then, might a man

d   provide himself to protect himself so that he has both these benefits, the one that comes from not doing what's unjust and the one that comes from not suffering it? Is it power or wish? What I mean is this: Is it when a person doesn't wish to suffer what's unjust that he will avoid suffering it, or when he procures a power to avoid suffering it?

CALLICLES: When he procures a power. That is obvious, at least.

SOCRATES: And what about doing what's unjust? Is it when he doesn't wish to

e   do it, is that sufficient—for he won't do it—or should he procure a power and a craft for this, too, so that unless he learns and practices it, he will commit injustice? Why don't you answer at least this question, Callicles? Do you think Polus and I were or were not correct in being compelled to agree in our previous discussion when we agreed that no one does what's unjust because he wants to, but that all who do so do it unwillingly?[20]

510   CALLICLES: Let it be so, Socrates, so you can finish up your argument.

SOCRATES: So we should procure a certain power and craft against this too, evidently, so that we won't do what's unjust.

CALLICLES: That's right.

SOCRATES: What, then, is the craft by which we make sure that we don't suffer anything unjust, or as little as possible? Consider whether you think it's the one I do. This is what I think it is: that one ought either to be a ruler himself in his city or even be a tyrant, or else to be a partisan of the regime in power.

b   CALLICLES: Do you see, Socrates, how ready I am to applaud you whenever you say anything right? I think that this statement of yours is right on the mark.

SOCRATES: Well, consider whether you think that the following statement of mine is a good one, too. I think that the one man who's a friend of another most of all is the one whom the men of old and the wise call a friend, the one who's like the other. Don't you think so, too?

CALLICLES: Yes, I do.

---

[20] Cf. 467c–468e.

SOCRATES: Now, if in the case of a tyrant who's a savage, uneducated ruler, there were in his city someone much better than he, wouldn't the tyrant no doubt be afraid of him and never be able to be a friend to him with all his heart?

CALLICLES: That's so.

SOCRATES: Nor would he, the tyrant, be a friend to a man much his inferior, if there were such a man, for the tyrant would despise him and would never take a serious interest in him as a friend.

CALLICLES: That's true, too.

SOCRATES: This leaves only a man of like character, one who approves and disapproves of the same thing and who is willing to be ruled by and be subject to the ruler, to be to such a man a friend worth mentioning. This man will have great power in that city, and no one will do him any wrong and get away with it. Isn't that so?

CALLICLES: Yes.

SOCRATES: So, if some young person in that city were to reflect, "In what way would I be able to have great power and no one treat me unjustly?" this, evidently, would be his way to go: to get himself accustomed from childhood on to like and dislike the same things as the master, and to make sure that he'll be as like him as possible. Isn't that so?

CALLICLES: Yes.

SOCRATES: Now won't this man have achieved immunity to unjust treatment and great power in his city, as you people say?

CALLICLES: Oh, yes.

SOCRATES: And also immunity to unjust action? Or is that far from the case, since he'll be like the ruler who's unjust, and he'll have his great power at the ruler's side? For my part, I think that, quite to the contrary, in this way he'll be making sure he'll have the ability to engage in as much unjust action as possible and to avoid paying what's due for acting so. Right?

CALLICLES: Apparently.

SOCRATES: So he'll have incurred the worst thing there is, when his soul is corrupt and mutilated on account of his imitation of the master and on account of his "power."

CALLICLES: I don't know how you keep twisting our discussion in every direction, Socrates. Or don't you know that this "imitator" will put to death, if he likes, your "non-imitator," and confiscate his property?

SOCRATES: I do know that, Callicles. I'm not deaf. I hear you say it, and heard Polus just now say it many times, and just about everyone else in the city. But now you listen to me, too. I say that, yes, he'll kill him, if he likes, but it'll be a wicked man killing one who's admirable and good.

CALLICLES: And isn't that just the most irritating thing about it?

SOCRATES: No, not for an intelligent person, anyway, as our discussion points out. Or do you think that a man ought to make sure that his life be as long as possible and that he practice those crafts that ever rescue us from dangers, like the oratory that you tell me to practice, the kind that preserves us in the law courts?

CALLICLES: Yes, and by Zeus, that's sound advice for you!

SOCRATES: Well, my excellent fellow, do you think that expertise in swimming is a grand thing?

CALLICLES: No, by Zeus, I don't.

SOCRATES: But it certainly does save people from death whenever they fall into the kind of situation that requires this expertise. But if you think this expertise is a trivial one, I'll give you one more important than it, that of helmsmanship, which saves not only souls but also bodies and valuables from the utmost dangers, just as oratory does. This expertise is unassuming and orderly, and does not make itself grand, posturing as though its accomplishment is so magnificent. But while its accomplishment is the same as that of the expertise practiced in the courts, it has earned two obols, I suppose, if it has brought people safely here from Aegina; and if it has brought them here from Egypt or the Pontus,[21] then, for that great service, having given safe passage to those I was mentioning just now, the man himself, his children, valuables, and womenfolk, and setting them ashore in the harbor, it has earned two drachmas, if that much.[22] And the man who possesses the craft and who has accomplished these feats, disembarks and goes for a stroll along the seaside and beside his ship, with a modest air. For he's enough of an expert, I suppose, to conclude that it isn't clear which ones of his fellow voyagers he has benefited by not letting them drown in the deep, and which ones he has harmed, knowing that they were no better in either body or soul when he set them ashore than they were when they embarked. So he concludes that if a man afflicted with serious incurable physical diseases did not drown, this man is miserable for not dying and has gotten no benefit from him. But if a man has many incurable diseases in what is more valuable than his body, his soul, life for that man is not worth living, and he won't do him any favor if he rescues him from the sea or from prison or from anywhere else. He knows that for a corrupt person it's better not to be alive, for he necessarily lives badly.

That is why it's not the custom for the helmsman to give himself glory even though he preserves us, and not the engineer either, who sometimes can preserve us no less well than a general or anyone else, not to mention a helmsman. For there are times when he preserves entire cities. You don't think that he's on a level with the advocate, do you? And yet if he wanted to say what you people do, Callicles, glorifying his occupation, he would smother you with speeches, telling you urgently that people should become engineers, because nothing else amounts to anything. And the speech would make his point. But you nonetheless despise him and his craft, and you'd call him "engineer" as a term of abuse. You'd be unwilling either to give your daughter to his son, or take his daughter yourself. And yet, given your grounds for applauding your own activities, what just reason do you have for despising the engineer and the others whom I was mentioning just now? I know that you'd say that you're a better man, one from better stock. But if "better" does not mean what I take it to mean, and if instead to preserve yourself and what belongs to you, no matter what sort of person you happen to be, is what excellence is, then your reproach against engineer, doctor, and all the other crafts which have been devised to preserve

---

[21] A region along the southern shore of the Black Sea.
[22] A drachma is six obols. In 409–406 B.C. the standard daily wage of a laborer was one drachma.

us will prove to be ridiculous. But, my blessed man, please see whether what's noble and what's good isn't something other than preserving and being preserved. Perhaps one who is truly a man should stop thinking about how long he will live. He should not be attached to life but should commit these concerns to the god and believe the women who say that not one single person can escape fate. He should thereupon give consideration to how he might live the part of his life still before him as well as possible. Should it be by becoming like the regime under which he lives? In that case you should now be making yourself as much like the Athenian people as possible if you expect to endear yourself to them and have great power in the city. Please see whether this profits you and me, my friend, so that what they say happens to the Thessalian witches when they pull down the moon[23] won't happen to us. Our choice of this kind of civic power will cost us what we hold most dear. If you think that some person or other will hand you a craft of the sort that will give you great power in this city while you are unlike the regime, whether for better or for worse, then in my opinion, Callicles, you're not well advised. You mustn't be their imitator but be naturally like them in your own person if you expect to produce any genuine result toward winning the friendship of the Athenian people [demos] and, yes, by Zeus, of Demos the son of Pyrilampes to boot. Whoever then turns you out to be most like these men, he'll make you a politician in the way you desire to be one, and an orator, too. For each group of people takes delight in speeches that are given in its own character, and resents those given in an alien manner—unless you say something else, my dear friend. Can we say anything in reply to this, Callicles?

CALLICLES: I don't know, Socrates—in a way you seem to me to be right, but the thing that happens to most people has happened to me: I'm not really persuaded by you.

SOCRATES: It's your love for the people, Callicles, existing in your soul, that stands against me. But if we closely examine these same matters often and in a better way, you'll be persuaded. Please recall that we said that there are two practices for caring for a particular thing, whether it's the body or the soul.[24] One of them deals with pleasure and the other with what's best and doesn't gratify it but struggles against it. Isn't this how we distinguished them then?

CALLICLES: Yes, that's right.

SOCRATES: Now one of them, the one dealing with pleasure, is ignoble and is actually nothing but flattery, right?

CALLICLES: Let it be so, if you like.

SOCRATES: Whereas the other one, the one that aims to make the thing we're caring for, whether it's a body or a soul, as good as possible, is the more noble one?

CALLICLES: Yes, that's so.

SOCRATES: Shouldn't we then attempt to care for the city and its citizens with the aim of making the citizens themselves as good as possible? For without this, as we discovered earlier, it does no good to provide any other service if the intentions of

23 That is, causing an eclipse.
24 At 500b.

514   those who are likely to make a great deal of money or take a position of rule over people or some other position of power aren't admirable and good. Are we to put this down as true?

CALLICLES: Certainly, if that pleases you more.

SOCRATES: Suppose, then, Callicles, that you and I were about to take up the public business of the city, and we called on each other to carry out building projects—the major works of construction: walls, or ships, or temples—would we have to

b   examine and check ourselves closely, first, to see if we are or are not experts in the building craft, and whom we've learned it from? Would we have to, or wouldn't we?

CALLICLES: Yes, we would.

SOCRATES: And, second, we'd have to check, wouldn't we, whether we've ever built a work of construction in private business, for a friend of ours, say, or for ourselves, and whether this structure is admirable or disgraceful. And if we discovered on examination that our teachers have proved to be good and reputable ones, and that

c   the works of construction built by us under their guidance were numerous and admirable, and those built by us on our own after we left our teachers were numerous, too, then, if that were our situation, we'd be wise to proceed to public projects. But if we could point out neither teacher nor construction works, either none at all or else many worthless ones, it would surely be stupid to undertake public projects and

d   to call each other on to them. Shall we say that this point is right, or not?

CALLICLES: Yes, we shall.

SOCRATES: Isn't it so in all cases, especially if we attempted to take up public practice and called on each other, thinking we were capable doctors? I'd have examined you, and you me, no doubt: "Well now, by the gods! What is Socrates' own physical state of health? Has there ever been anyone else, slave or free man, whose deliverance from illness has been due to Socrates?" And I'd be considering other

e   similar questions about you, I suppose. And if we found no one whose physical improvement has been due to us, among either visitors or townspeople, either a man or a woman, then by Zeus, Callicles, wouldn't it be truly ridiculous that people should advance to such a height of folly that, before producing many mediocre as well as many successful results in private practice and before having had sufficient exercise at the craft, they should attempt to "learn pottery on the big jar," as that saying goes, and attempt both to take up public practice themselves and to call on others like them to do so as well? Don't you think it would be stupid to proceed like that?

CALLICLES: Yes, I do.

515   SOCRATES: But now, my most excellent fellow, seeing that you yourself are just now beginning to be engaged in the business of the city and you call on me and take me to task for not doing so, shall we not examine each other? "Well now, has Callicles ever improved any of the citizens? Is there anyone who was wicked before, unjust, undisciplined, and foolish, a visitor or townsman, a slave or free man, who because of Callicles has turned out admirable and good?" Tell me, Callicles, what

b   will you say if somebody asks you these scrutinizing questions? Whom will you say you've made a better person through your association with him? Do you shrink back from answering—if there even *is* anything you produced while still in private practice before attempting a public career?

CALLICLES: You love to win, Socrates.

SOCRATES: But it's not for love of winning that I'm asking you. It's rather because I really do want to know the way, whatever it is, in which you suppose the city's business ought to be conducted among us. Now that you've advanced to the business of the city, are we to conclude that you're devoted to some objective other than that we, the citizens, should be as good as possible? Haven't we agreed many times already that this is what a man active in politics should be doing? Have we or haven't we? Please answer me. Yes we have. (I'll answer for you.) So, if this is what a good man should make sure about for his own city, think back now to those men whom you were mentioning a little earlier and tell me whether you still think that Pericles, Cimon, Miltiades, and Themistocles have proved to be good citizens.

CALLICLES: Yes, I do.

SOCRATES: So if they were good ones, each of them was obviously making the citizens better than they were before. Was he or wasn't he?

CALLICLES: Yes.

SOCRATES: So when Pericles first began giving speeches among the people, the Athenians were worse than when he gave his last ones?

CALLICLES: Presumably.

SOCRATES: Not "presumably," my good man. It necessarily follows from what we've agreed, if he really was a good citizen.

CALLICLES: So what?

SOCRATES: Nothing. But tell me this as well. Are the Athenians said to have become better because of Pericles, or, quite to the contrary, are they said to have been corrupted by him? That's what *I* hear, anyhow, that Pericles made the Athenians idle and cowardly, chatterers and moneygrubbers, since he was the first to institute wages for them.

CALLICLES: The people you hear say this have cauliflower ears, Socrates.

SOCRATES: Here, though, is something I'm not just hearing. I do know clearly and you do, too, that at first Pericles had a good reputation, and when they were worse, the Athenians never voted to convict him in any shameful deposition. But after he had turned them into "admirable and good" people, near the end of his life, they voted to convict Pericles of embezzlement and came close to condemning him to death, because they thought he was a wicked man, obviously.

CALLICLES: Well? Did that make Pericles a bad man?

SOCRATES: A man like that who cared for donkeys or horses or cattle would at least look bad if he showed these animals kicking, butting, and biting him because of their wildness, when they had been doing none of these things when he took them over. Or don't you think that any caretaker of any animal is a bad one who will show his animals to be wilder than when he took them over, when they were gentler? Do you think so or not?

CALLICLES: Oh yes, so I may gratify you.

SOCRATES: In that case gratify me now with your answer, too. Is man one of the animals, too?

CALLICLES: Of course he is.

SOCRATES: Wasn't Pericles a caretaker of men?

CALLICLES: Yes.

SOCRATES: Well? Shouldn't he, according to what we agreed just now, have turned them out more just instead of more unjust, if while he cared for them he really was good at politics?

c

CALLICLES: Yes, he should have.

SOCRATES: Now as Homer says, the just are gentle.25 What do you say? Don't you say the same?

CALLICLES: Yes.

SOCRATES: But Pericles certainly showed them to be wilder than they were when he took them over, and that toward himself, the person he'd least want this to happen to.

CALLICLES: Do you want me to agree with you?

SOCRATES: Yes, if you think that what I say is true.

CALLICLES: So be it, then.

SOCRATES: And if wilder, then both more unjust and worse?

d

CALLICLES: So be it.

SOCRATES: So on this reasoning Pericles wasn't good at politics.

CALLICLES: You at least deny that he was.

SOCRATES: By Zeus, you do, too, given what you were agreeing to. Let's go back to Cimon. Tell me: didn't the people he was serving ostracize him so that they wouldn't hear his voice for ten years? And didn't they do the very same thing to Themistocles, punishing him with exile besides? And didn't they vote to throw

e

Miltiades, of Marathon fame, into the pit, and if it hadn't been for the prytanis he would have been thrown in?26 And yet these things would not have happened to these men if they were good men, as you say they were. At least it's not the case that good drivers are the ones who at the start don't fall out of their chariots but who do fall out after they've cared for their horses and become better drivers themselves. This doesn't happen either in driving or in any other work. Or do you think it does?

CALLICLES: No, I don't.

517

SOCRATES: So it looks as though our earlier statements were true, that we don't know any man who has proved to be good at politics in this city. You were agreeing that none of our present-day ones has, though you said that some of those of times past had, and you gave preference to these men. But these have been shown to be on equal footing with the men of today. The result is that if these men were orators, they practiced neither the true oratory—for in that case they wouldn't have been thrown out—nor the flattering kind.

CALLICLES: But surely, Socrates, any accomplishment that any of our present-

b

day men produces is a far cry from the sorts of accomplishments produced by any one of the others you choose.

25 Apparently a reference to the formulaic expression, "wild and not just," which occurs three times in the *Odyssey* (vi.120; ix.175; xiii.201).

26 The *prytanis* was that member of the officiating tribe in the Council chosen daily by lot to preside over the Council and the Assembly.

SOCRATES: No, my strange friend, I'm not criticizing these men either, insofar as they were servants of the city. I think rather that they proved to be better servants than the men of today, and more capable than they of satisfying the city's appetites. But the truth is that in redirecting its appetites and not giving in to them, using persuasion or constraint to get the citizens to become better, they were really not much c different from our contemporaries. That alone is the task of a good citizen. Yes, I too agree with you that they were more clever than our present leaders at supplying ships and walls and dockyards and many other things of the sort.

Now you and I are doing an odd thing in our conversation. The whole time we've been discussing, we constantly keep drifting back to the same point, neither of us recognizing what the other is saying. For my part, I believe you've agreed many times and recognized that after all this subject of ours has two parts, both in the case of the body and the soul. The one part of it is the servient one, enabling us to provide d our bodies with food whenever they're hungry or with drink whenever they're thirsty, and whenever they're cold, with clothes, wraps, shoes, and other things our bodies come to have an appetite for. I'm purposely using the same examples in speaking to you, so that you'll understand more easily. For these, I think you agree, are the very things a shopkeeper, importer, or producer can provide, a breadbaker or pastrychef, a weaver or cobbler or tanner, so it isn't at all surprising that such a per- e son should think himself and be thought by others to be a caretaker of the body—by everyone who doesn't know that over and above all these practices there's a craft, that of gymnastics and medicine, that really does care for the body and is entitled to rule all these crafts and use their products because of its knowledge of what food or drink is good or bad for bodily excellence, a knowledge which all of the others lack. 518 That's why the other crafts are slavish and servient and ill-bred, and why gymnastics and medicine are by rights mistresses over them. Now, when I say that these same things hold true of the soul, too, I think you sometimes understand me, and you agree as one who knows what I'm saying. But then a little later you come along saying that there have been persons whove proved to be admirable and good citizens in the city, b and when I ask who they are, you seem to me to produce people who in the area of politics are very much the same sort you would produce if I asked you, "Who have proved to be or are good caretakers of bodies?" and you replied in all seriousness, "Thearion the breadbaker, and Mithaecus the author of the book on Sicilian pastry baking, and Sarambus the shopkeeper, because these men have proved to be wonderful caretakers of bodies, the first by providing wonderful loaves of bread, the second pastry, and the third wine." c

Perhaps you'd be upset if I said to you, "My man, you don't have the slightest understanding of gymnastics. The men you're mentioning to me are servants, satisfiers of appetites! They have no understanding whatever of anything that's admirable and good in these cases. They'll fill and fatten people's bodies, if they get the chance, and besides that, destroy their original flesh as well, all the while receiving their praise! These people, in their turn, thanks to their inexperience, will lay the blame for their illnesses and the destruction of their original flesh not on those who threw the d parties, but on any people who happen to be with them at the time giving them advice. Yes, when that earlier stuffing has come bringing sickness in its train much later, then, because it's proved to be unhealthy, they'll blame these people and scold them and do something bad to them if they can, and they'll sing the praises of those

e   earlier people, the ones responsible for their ills. Right now you're operating very much like that, too, Callicles. You sing the praises of those who threw parties for these people, and who feasted them lavishly with what they had an appetite for. And they say that *they* have made the city great! But that the city is swollen and festering,

519 thanks to those early leaders, that they don't notice. For they filled the city with harbors and dockyards, walls, and tribute payments and such trash as that, but did so without justice and self-control. So, when that fit of sickness comes on, they'll blame their advisers of the moment and sing the praises of Themistocles and Cimon and Pericles, the ones who are to blame for their ills. Perhaps, if you're not careful,

b   they'll lay their hands on you, and on my friend Alcibiades, when they lose not only what they gained but what they had originally as well, even though you aren't responsible for their ills but perhaps accessories to them.

And yet there's a foolish business that I, for one, both see happening now and hear about in connection with our early leaders. For I notice that whenever the city lays its hands on one of its politicians because he does what's unjust, they resent it and complain indignantly that they're suffering terrible things. They've done many good

c   things for the city, and so they're being unjustly brought to ruin by it, so their argument goes. But that's completely false. Not a single city leader could ever be brought to ruin by the very city he's the leader of. It looks as though those who profess to be politicians are just like those who profess to be sophists. For sophists, too, even though they're wise in other matters, do this absurd thing: while they claim to be teachers of excellence, they frequently accuse their students of doing them wrong, depriving them of their fees and withholding other forms of thanks from them, even though the students have been well served by them. Yet what could be a more illogi-

d   cal business than this statement, that people who've become good and just, whose injustice has been removed by their teacher and who have come to possess justice, should wrong him—something they can't do? Don't you think that's absurd, my friend? You've made me deliver a real popular harangue, Callicles, because you aren't willing to answer.

CALLICLES: And you couldn't speak unless somebody answered you?

e   SOCRATES: Evidently I could. Anyhow I *am* stretching my speeches out at length now, since you're unwilling to answer me. But, my good man, tell me, by the god of friendship: don't you think it's illogical that someone who says he's made someone else good should find fault with that person, charging that he, whom he himself made to become and to be good, is after all wicked?

CALLICLES: Yes, I do think so.

SOCRATES: Don't you hear people who say they're educating people for excellence saying things like that?

520 CALLICLES: Yes, I do. But why would you mention completely worthless people?

SOCRATES: Why would you talk about those people who, although they say they're the city's leaders and devoted to making it as good as possible, turn around and accuse it, when the time comes, of being the most wicked? Do you think they're any different from those others? Yes, my blessed man, they are one and the same, the sophist and the orator, or nearly so and pretty similar, as I was telling Polus. But because you don't see this, you suppose that one of them, oratory, is something wonderful, while you sneer at the other. In actuality, however, sophistry is more to be admired than oratory, insofar as legislation is more admirable than the administration of justice, and gymnastics more than medicine. And I, for one, should have supposed that public speakers and sophists are the only people not in a position to charge the creature they themselves educate with being wicked to them, or else they simultaneously accuse themselves as well, by this same argument, of having entirely failed to benefit those whom they say they benefit. Isn't this so?

CALLICLES: Yes, it is.

SOCRATES: And if what I was saying is true, then they alone, no doubt, are in a position to offer on terms of honor the benefit they provide—without charge, as is reasonable. For somebody who had another benefit conferred on him, one who, for example, had been turned into a fast runner by a physical trainer, could perhaps deprive the man of his compensation if the trainer offered him that benefit on his honor, instead of agreeing on a fixed fee and taking his money as closely as possible to the time he imparts the speed. For I don't suppose that it's by slowness that people act unjustly, but by injustice. Right?

CALLICLES: Yes.

SOCRATES: So if somebody removes that very thing, injustice, he shouldn't have any fear of being treated unjustly. For him alone is it safe to offer this benefit on terms of honor, if it's really true that one can make people good. Isn't that so?

CALLICLES: I agree.

SOCRATES: This, then, is evidently why there's nothing shameful in taking money for giving advice concerning other matters such as housebuilding or the other crafts.

CALLICLES: Yes, evidently.

SOCRATES: But as for this activity, which is concerned with how a person might be as good as possible and manage his own house or his city in the best possible way, it's considered shameful to refuse to give advice concerning it unless somebody pays you money. Right?

CALLICLES: Yes.

SOCRATES: For it's clear that what accounts for this is the fact that of all the benefits this one alone makes the one who has had good done to him have the desire to do good in return, so that we think it's a good sign of someone's having done good by conferring this benefit that he'll have good done to him in return, and not a good sign if he won't. Is this how it is?

CALLICLES: It is.

SOCRATES: Now, please describe for me precisely the type of care for the city to which you are calling me. Is it that of striving valiantly with the Athenians to make them as good as possible, like a doctor, or is it like one ready to serve them and to associate with them for their gratification? Tell me the truth, Callicles. For just as you began by speaking candidly to me, it's only fair that you should continue speaking your mind. Tell me now, too, well and nobly.

CALLICLES: In that case I say it's like one ready to serve.

b   SOCRATES: So, noblest of men, you're calling on me to be ready to flatter.

CALLICLES: Yes, if you find it more pleasant not to mince words, Socrates. Because if you don't do this—

SOCRATES: I hope you won't say what you've said many times, that anyone who wants to will put me to death. That way I, too, won't repeat my claim that it would be a wicked man doing this to a good man. And don't say that he'll confiscate any of my possessions, either, so I won't reply that when he's done so he won't know how to use them. Rather, just as he unjustly confiscated them from me, so, having

c   gotten them, he'll use them unjustly too, and if unjustly, shamefully, and if shamefully, badly.

CALLICLES: How sure you seem to me to be, Socrates, that not even one of these things will happen to you! You think that you live out of their way and that you wouldn't be brought to court perhaps by some very corrupt and mean man.

SOCRATES: In that case I really am a fool, Callicles, if I don't suppose that any-

d   thing might happen to anybody in this city. But I know this well: that if I do come into court involved in one of those perils which you mention, the man who brings me in will be a wicked man—for no good man would bring in a man who is not a wrongdoer—and it wouldn't be at all strange if I were to be put to death. Would you like me to tell you my reason for expecting this?

CALLICLES: Yes, I would.

SOCRATES: I believe that I'm one of a few Athenians—so as not to say I'm the only one, but the only one among our contemporaries—to take up the true political craft and practice the true politics. This is because the speeches I make on each occa-

e   sion do not aim at gratification but at what's best. They don't aim at what's most pleasant. And because I'm not willing to do those clever things you recommend, I won't know what to say in court. And the same account I applied to Polus comes back to me. For I'll be judged the way a doctor would be judged by a jury of children if a pastry chef were to bring accusations against him. Think about what a man like that, taken captive among these people, could say in his defense, if somebody were to accuse him and say, "Children, this man has worked many great evils on you, yes,

522   on you. He destroys the youngest among you by cutting and burning them, and by slimming them down and choking them he confuses them. He gives them the most bitter potions to drink and forces hunger and thirst on them. He doesn't feast you on a great variety of sweets the way I do!" What do you think a doctor, caught in such an evil predicament, could say? Or if he should tell them the truth and say, "Yes, children, I was doing all those things in the interest of health," how big an uproar do you think such "judges" would make? Wouldn't it be a loud one?

CALLICLES: Perhaps so.

SOCRATES: I should think so! Don't you think he'd be at a total loss as to what

b   he should say?

CALLICLES: Yes, he would be.

SOCRATES: That's the sort of thing I know would happen to me, too, if I came into court. For I won't be able to point out any pleasures that I've provided for them,

ones they believe to be services and benefits, while I envy neither those who provide them nor the ones for whom they're provided. Nor will I be able to say what's true if someone charges that I ruin younger people by confusing them or abuse older ones by speaking bitter words against them in public or private. I won't be able to say, that is, "Yes, I say and do all these things in the interest of justice, my 'honored judges'"—to use that expression you people use—nor anything else. So presumably   c
I'll get whatever comes my way.

CALLICLES: Do you think, Socrates, that a man in such a position in his city, a man who's unable to protect himself, is to be admired?

SOCRATES: Yes, Callicles, as long as he has that one thing that you've often agreed he should have: as long as he has protected himself against having spoken or done anything unjust relating to either men or gods. For this is the self-protection that you and I often have agreed avails the most. Now if someone were to refute me   d
and prove that I am unable to provide *this* protection for myself or for anyone else, I would feel shame at being refuted, whether this happened in the presence of many or of a few, or just between the two of us; and if I were to be put to death for lack of this ability, I really would be upset. But if I came to my end because of a deficiency in flattering oratory, I know that you'd see me bear my death with ease. For no one who isn't totally bereft of reason and courage is afraid to die; doing what's unjust is what   e
he's afraid of. For to arrive in Hades with one's soul stuffed full of unjust actions is the ultimate of all bad things. If you like, I'm willing to give you an account showing that this is so.

CALLICLES: All right, since you've gone through the other things, go through this, too.

SOCRATES: Give ear then—as they put it—to a very fine account. You'll think   523
that it's a mere tale, I believe, although I think it's an account, for what I'm about to say I will tell you as true. As Homer tells it, after Zeus, Posidon, and Pluto took over the sovereignty from their father, they divided it among themselves. Now there was a law concerning human beings during Cronus' time, one that gods even now continue to observe, that when a man who has lived a just and pious life comes to his end, he goes to the Isles of the Blessed, to make his abode in complete happiness, beyond the reach of evils, but when one who has lived in an unjust and godless way   b
dies, he goes to the prison of payment and retribution, the one they call Tartarus. In Cronus' time, and even more recently during Zeus' tenure of sovereignty, these men faced living judges while they were still alive, who judged them on the day they were going to die. Now the cases were badly decided, so Pluto and the keepers from the Isles of the Blessed came to Zeus and told him that people were undeservingly making their way in both directions. So Zeus said, "All right, I'll put a stop to that. The   c
cases are being badly decided at this time because those being judged are judged fully dressed. They're being judged while they're still alive. Many," he said, "whose souls are wicked are dressed in handsome bodies, good stock and wealth, and when the judgment takes place they have many witnesses appear to testify that they have lived just lives. Now the judges are awestruck by these things and pass judgment at a   d
time when they themselves are fully dressed, too, having put their eyes and ears and

their whole bodies up as screens in front of their souls. All these things, their own clothing and that of those being judged, have proved to be obstructive to them. What we must do first," he said, "is to stop them from knowing their death ahead of time.
e   Now they do have that knowledge. This is something that Prometheus has already been told to put a stop to. Next, they must be judged when they're stripped naked of all these things, for they should be judged when they're dead. The judge, too, should be naked, and dead, and with only his soul he should study only the soul of each person immediately upon his death, when he's isolated from all his kinsmen and has left behind on earth all that adornment, so that the judgment may be a just one. Now I, realizing this before you did, have already appointed my sons as judges, two from
524 Asia, Minos and Rhadamanthus, and one from Europe, Aeacus. After they've died, they'll serve as judges in the meadow, at the three-way crossing from which the two roads go on, the one to the Isles of the Blessed and the other to Tartarus. Rhadamanthus will judge the people from Asia and Aeacus those from Europe. I'll give seniority to Minos to render final judgment if the other two are at all perplexed, so that the judgment concerning the passage of humankind may be as just as possible."
b   This, Callicles, is what I've heard, and I believe that it's true. And on the basis of these accounts I conclude that something like this takes place: Death, I think, is actually nothing but the separation of two things from each other, the soul and the body. So, after they're separated, each of them stays in a condition not much worse than what it was in when the person was alive. The body retains its nature, and the care it
c   had received as well as the things that have happened to it are all evident. If a man had a body, for instance, which was large (either by nature or through nurture, or both) while he was alive, his corpse after he has died is large, too. And if it was fat, so is the corpse of the dead man, and so on. And if a man took care to grow his hair long, his corpse will have long hair, too. And again, if a man had been a criminal whipped for his crime and showed scars, traces of beatings on his body inflicted by whips or other blows while he was alive, his body can be seen to have these marks, too, when he is dead. And if a man's limbs were broken or twisted while he was
d   alive, these very things will be evident, too, when he is dead. In a word, however a man treated his body while he was alive, all the marks of that treatment, or most of them, are evident for some time even after he is dead. And I think that the same thing, therefore, holds true also for the soul, Callicles. All that's in the soul is evident after it has been stripped naked of the body, both things that are natural to it and things that have happened to it, things that the person came to have in his soul as a result of his pursuit of each objective. So when they arrive before their judge—the people from
e   Asia before Rhadamanthus—Rhadamanthus brings them to a halt and studies each person's soul without knowing whose it is. He's often gotten hold of the Great King, or some other king or potentate, and noticed that there's nothing sound in his soul but
525 that it's been thoroughly whipped and covered with scars, the results of acts of perjury and of injustice, things that each of his actions has stamped upon his soul. Everything was warped as a result of deception and pretense, and nothing was straight, all because the soul had been nurtured without truth. And he saw that the

soul was full of distortion and ugliness due to license and luxury, arrogance and incontinence in its actions. And when he had seen it, he dismissed this soul in dishonor straight to the guardhouse, where it went to await suffering its appropriate fate.

It is appropriate for everyone who is subject to punishment rightly inflicted by   b
another either to become better and profit from it, or else to be made an example for others, so that when they see him suffering whatever it is he suffers, they may be afraid and become better. Those who are benefited, who are made to pay their due by gods and men, are the ones whose errors are curable; even so, their benefit comes to them, both here and in Hades, by way of pain and suffering, for there is no other possible way to get rid of injustice. From among those who have committed the ultimate   c
wrongs and who because of such crimes have become incurable come the ones who are made examples of. These persons themselves no longer derive any profit from their punishment, because they're incurable. Others, however, do profit from it when they see them undergoing for all time the most grievous, intensely painful and frightening sufferings for their errors, simply strung up there in the prison in Hades as examples, visible warnings to unjust men who are ever arriving. I claim that Archelaus, too, will be one of their number, if what Polus says is true, and anyone   d
else who's a tyrant like him. I suppose that in fact the majority of these examples have come from the ranks of tyrants, kings, potentates, and those active in the affairs of cities, for these people commit the most grievous and impious errors because they're in a position to do so. Homer, too, is a witness on these matters, for he has depicted those undergoing eternal punishment in Hades as kings and potentates: Tantalus, Sisyphus and Tityus. As for Thersites and any other private citizen who   e
was wicked, no one has depicted him as surrounded by the most grievous punishments, as though he were incurable; he wasn't in that position, I suppose, and for that reason he's also happier than those who were. The fact is, Callicles, that those persons who become extremely wicked do come from the ranks of the powerful,   526
although there's certainly nothing to stop good men from turning up even among the powerful, and those who do turn up there deserve to be enthusiastically admired. For it's a difficult thing, Callicles, and one that merits much praise, to live your whole life justly when you've found yourself having ample freedom to do what's unjust. Few are those who prove to be like that. But since there *have* proved to be such people, both here and elsewhere, I suppose that there'll be others, too, men admirable and good in that excellence of justly carrying out whatever is entrusted to them. One   b
of these, Aristides the son of Lysimachus, has proved to be very illustrious indeed, even among the rest of the Greeks. But the majority of our potentates, my good man, prove to be bad.

So as I was saying, when Rhadamanthus the judge gets hold of someone like that, he doesn't know a thing about him, neither who he is nor who his people are, except that he's somebody wicked. And once he's noticed that, he brands the man as either curable or incurable, as he sees fit, and dismisses the man to Tartarus, and once the man has arrived there, he undergoes the appropriate sufferings. Once in a while he   c
inspects another soul, one who has lived a pious life, one devoted to truth, the soul of a private citizen or someone else, especially—and I at any rate say this, Callicles—

that of a philosopher who has minded his own affairs and hasn't been meddlesome in the course of his life. He admires the man and sends him off to the Isles of the Blessed. And Aeacus, too, does the very same things. Each of them with staff in hand renders judgments. And Minos is seated to oversee them. He alone holds the golden

d   scepter the way Homer's Odysseus claims to have seen him,

holding his golden scepter, decreeing right among the dead.[27]

For my part, Callicles, I'm convinced by these accounts, and I think about how I'll reveal to the judge a soul that's as healthy as it can be. So I disregard the things held in honor by the majority of people, and by practicing truth I really try, to the best

e   of my ability, to be and to live as a very good man, and when I die, to die like that. And I call on all other people as well, as far as I can—and you especially I call on in response to your call—to this way of life, this contest, that I hold to be worth all the other contests in this life. And I take you to task, because you won't be able to come to protect yourself when you appear at the trial and judgment I was talking about just

527 now. When you come before that judge, the son of Aegina, and he takes hold of you and brings you to trial, your mouth will hang open and you'll get dizzy there just as much as I will here, and maybe somebody'll give you a demeaning knock on the jaw and throw all sorts of dirt at you.

Maybe you think this account is told as an old wives' tale, and you feel contempt for it. And it certainly wouldn't be a surprising thing to feel contempt for it if we could look for and somehow find one better and truer than it. As it is, you see that there are three of you, the wisest of the Greeks of today—you, Polus, and Gorgias—

b   and you're not able to prove that there's any other life one should live than the one which will clearly turn out to be advantageous in that world, too. But among so many arguments this one alone survives refutation and remains steady: that doing what's unjust is more to be guarded against than suffering it, and that it's not *seeming* to be good but *being* good that a man should take care of more than anything, both in his public and his private life; and that if a person proves to be bad in some respect, he's to be disciplined, and that the second best thing after being just is to become just by

c   paying one's due, by being disciplined; and that every form of flattery, both the form concerned with oneself and that concerned with others, whether they're few or many, is to be avoided, and that oratory and every other activity is always to be used in support of what's just.

So, listen to me and follow me to where I am, and when you've come here you'll be happy both during life and at its end, as the account indicates. Let someone despise you as a fool and throw dirt on you, if he likes. And, yes, by Zeus, confi-

d   dently let him deal you that demeaning blow. Nothing terrible will happen to you if you really are an admirable and good man, one who practices excellence. And then, after we've practiced it together, then at last, if we think we should, we'll turn to politics, or then we'll deliberate about whatever subject we please, when we're better at

[27] *Odyssey* xi.569.

deliberating than we are now. For it's a shameful thing for us, being in the condition we appear to be in at present—when we never think the same about the same subjects, the most important ones at that—to sound off as though we're somebodies. That's how far behind in education we've fallen. So let's use the account that has now been disclosed to us as our guide, one that indicates to us that this way of life is the best, to practice justice and the rest of excellence both in life and in death. Let us follow it, then, and call on others to do so, too, and let's not follow the one that you believe in and call on me to follow. For that one is worthless, Callicles.

e

4

MENO

Meno's is one of the leading aristocratic families of Thessaly, traditionally friendly to Athens and Athenian interests. Here he is a young man, about to embark on an unscrupulous military and political career, leading to an early death at the hands of the Persian king. To his aristocratic 'virtue' (Plato's ancient readers would know what that ultimately came to) he adds an admiration for ideas on the subject he has learned from the rhetorician Gorgias (about whom we learn more in the dialogue named after him). What brings him to Athens we are not told. His family's local sponsor is the democratic politician Anytus, one of Socrates' accusers at his trial, and apparently Anytus is his host. The dialogue begins abruptly, without stage-setting preliminaries of the sort we find in the 'Socratic' dialogues, and with no context of any kind being provided for the conversation. Meno wants to know Socrates' position on the then much-debated question whether virtue can be taught, or whether it comes rather by practice, or else is acquired by one's birth and nature, or in some other way? Socrates and Meno pursue that question, and the preliminary one of what virtue indeed is, straight through to the inconclusive conclusion characteristic of 'Socratic' dialogues. (Anytus joins the conversation briefly. He bristles when, to support his doubts that virtue can be taught, Socrates points to the failure of famous Athenian leaders to pass their own virtue on to their sons, and he issues a veiled threat of the likely consequences to Socrates of such 'slanderous' attacks.)

The dialogue is best remembered, however, for the interlude in which Socrates questions Meno's slave about a problem in geometry—how to find a square double in area to any given square. Having determined that Meno does not know what virtue is, and recognizing that he himself does not know either, Socrates has proposed to Meno that they inquire into this together. Meno protests that that is impossible, challenging Socrates with the 'paradox' that one logically cannot inquire productively into what one does not already know—nor of course into what one already does! Guided by Socrates' questions, the slave (who has never studied geometry before) comes to see for himself, to recognize, what the right answer to the geometrical problem must be. Socrates argues that this confirms something he has heard from certain wise priests and priestesses—that the soul is immortal and that at our birth we already possess all theoretical knowledge (he includes here not just mathematical theory but moral knowledge as well). Prodded by Socrates' questions, the slave was 'recollecting' this prior knowledge, not drawing new conclusions from data being presented to him for the first time. So in moral inquiry, as well, there is hope that, if we question ourselves rightly, 'recollection' can progressively improve our understanding of moral truth and eventually lead us to full knowledge of it. The examination of the slave assuages Meno's doubt about the possibility of such inquiry. He and Socrates proceed to inquire together what virtue is—but now they follow a new method of 'hypothesis', introduced by Socrates again by analogy with procedures in geometry. Socrates no longer asks Meno for his views and criticizes those. Among other 'hypotheses' that he now works with, he advances and argues for an hypothesis of his own, that virtue is knowledge (in which case it must be teachable). But he also considers weaknesses in his own argument, leading to the alternative possible hypothesis, that virtue is god-granted right opinion (and so, not teachable). In the second half of the dialogue we thus see a new Socrates, with new methods of argument and inquiry, not envisioned in such 'Socratic' dialogues as Euthyphro, Laches, *and* Charmides. Meno *points forward to* Phaedo, *where the thesis that theoretical knowledge comes by recollection is discussed again, with a clear reference back to the* Meno, *but now expanded by the addition of Platonic Forms as objects of recollection and knowledge.*

J.M.C.

70   MENO: Can you tell me, Socrates, can virtue be taught? Or is it not teachable but the result of practice, or is it neither of these, but men possess it by nature or in some other way?

SOCRATES: Before now, Meno, Thessalians had a high reputation among the Greeks and were admired for their horsemanship and their wealth, but now, it seems

b   to me, they are also admired for their wisdom, not least the fellow citizens of your friend Aristippus of Larissa. The responsibility for this reputation of yours lies with Gorgias, for when he came to your city he found that the leading Aleuadae, your lover Aristippus among them, loved him for his wisdom, and so did the other leading Thessalians. In particular, he accustomed you to give a bold and grand answer to any

c   question you may be asked, as experts are likely to do. Indeed, he himself was ready to answer any Greek who wished to question him, and every question was answered. But here in Athens, my dear Meno, the opposite is the case, as if there were a dearth of wisdom, and wisdom seems to have departed hence to go to you. If then you want

71   to ask one of us that sort of question, everyone will laugh and say: "Good stranger, you must think me happy indeed if you think I know whether virtue can be taught or how it comes to be; I am so far from knowing whether virtue can be taught or not that I do not even have any knowledge of what virtue itself is."

b   I myself, Meno, am as poor as my fellow citizens in this matter, and I blame myself for my complete ignorance about virtue. If I do not know what something is, how could I know what qualities it possesses? Or do you think that someone who does not know at all who Meno is could know whether he is good-looking or rich or well-born, or the opposite of these? Do you think that is possible?

c   MENO: I do not; but, Socrates, do you really not know what virtue is? Are we to report this to the folk back home about you?

SOCRATES: Not only that, my friend, but also that, as I believe, I have never yet met anyone else who did know.

Translated by G.M.A. Grube.

MENO: How so? Did you not meet Gorgias when he was here?

SOCRATES: I did.

MENO: Did you then not think that he knew?

SOCRATES: I do not altogether remember, Meno, so that I cannot tell you now what I thought then. Perhaps he does know; you know what he used to say, so you remind me of what he said. You tell me yourself, if you are willing, for surely you share his views.—I do.

SOCRATES: Let us leave Gorgias out of it, since he is not here. But Meno, by the gods, what do you yourself say that virtue is? Speak and do not begrudge us, so that I may have spoken a most unfortunate untruth when I said that I had never met anyone who knew, if you and Gorgias are shown to know.

MENO: It is not hard to tell you, Socrates. First, if you want the virtue of a man, it is easy to say that a man's virtue consists of being able to manage public affairs and in so doing to benefit his friends and harm his enemies and to be careful that no harm comes to himself; if you want the virtue of a woman, it is not difficult to describe: she must manage the home well, preserve its possessions, and be submissive to her husband; the virtue of a child, whether male or female, is different again, and so is that of an elderly man, if you want that, or if you want that of a free man or a slave. And there are very many other virtues, so that one is not at a loss to say what virtue is. There is virtue for every action and every age, for every task of ours and every one of us—and Socrates, the same is true for wickedness.

SOCRATES: I seem to be in great luck, Meno; while I am looking for one virtue, I have found you to have a whole swarm of them. But, Meno, to follow up the image of swarms, if I were asking you what is the nature of bees, and you said that they are many and of all kinds, what would you answer if I asked you: "Do you mean that they are many and varied and different from one another in so far as they are bees? Or are they no different in that regard, but in some other respect, in their beauty, for example, or their size or in some other such way?" Tell me, what would you answer if thus questioned?

MENO: I would say that they do not differ from one another in being bees.

SOCRATES: If I went on to say: "Tell me, what is this very thing, Meno, in which they are all the same and do not differ from one another?" Would you be able to tell me?

MENO: I would.

SOCRATES: The same is true in the case of the virtues. Even if they are many and various, all of them have one and the same form which makes them virtues, and it is right to look to this when one is asked to make clear what virtue is. Or do you not understand what I mean?

MENO: I think I understand, but I certainly do not grasp the meaning of the question as fully as I want to.

SOCRATES: I am asking whether you think it is only in the case of virtue that there is one for man, another for woman and so on, or is the same true in the case of health and size and strength? Do you think that there is one health for man and another for woman? Or, if it is health, does it have the same form everywhere, whether in man or in anything else whatever?

MENO: The health of a man seems to me the same as that of a woman.

SOCRATES: And so with size and strength? If a woman is strong, that strength will be the same and have the same form, for by "the same" I mean that strength is no different as far as being strength, whether in a man or a woman. Or do you think there is a difference?

MENO: I do not think so.

SOCRATES: And will there be any difference in the case of virtue, as far as being
73   virtue is concerned, whether it be in a child or an old man, in a woman or in a man?

MENO: I think, Socrates, that somehow this is no longer like those other cases.

SOCRATES: How so? Did you not say that the virtue of a man consists of managing the city well, and that of a woman of managing the household?—I did.

SOCRATES: Is it possible to manage a city well, or a household, or anything else, while not managing it moderately and justly?—Certainly not.

b   SOCRATES: Then if they manage justly and moderately, they must do so with justice and moderation?—Necessarily.

SOCRATES: So both the man and the woman, if they are to be good, need the same things, justice and moderation.—So it seems.

SOCRATES: What about a child and an old man? Can they possibly be good if they are intemperate and unjust?—Certainly not.

SOCRATES: But if they are moderate and just?—Yes.

SOCRATES: So all human beings are good in the same way, for they become
c   good by acquiring the same qualities.—It seems so.

SOCRATES: And they would not be good in the same way if they did not have the same virtue.—They certainly would not be.

SOCRATES: Since then the virtue of all is the same, try to tell me and to remember what Gorgias, and you with him, said that that same thing is.

d   MENO: What else but to be able to rule over people, if you are seeking one description to fit them all.

SOCRATES: That is indeed what I am seeking, but Meno, is virtue the same in the case of a child or a slave, namely, for them to be able to rule over a master, and do you think that he who rules is still a slave?—I do not think so at all, Socrates.

SOCRATES: It is not likely, my good man. Consider this further point: you say that virtue is to be able to rule. Shall we not add to this *justly and not unjustly?*

MENO: I think so, Socrates, for justice is virtue.

e   SOCRATES: Is it virtue, Meno, or a virtue?—What do you mean?

SOCRATES: As with anything else. For example, if you wish, take roundness, about which I would say that it is a shape, but not simply that it is shape. I would not so speak of it because there are other shapes.

MENO: You are quite right. So I too say that not only justice is a virtue but there are many other virtues.

74   SOCRATES: What are they? Tell me, as I could mention other shapes to you if you bade me do so, so do you mention other virtues.

MENO: I think courage is a virtue, and moderation, wisdom, and munificence, and very many others.

SOCRATES: We are having the same trouble again, Meno, though in another way; we have found many virtues while looking for one, but we cannot find the one which covers all the others.

MENO: I cannot yet find, Socrates, what you are looking for, one virtue for them all, as in the other cases.

SOCRATES: That is likely, but I am eager, if I can, that we should make progress, for you understand that the same applies to everything. If someone asked you what I mentioned just now: "What is shape, Meno?" and you told him that it was roundness, and if then he said to you what I did: "Is roundness shape or a shape?" you would surely tell him that it is a shape?—I certainly would.

SOCRATES: That would be because there are other shapes?—Yes.

SOCRATES: And if he asked you further what they were, you would tell him?—I would.

SOCRATES: So too, if he asked you what color is, and you said it is white, and your questioner interrupted you, "Is white color or a color?" you would say that it is a color, because there are also other colors?—I would.

SOCRATES: And if he bade you mention other colors, you would mention others that are no less colors than white is?—Yes.

SOCRATES: Then if he pursued the argument as I did and said: "We always arrive at the many; do not talk to me in that way, but since you call all these many by one name, and say that no one of them is not a shape even though they are opposites, tell me what this is which applies as much to the round as to the straight and which you call shape, as you say the round is as much a shape as the straight." Do you not say that?—I do.

SOCRATES: When you speak like that, do you assert that the round is no more round than it is straight, and that the straight is no more straight than it is round?

MENO: Certainly not, Socrates.

SOCRATES: Yet you say that the round is no more a shape than the straight is, nor the one more than the other.—That is true.

SOCRATES: What then is this to which the name shape applies? Try to tell me. If then you answered the man who was questioning about shape or color: "I do not understand what you want, my man, nor what you mean," he would probably wonder and say: "You do not understand that I am seeking that which is the same in all these cases?" Would you still have nothing to say, Meno, if one asked you: "What is this which applies to the round and the straight and the other things which you call shapes and which is the same in them all?" Try to say, that you may practice for your answer about virtue.

MENO: No, Socrates, but you tell me.

SOCRATES: Do you want me to do you this favor?

MENO: I certainly do.

SOCRATES: And you will then be willing to tell me about virtue?

MENO: I Will.

SOCRATES: We must certainly press on. The subject is worth it.

MENO: It surely is.

SOCRATES: Come then, let us try to tell you what shape is. See whether you will accept that it is this: Let us say that shape is that which alone of existing things always follows color. Is that satisfactory to you, or do you look for it in some other way? I should be satisfied if you defined virtue in this way.

MENO: But that is foolish, Socrates.

SOCRATES: How do you mean?

MENO: That shape, you say, always follows color. Well then, if someone were to say that he did not know what color is, but that he had the same difficulty as he had about shape, what do you think your answer would be?

SOCRATES: A true one, surely, and if my questioner was one of those clever and disputatious debaters, I would say to him: "I have given my answer; if it is wrong, it is your job to refute it." Then, if they are friends as you and I are, and want to discuss with each other, they must answer in a manner more gentle and more proper to discussion. By this I mean that the answers must not only be true, but in terms admittedly known to the questioner. I too will try to speak in these terms. Do you call something "the end?" I mean such a thing as a limit or boundary, for all those are, I say, the same thing. Prodicus[1] might disagree with us, but you surely call something "finished" or "completed"—that is what I want to express, nothing elaborate.

MENO: I do, and I think I understand what you mean.

SOCRATES: Further, you call something a plane, and something else a solid, as in geometry?

MENO: I do.

SOCRATES: From this you may understand what I mean by shape, for I say this of every shape, that a shape is that which limits a solid; in a word, a shape is the limit of a solid.

MENO: And what do you say color is, Socrates?

SOCRATES: You are outrageous, Meno. You bother an old man to answer questions, but you yourself are not willing to recall and to tell me what Gorgias says that virtue is.

MENO: After you have answered this, Socrates, I will tell you.

SOCRATES: Even someone who was blindfolded would know from your conversation that you are handsome and still have lovers.

MENO: Why so?

SOCRATES: Because you are forever giving orders in a discussion, as spoiled people do, who behave like tyrants as long as they are young. And perhaps you have recognized that I am at a disadvantage with handsome people, so I will do you the favor of an answer.

MENO: By all means do me that favor.

SOCRATES: Do you want me to answer after the manner of Gorgias, which you would most easily follow?

MENO: Of course I want that.

---

[1] Prodicus was a well-known sophist who was especially keen on the exact meaning of words.

SOCRATES: Do you both say there are effluvia of things, as Empedocles[2] does?—Certainly.

SOCRATES: And that there are channels through which the effluvia make their way?—Definitely.

SOCRATES: And some effluvia fit some of the channels, while others are too small or too big?—That is so.

d

SOCRATES: And there is something which you call sight?—There is.

SOCRATES: From this, "comprehend what I state," as Pindar said;[3] for color is an effluvium from shapes which fits the sight and is perceived.

MENO: That seems to me to be an excellent answer, Socrates.

SOCRATES: Perhaps it was given in the manner to which you are accustomed. At the same time I think that you can deduce from this answer what sound is, and smell, and many such things.—Quite so.

e

SOCRATES: It is a theatrical answer so it pleases you, Meno, more than that about shape.—It does.

SOCRATES: It is not better, son of Alexidemus, but I am convinced that the other is, and I think you would agree, if you did not have to go away before the mysteries as you told me yesterday, but could remain and be initiated.

MENO: I would stay, Socrates, if you could tell me many things like these.

77

SOCRATES: I shall certainly not be lacking in eagerness to tell you such things, both for your sake and my own, but I may not be able to tell you many. Come now, you too try to fulfill your promise to me and tell me the nature of virtue as a whole and stop making many out of one, as jokers say whenever someone breaks something; but allow virtue to remain whole and sound, and tell me what it is, for I have given you examples.

b

MENO: I think, Socrates, that virtue is, as the poet says, "to find joy in beautiful things and have power." So I say that virtue is to desire beautiful things and have the power to acquire them.

SOCRATES: Do you mean that the man who desires beautiful things desires good things?—Most certainly.

SOCRATES: Do you assume that there are people who desire bad things, and others who desire good things? Do you not think, my good man, that all men desire good things?

c

MENO: I do not.

SOCRATES: But some desire bad things?—Yes.

SOCRATES: Do you mean that they believe the bad things to be good, or that they know they are bad and nevertheless desire them?—I think there are both kinds.

SOCRATES: Do you think, Meno, that anyone, knowing that bad things are bad, nevertheless desires them?—I certainly do.

---

[2] Empedocles (c. 493–433 B.C.) of Acragas in Sicily was a philosopher famous for his theories about the world of nature and natural phenomena (including sense-perception).

[3] Frg. 105 (Snell).

SOCRATES: What do you mean by desiring? Is it to secure for oneself?—What else?

d   SOCRATES: Does he think that the bad things benefit him who possesses them, or does he know they harm him?

MENO: There are some who believe that the bad things benefit them, others who know that the bad things harm them.

SOCRATES: And do you think that those who believe that bad things benefit them know that they are bad?

MENO: No, that I cannot altogether believe.

SOCRATES: It is clear then that those who do not know things to be bad do not
e   desire what is bad, but they desire those things that they believe to be good but that are in fact bad. It follows that those who have no knowledge of these things and believe them to be good clearly desire good things. Is that not so?—It is likely.

SOCRATES: Well then, those who you say desire bad things, believing that bad things harm their possessor, know that they will be harmed by them?—Necessarily.

78   SOCRATES: And do they not think that those who are harmed are miserable to the extent that they are harmed?—That too is inevitable.

SOCRATES: And that those who are miserable are unhappy?—I think so.

SOCRATES: Does anyone wish to be miserable and unhappy?—I do not think so, Socrates.

SOCRATES: No one then wants what is bad, Meno, unless he wants to be such. For what else is being miserable but to desire bad things and secure them?

b   MENO: You are probably right, Socrates, and no one wants what is bad.

SOCRATES: Were you not saying just now that virtue is to desire good things and have the power to secure them?—Yes, I was.

SOCRATES: The desiring part of this statement is common to everybody, and one man is no better than another in this?—So it appears.

SOCRATES: Clearly then, if one man is better than another, he must be better at securing them.—Quite so.

SOCRATES: This then is virtue according to your argument, the power of
c   securing good things.

MENO: I think, Socrates, that the case is altogether as you now understand it.

SOCRATES: Let us see then whether what you say is true, for you may well be right. You say that the capacity to acquire good things is virtue?—I do.

SOCRATES: And by good things you mean, for example, health and wealth?

MENO: Yes, and also to acquire gold and silver, also honors and offices in the city.

SOCRATES: By good things you do not mean other goods than these?

MENO: No, but I mean all things of this kind.

d   SOCRATES: Very well. According to Meno, the hereditary guest friend of the Great King, virtue is the acquisition of gold and silver. Do you add to this acquiring, Meno, the words justly and piously, or does it make no difference to you but even if one secures these things unjustly, you call it virtue none the less?

MENO: Certainly not, Socrates.

SOCRATES: You would then call it wickedness?—Indeed I would.

SOCRATES: It seems then that the acquisition must be accompanied by justice or moderation or piety or some other part of virtue; if it is not, it will not be virtue, even though it provides good things.

MENO: How could there be virtue without these?

SOCRATES: Then failing to secure gold and silver, whenever it would not be just to do so, either for oneself or another, is not this failure to secure them also virtue?

MENO: So it seems.

SOCRATES: Then to provide these goods would not be virtue any more than not to provide them, but apparently whatever is done with justice will be virtue, and what is done without anything of the kind is wickedness.

MENO: I think it must necessarily be as you say.

SOCRATES: We said a little while ago that each of these things was a part of virtue, namely, justice and moderation and all such things?—Yes.

SOCRATES: Then you are playing with me, Meno.—How so, Socrates?

SOCRATES: Because I begged you just now not to break up or fragment virtue, and I gave examples of how you should answer. You paid no attention, but you tell me that virtue is to be able to secure good things with justice, and this, you say, is a part of virtue.

MENO: I do.

SOCRATES: It follows then from what you agree to, that to act in whatever you do with a part of virtue is virtue, for you say that justice is a part of virtue, as are all such qualities. Why do I say this? Because when I begged you to tell me about virtue as a whole, you are far from telling me what it is. Rather, you say that every action is virtue if it is performed with a part of virtue, as if you had told me what virtue as a whole is, and I would already know that, even if you fragment it into parts. I think you must face the same question from the beginning, my dear Meno, namely, what is virtue, if every action performed with a part of virtue is virtue? For that is what one is saying when he says that every action performed with justice is virtue. Do you not think you should face the same question again, or do you think one knows what a part of virtue is if one does not know virtue itself?—I do not think so.

SOCRATES: If you remember, when I was answering you about shape, we rejected the kind of answer that tried to answer in terms still being the subject of inquiry and not yet agreed upon.—And we were right to reject them.

SOCRATES: Then surely, my good sir, you must not think, while the nature of virtue as a whole is still under inquiry, that by answering in terms of the parts of virtue you can make its nature clear to anyone or make anything else clear by speaking in this way, but only that the same question must be put to you again—what do you take the nature of virtue to be when you say what you say? Or do you think there is no point in what I am saying?—I think what you say is right.

SOCRATES: Answer me again then from the beginning: What do you and your friend say that virtue is?

MENO: Socrates, before I even met you I used to hear that you are always in a state of perplexity and that you bring others to the same state, and now I think you are bewitching and beguiling me, simply putting me under a spell, so that I am quite perplexed. Indeed, if a joke is in order, you seem, in appearance and in every other way, to be like the broad torpedo fish, for it too makes anyone who comes close and touches it feel numb, and you now seem to have had that kind of effect on me, for

b   both my mind and my tongue are numb, and I have no answer to give you. Yet I have made many speeches about virtue before large audiences on a thousand occasions, very good speeches as I thought, but now I cannot even say what it is. I think you are wise not to sail away from Athens to go and stay elsewhere, for if you were to behave like this as a stranger in another city, you would be driven away for practising sorcery.

SOCRATES: You are a rascal, Meno, and you nearly deceived me.

MENO: Why so particularly, Socrates?

c   SOCRATES: I know why you drew this image of me.

MENO: Why do you think I did?

SOCRATES: So that I should draw an image of you in return. I know that all handsome men rejoice in images of themselves; it is to their advantage, for I think that the images of beautiful people are also beautiful, but I will draw no image of you in turn. Now if the torpedo fish is itself numb and so makes others numb, then I resemble it, but not otherwise, for I myself do not have the answer when I perplex others, but I am more perplexed than anyone when I cause perplexity in others. So now I do not know what virtue is; perhaps you knew before you contacted me, but

d   now you are certainly like one who does not know. Nevertheless, I want to examine and seek together with you what it may be.

MENO: How will you look for it, Socrates, when you do not know at all what it is? How will you aim to search for something you do not know at all? If you should meet with it, how will you know that this is the thing that you did not know?

e   SOCRATES: I know what you want to say, Meno. Do you realize what a debater's argument you are bringing up, that a man cannot search either for what he knows or for what he does not know? He cannot search for what he knows—since he knows it, there is no need to search—nor for what he does not know, for he does not know what to look for.

81   MENO: Does that argument not seem sound to you, Socrates?

SOCRATES: Not to me.

MENO: Can you tell me why?

SOCRATES: I can. I have heard wise men and women talk about divine matters . . .

MENO: What did they say?

SOCRATES: What was, I thought, both true and beautiful.

MENO: What was it, and who were they?

b   SOCRATES: The speakers were among the priests and priestesses whose care it is to be able to give an account of their practices. Pindar too says it, and many others of the divine among our poets. What they say is this; see whether you think they speak the truth: They say that the human soul is immortal; at times it comes to an end, which they call dying, at times it is reborn, but it is never destroyed, and one must therefore live one's life as piously as possible:

Persephone will return to the sun above in the ninth year
the souls of those from whom

she will exact punishment for old miseries,
and from these come noble kings,   c
mighty in strength and greatest in wisdom,
and for the rest of time men will call them sacred heroes[4]

As the soul is immortal, has been born often and has seen all things here and in the underworld, there is nothing which it has not learned; so it is in no way surprising that it can recollect the things it knew before, both about virtue and other things. As   d
the whole of nature is akin, and the soul has learned everything, nothing prevents a man, after recalling one thing only—a process men call learning—discovering everything else for himself, if he is brave and does not tire of the search, for searching and learning are, as a whole, recollection. We must, therefore, not believe that debater's argument, for it would make us idle, and fainthearted men like to hear it, whereas my argument makes them energetic and keen on the search. I trust that   e
this is true, and I want to inquire along with you into the nature of virtue.

MENO: Yes, Socrates, but how do you mean that we do not learn, but that what we call learning is recollection? Can you teach me that this is so?

SOCRATES: As I said just now, Meno, you are a rascal. You now ask me if I can teach you, when I say there is no teaching but recollection, in order to show me up   82
at once as contradicting myself.

MENO: No, by Zeus, Socrates, that was not my intention when I spoke, but just a habit. If you can somehow show me that things are as you say, please do so.

SOCRATES: It is not easy, but I am nevertheless willing to do my best for your sake. Call one of these many attendants of yours, whichever you like, that I may   b
prove it to you in his case.

MENO: Certainly. You there come forward.

SOCRATES: Is he a Greek? Does he speak Greek?

MENO: Very much so. He was born in my household.

SOCRATES: Pay attention then whether you think he is recollecting or learning from me.

MENO: I will pay attention.

SOCRATES: Tell me now, boy, you know that a square figure is like this?—I do.

SOCRATES: A square then is a figure in which all these four sides are equal?—   c
Yes indeed.

SOCRATES: And it also has these lines through the middle equal?[5]—Yes.

---

[4] Frg. 133 (Snell).

[5] Socrates draws a square ABCD. The "lines through the middle" are the lines joining the middle of these sides, which also go through the center of the square, namely EF and GH.

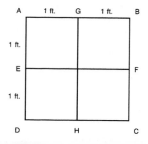

SOCRATES: And such a figure could be larger or smaller?—Certainly.

SOCRATES: If then this side were two feet, and this other side two feet, how many feet would the whole be? Consider it this way: if it were two feet this way, and only one foot that way, the figure would be once two feet?—Yes.

d   SOCRATES: But if it is two feet also that way, it would surely be twice two feet?—Yes.

SOCRATES: How many feet is twice two feet? Work it out and tell me.—Four, Socrates.

SOCRATES: Now we could have another figure twice the size of this one, with the four sides equal like this one.—Yes.

SOCRATES: How many feet will that be?—Eight.

e   SOCRATES: Come now, try to tell me how long each side of this will be. The side of this is two feet. What about each side of the one which is its double?—Obviously, Socrates, it will be twice the length.

SOCRATES: You see, Meno, that I am not teaching the boy anything, but all I do is question him. And now he thinks he knows the length of the line on which an eight-foot figure is based. Do you agree?

MENO: I do.

SOCRATES: And does he know?

MENO: Certainly not.

SOCRATES: He thinks it is a line twice the length?

MENO: Yes.

SOCRATES: Watch him now recollecting things in order, as one must recollect.
83   Tell me, boy, do you say that a figure double the size is based on a line double the length? Now I mean such a figure as this, not long on one side and short on the other, but equal in every direction like this one, and double the size, that is, eight feet. See whether you still believe that it will be based on a line double the length.—I do.

SOCRATES: Now the line becomes double its length if we add another of the same length here?—Yes indeed.

SOCRATES: And the eight-foot square will be based on it, if there are four lines of that length?—Yes.

b   SOCRATES: Well, let us draw from it four equal lines, and surely that is what you say is the eight-foot square?—Certainly.

SOCRATES: And within this figure are four squares, each of which is equal to the four-foot square?—Yes.

SOCRATES: How big is it then? Is it not four times as big?—Of course.

SOCRATES: Is this square then, which is four times as big, its double?—No, by Zeus.

SOCRATES: How many times bigger is it?—Four times.

c   SOCRATES: Then, my boy, the figure based on a line twice the length is not double but four times as big?—You are right.

SOCRATES: And four times four is sixteen, is it not?—Yes.

SOCRATES: On how long a line should the eight-foot square be based? On *this* line we have a square that is four times bigger, do we not?—Yes.

SOCRATES: Now this four-foot square is based on this line here, half the length?—Yes.

SOCRATES: Very well. Is the eight-foot square not double this one and half that one?[6]—Yes.

SOCRATES: Will it not be based on a line longer than this one and shorter than that one? Is that not so?—I think so.

d

SOCRATES: Good, you answer what you think. And tell me, was this one not two-feet long, and that one four feet?—Yes.

SOCRATES: The line on which the eight-foot square is based must then be longer than this one of two feet, and shorter than that one of four feet?—It must be.

SOCRATES: Try to tell me then how long a line you say it is.—Three feet.

e

SOCRATES: Then if it is three feet, let us add the half of this one, and it will be three feet? For these are two feet, and the other is one. And here, similarly, these are two feet and that one is one foot, and so the figure you mention comes to be?—Yes.

SOCRATES: Now if it is three feet this way and three feet that way, will the whole figure be three times three feet?—So it seems.

SOCRATES: How much is three times three feet?—Nine feet.

SOCRATES: And the double square was to be how many feet?—Eight.

SOCRATES: So the eight-foot figure cannot be based on the three-foot line?—Clearly not.

SOCRATES: But on how long a line? Try to tell us exactly, and if you do not want to work it out, show me from what line.—By Zeus, Socrates, I do not know.

84

SOCRATES: You realize, Meno, what point he has reached in his recollection. At first he did not know what the basic line of the eight-foot square was; even now he does not yet know, but then he thought he knew, and answered confidently as if he did know, and he did not think himself at a loss, but now he does think himself at a loss, and as he does not know, neither does he think he knows.

b

MENO: That is true.

SOCRATES: So he is now in a better position with regard to the matter he does not know?

MENO: I agree with that too.

SOCRATES: Have we done him any harm by making him perplexed and numb as the torpedo fish does?

MENO: I do not think so.

SOCRATES: Indeed, we have probably achieved something relevant to finding out how matters stand, for now, as he does not know, he would be glad to find out, whereas before he thought he could easily make many fine speeches to large audiences about the square of double size and said that it must have a base twice as long.

c

MENO: So it seems.

SOCRATES: Do you think that before he would have tried to find out that which he thought he knew though he did not, before he fell into perplexity and realized he did not know and longed to know?

MENO: I do not think so, Socrates.

---

[6] I.e., the eight-foot square is double the four-foot square and half the sixteen-foot square—double the square based on a line two feet long, and half the square based on a four-foot side.

SOCRATES: Has he then benefitted from being numbed?

MENO: I think so.

d   SOCRATES: Look then how he will come out of his perplexity while searching along with me. I shall do nothing more than ask questions and not teach him. Watch whether you find me teaching and explaining things to him instead of asking for his opinion.

SOCRATES: You tell me, is this not a four-foot figure? You understand?—I do.

SOCRATES: We add to it this figure which is equal to it?—Yes.

SOCRATES: And we add this third figure equal to each of them?—Yes.

SOCRATES: Could we then fill in the space in the corner?—Certainly.[7]

SOCRATES: So we have these four equal figures?—Yes.

e   SOCRATES: Well then, how many times is the whole figure larger than this one?[8]—Four times.

SOCRATES: But we should have had one that was twice as large, or do you not remember?—I certainly do.

85   SOCRATES: Does not this line from one corner to the other cut each of these figures in two?[9]—Yes.

SOCRATES: So these are four equal lines which enclose this figure?[10]— They are.

---

7 Socrates now builds up his sixteen-foot square by joining two four-foot squares, then a third, like this:

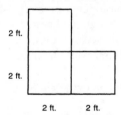

2 ft.

2 ft.

2 ft.   2 ft.

Filling "the space in the corner" will give another four-foot square, which completes the sixteen-foot square containing four four-foot squares.

8 "This one" is any one of the inside squares of four feet.

9 Socrates now draws the diagonals of the four inside squares, namely, FH, HE, EG, and GF, which together form the square GFHE.

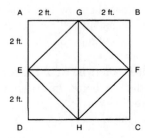

10 I.e., GFHE.

SOCRATES: Consider now: how large is the figure?—I do not understand.

SOCRATES: Within these four figures, each line cuts off half of each, does it not?—Yes.

SOCRATES: How many of this size are there in this figure?[11]—Four.

SOCRATES: How many in this[12]—Two.

SOCRATES: What is the relation of four to two?—Double.

b

SOCRATES: How many feet in this?[13]—Eight.

SOCRATES: Based on what line?—This one.

SOCRATES: That is, on the line that stretches from corner to corner of the four-foot figure?—Yes.—Clever men call this the diagonal, so that if diagonal is its name, you say that the double figure would be that based on the diagonal?—Most certainly, Socrates.

SOCRATES: What do you think, Meno? Has he, in his answers, expressed any opinion that was not his own?

c

MENO: No, they were all his own.

SOCRATES: And yet, as we said a short time ago, he did not know?—That is true.

SOCRATES: So these opinions were in him, were they not?—Yes.

SOCRATES: So the man who does not know has within himself true opinions about the things that he does not know?—So it appears.

SOCRATES: These opinions have now just been stirred up like a dream, but if he were repeatedly asked these same questions in various ways, you know that in the end his knowledge about these things would be as accurate as anyone's.—It is likely.

d

SOCRATES: And he will know it without having been taught but only questioned, and find the knowledge within himself?—Yes.

SOCRATES: And is not finding knowledge within oneself recollection?—Certainly.

SOCRATES: Must he not either have at some time acquired the knowledge he now possesses, or else have always possessed it?—Yes.

SOCRATES: If he always had it, he would always have known. If he acquired it, he cannot have done so in his present life. Or has someone taught him geometry? For he will perform in the same way about all geometry, and all other knowledge. Has someone taught him everything? You should know, especially as he has been born and brought up in your house.

e

MENO: But I know that no one has taught him.

SOCRATES: Yet he has these opinions, or doesn't he?

MENO: That seems indisputable, Socrates.

---

[11] Again, GFHE: Socrates is asking how many of the triangles "cut off from inside" there are inside GFHE.

[12] I.e., any of the interior squares.

[13] GFHE again.

86   SOCRATES: If he has not acquired them in his present life, is it not clear that he had them and had learned them at some other time?—It seems so.

SOCRATES: Then that was the time when he was not a human being?—Yes.

SOCRATES: If then, during the time he exists and is not a human being he will have true opinions which, when stirred by questioning, become knowledge, will not his soul have learned during all time? For it is clear that during all time he exists, either as a man or not.—So it seems.

b   SOCRATES: Then if the truth about reality is always in our soul, the soul would be immortal so that you should always confidently try to seek out and recollect what you do not know at present—that is, what you do not recollect?

MENO: Somehow, Socrates, I think that what you say is right.

SOCRATES: I think so too, Meno. I do not insist that my argument is right in all other respects, but I would contend at all costs both in word and deed as far as I could that we will be better men, braver and less idle, if we believe that one must search

c   for the things one does not know, rather than if we believe that it is not possible to find out what we do not know and that we must not look for it.

MENO: In this too I think you are right, Socrates.

SOCRATES: Since we are of one mind that one should seek to find out what one does not know, shall we try to find out together what virtue is?

MENO: Certainly. But Socrates, I should be most pleased to investigate and hear

d   your answer to my original question, whether we should try on the assumption that virtue is something teachable, or is a natural gift, or in whatever way it comes to men.

SOCRATES: If I were directing you, Meno, and not only myself, we would not have investigated whether virtue is teachable or not before we had investigated what virtue itself is. But because you do not even attempt to rule yourself, in order that you may be free, but you try to rule me and do so, I will agree with you—for what can I do? So we must, it appears, inquire into the qualities of something the nature

e   of which we do not yet know. However, please relax your rule a little bit for me and agree to investigate whether it is teachable or not by means of a hypothesis. I mean the way geometers often carry on their investigations. For example, if they are asked

87   whether a specific area can be inscribed in the form of a triangle within a given circle, one of them might say: "I do not yet know whether that area has that property, but I think I have, as it were, a hypothesis that is of use for the problem, namely this: If that area is such that when one has applied it as a rectangle to the given straight

b   line in the circle it is deficient by a figure similar to the very figure which is applied, then I think one alternative results, whereas another results if it is impossible for this to happen. So, by using this hypothesis, I am willing to tell you what results with regard to inscribing it in the circle—that is, whether it is impossible or not."[14] So let us speak about virtue also, since we do not know either what it is or what qualities it possesses, and let us investigate whether it is teachable or not by means of a hypothesis, and say this: Among the things existing in the soul, of what sort is virtue, that it should be teachable or not? First, if it is another sort than knowledge, is it

[14] The translation here follows the interpretation of T. L. Heath, *A History of Greek Mathematics* (Oxford: Clarendon Press, 1921), vol. I pp. 298 ff.

teachable or not, or, as we were just saying, recollectable? Let it make no difference   c
to us which term we use: is it teachable? Or is it plain to anyone that men cannot be
taught anything but knowledge?—I think so.

SOCRATES: But, if virtue is a kind of knowledge, it is clear that it could be
taught.—Of course.

SOCRATES: We have dealt with that question quickly, that if it is of one kind it
can be taught, if it is of a different kind, it cannot.—We have indeed.

SOCRATES: The next point to consider seems to be whether virtue is knowledge
or something else.—That does seem to be the next point to consider.   d

SOCRATES: Well now, do we say that virtue is itself something good, and will
this hypothesis stand firm for us, that it is something good?—Of course.

SOCRATES: If then there is anything else good that is different and separate from
knowledge, virtue might well not be a kind of knowledge; but if there is nothing
good that knowledge does not encompass, we would be right to suspect that it is a
kind of knowledge.—That is so.

SOCRATES: Surely virtue makes us good?—Yes.   e

SOCRATES: And if we are good, we are beneficent, for all that is good is
beneficial. Is that not so?—Yes.

SOCRATES: So virtue is something beneficial?

MENO: That necessarily follows from what has been agreed.

SOCRATES: Let us then examine what kinds of things benefit us, taking them up
one by one: health, we say, and strength, and beauty, and also wealth. We say that
these things, and others of the same kind, benefit us, do we not?—We do.

SOCRATES: Yet we say that these same things also sometimes harm one. Do you   88
agree or not?—I do.

SOCRATES: Look then, what directing factor determines in each case whether
these things benefit or harm us? Is it not the right use of them that benefits us, and
the wrong use that harms us?—Certainly.

SOCRATES: Let us now look at the qualities of the soul. There is something you
call moderation, and justice, courage, intelligence, memory, munificence, and all
such things?—There is.

SOCRATES: Consider whichever of these you believe not to be knowledge but   b
different from it; do they not at times harm us, at other times benefit us? Courage,
for example, when it is not wisdom but like a kind of recklessness: when a man is
reckless without understanding, he is harmed; when with understanding, he is
benefitted.—Yes.

SOCRATES: The same is true of moderation and mental quickness; when they
are learned and disciplined with understanding they are beneficial, but without
understanding they are harmful?—Very much so.

SOCRATES: Therefore, in a word, all that the soul undertakes and endures, if   c
directed by wisdom, ends in happiness, but if directed by ignorance, it ends in the
opposite?—That is likely.

SOCRATES: If then virtue is something in the soul and it must be beneficial, it
must be knowledge, since all the qualities of the soul are in themselves neither   d

beneficial nor harmful, but accompanied by wisdom or folly they become harmful or beneficial. This argument shows that virtue, being beneficial, must be a kind of wisdom.—I agree.

SOCRATES: Furthermore, those other things we were mentioning just now, wealth and the like, are at times good and at times harmful. Just as for the rest of the

e   soul the direction of wisdom makes things beneficial, but harmful if directed by folly, so in these cases, if the soul uses and directs them right it makes them beneficial, but bad use makes them harmful?—Quite so.

SOCRATES: The wise soul directs them right, the foolish soul wrongly?—That is so.

SOCRATES: So one may say this about everything; all other human activities

89   depend on the soul, and those of the soul itself depend on wisdom if they are to be good. According to this argument the beneficial would be wisdom, and we say that virtue is beneficial?—Certainly.

SOCRATES: Then we say that virtue is wisdom, either the whole or a part of it?

MENO: What you say, Socrates, seems to me quite right.

SOCRATES: Then, if that is so, the good are not so by nature?—I do not think

b   they are.

SOCRATES: For if they were, this would follow: if the good were so by nature, we would have people who knew which among the young were by nature good; we would take those whom they had pointed out and guard them in the Acropolis, sealing them up there much more carefully than gold so that no one could corrupt them, and when they reached maturity they would be useful to their cities.— Reasonable enough, Socrates.

c   SOCRATES: Since the good are not good by nature, does learning make them so?

MENO: Necessarily, as I now think, Socrates, and clearly, on our hypothesis, if virtue is knowledge, it can be taught.

SOCRATES: Perhaps, by Zeus, but may it be that we were not right to agree to this?

MENO: Yet it seemed to be right at the time.

d   SOCRATES: We should not only think it right at the time, but also now and in the future if it is to be at all sound.

MENO: What is the difficulty? What do you have in mind that you do not like about it and doubt that virtue is knowledge?

SOCRATES: I will tell you, Meno. I am not saying that it is wrong to say that virtue is teachable if it is knowledge, but look whether it is reasonable of me to doubt whether it is knowledge. Tell me this: if not only virtue but anything whatever can be taught, should there not be of necessity people who teach it and people who learn it?—I think so.

e   SOCRATES: Then again, if on the contrary there are no teachers or learners of something, we should be right to assume that the subject cannot be taught?

MENO: Quite so, but do you think that there are no teachers of virtue?

SOCRATES: I have often tried to find out whether there were any teachers of it, but in spite of all my efforts I cannot find any. And yet I have searched for them with the help of many people, especially those whom I believed to be most experienced in this matter. And now, Meno, Anytus[15] here has opportunely come to sit down by us. Let us share our search with him. It would be reasonable for us to do so, for Anytus, in the first place, is the son of Anthemion, a man of wealth and wisdom, who   90 did not become rich automatically or as the result of a gift like Ismenias the Theban, who recently acquired the possessions of Polycrates, but through his own wisdom and efforts. Further, he did not seem to be an arrogant or puffed up or offensive citizen in other ways, but he was a well-mannered and well-behaved man. Also he gave our friend here a good upbringing and education, as the majority of Athenians   b believe, for they are electing him to the highest offices. It is right then to look for the teachers of virtue with the help of men such as he, whether there are any and if so who they are. Therefore, Anytus, please join me and your guest friend Meno here, in our inquiry as to who are the teachers of virtue. Look at it in this way: if we wanted Meno to become a good physician, to what teachers would we send him? Would we   c not send him to the physicians?

ANYTUS: Certainly.

SOCRATES: And if we wanted him to be a good shoemaker, to shoe-makers?—Yes.

SOCRATES: And so with other pursuits?—Certainly.

SOCRATES: Tell me again on this same topic, like this: we say that we would be right to send him to the physicians if we want him to become a physician; whenever   d we say that, we mean that it would be reasonable to send him to those who practice the craft rather than to those who do not, and to those who exact fees for this very practice and have shown themselves to be teachers of anyone who wishes to come to them and learn. Is it not with this in mind that we would be right to send him?—Yes.

SOCRATES: And the same is true about flute-playing and the other crafts? It   e would be very foolish for those who want to make someone a fluteplayer to refuse to send him to those who profess to teach the craft and make money at it, but to send him to make trouble for others by seeking to learn from those who do not claim to be teachers or have a single pupil in that subject which we want the one we send to learn from them? Do you not think it very unreasonable to do so?—By Zeus I do, and also very ignorant.

SOCRATES: Quite right. However, you can now deliberate with me about our guest friend Meno here. He has been telling me for some time, Anytus, that he longs   91 to acquire that wisdom and virtue which enables men to manage their households and their cities well, to take care of their parents, to know how to welcome and to send away both citizens and strangers as a good man should. Consider to whom we   b should be right to send him to learn this virtue. Or is it obvious in view of what was said just now that we should send him to those who profess to be teachers of virtue and have shown themselves to be available to any Greek who wishes to learn, and for this fix a fee and exact it?

ANYTUS: And who do you say these are, Socrates?

SOCRATES: You surely know yourself that they are those whom men call sophists.

---

[15] Anytus was one of Socrates' accusers at his trial. See *Apology* 23e.

c   ANYTUS: By Heracles, hush, Socrates. May no one of my household or friends, whether citizen or stranger, be mad enough to go to these people and be harmed by them, for they clearly cause the ruin and corruption of their followers.

         SOCRATES: How do you mean, Anytus? Are these people, alone of those who claim the knowledge to benefit one, so different from the others that they not only

d   do not benefit what one entrusts to them but on the contrary corrupt it, even though they obviously expect to make money from the process? I find I cannot believe you, for I know that one man, Protagoras, made more money from this knowledge of his than Phidias who made such notably fine works, and ten other sculptors. Surely what you say is extraordinary, if those who mend old sandals and restore clothes would be

e   found out within the month if they returned the clothes and sandals in a worse state than they received them; if they did this they would soon die of starvation, but the whole of Greece has not noticed for forty years that Protagoras corrupts those who frequent him and sends them away in a worse moral condition than he received them. I believe that he was nearly seventy when he died and had practiced his craft for forty years. During all that time to this very day his reputation has stood high; and not only Protagoras but a great many others, some born before him and some still alive today.

92   Are we to say that you maintain that they deceive and harm the young knowingly, or that they themselves are not aware of it? Are we to deem those whom some people consider the wisest of men to be so mad as that?

         ANYTUS: They are far from being mad, Socrates. It is much rather those among the young who pay their fees who are mad, and even more the relatives who entrust

b   their young to them and most of all the cities who allow them to come in and do not drive out any citizen or stranger who attempts to behave in this manner.

         SOCRATES: Has some sophist wronged you, Anytus, or why are you so hard on them?

         ANYTUS: No, by Zeus, I have never met one of them, nor would I allow any one of my people to do so.

         SOCRATES: Are you then altogether without any experience of these men?

         ANYTUS: And may I remain so.

c   SOCRATES: How then, my good sir, can you know whether there is any good in their instruction or not, if you are altogether without experience of it?

         ANYTUS: Easily, for I know who they are, whether I have experience of them or not.

         SOCRATES: Perhaps you are a wizard, Anytus, for I wonder, from what you yourself say, how else you know about these things. However, let us not try to find

d   out who the men are whose company would make Meno wicked—let them be the sophists if you like—but tell us, and benefit your family friend here by telling him, to whom he should go in so large a city to acquire, to any worthwhile degree, the virtue I was just now describing.

         ANYTUS: Why did you not tell him yourself?

         SOCRATES: I did mention those whom I thought to be teachers of it, but you say

e   I am wrong, and perhaps you are right. You tell him in your turn to whom among the Athenians he should go. Tell him the name of anyone you want.

ANYTUS: Why give him the name of one individual? Any Athenian gentleman he may meet, if he is willing to be persuaded, will make him a better man than the sophists would.

SOCRATES: And have these gentlemen become virtuous automatically, without learning from anyone, and are they able to teach others what they themselves never learned?   93

ANYTUS: I believe that these men have learned from those who were gentlemen before them; or do you not think that there are many good men in this city?

SOCRATES: I believe, Anytus, that there are many men here who are good at public affairs, and that there have been as many in the past, but have they been good teachers of their own virtue? That is the point we are discussing, not whether there are good men here or not, or whether there have been in the past, but we have been investigating for some time whether virtue can be taught. And in the course of that investigation we are inquiring whether the good men of today and of the past knew how to pass on to another the virtue they themselves possessed, or whether a man cannot pass it on or receive it from another. This is what Meno and I have been investigating for some time. Look at it this way, from what you yourself have said. Would you not say that Themistocles[16] was a good man?—Yes. Even the best of men.   b   c

SOCRATES: And therefore a good teacher of his own virtue if anyone was?

ANYTUS: I think so, if he wanted to be.

SOCRATES: But do you think he did not want some other people to be worthy men, and especially his own son? Or do you think he begrudged him this, and deliberately did not pass on to him his own virtue? Have you not heard that Themistocles taught his son Cleophantus to be a good horseman? He could remain standing upright on horseback and shoot javelins from that position and do many other remarkable things which his father had him taught and made skillful at, all of which required good teachers. Have you not heard this from your elders?—I have.   d

SOCRATES: So one could not blame the poor natural talents of the son for his failure in virtue?—Perhaps not.   e

SOCRATES: But have you ever heard anyone, young or old, say that Cleophantus, the son of Themistocles, was a good and wise man at the same pursuits as his father?—Never.

SOCRATES: Are we to believe that he wanted to educate his son in those other things but not to do better than his neighbors in that skill which he himself possessed, if indeed virtue can be taught?—Perhaps not, by Zeus.

SOCRATES: And yet he was, as you yourself agree, among the best teachers of virtue in the past. Let us consider another man, Aristides, the son of Lysimachus. Do you not agree that he was good?—I very definitely do.   94

SOCRATES: He too gave his own son Lysimachus the best Athenian education in matters which are the business of teachers, and do you think he made him a better

[16] Famous Athenian statesman and general of the early fifth century, a leader in the victorious war against the Persians.

b   man than anyone else? For you have been in his company and seen the kind of man
      he is. Or take Pericles, a man of such magnificent wisdom. You know that he brought
      up two sons, Paralus and Xanthippus?—I know.
            SOCRATES: You also know that he taught them to be as good horsemen as any
      Athenian, that he educated them in the arts, in gymnastics, and in all else that was a
      matter of skill not to be inferior to anyone, but did he not want to make them good
      men? I think he did, but this could not be taught. And lest you think that only a few
      most inferior Athenians are incapable in this respect, reflect that Thucydides[17] too
      brought up two sons, Melesias and Stephanus, that he educated them well in all other
c   things. They were the best wrestlers in Athens—he entrusted the one to Xanthias and
      the other to Eudorus, who were thought to be the best wrestlers of the day, or do you
      not remember?
            ANYTUS: I remember I have heard that said.
d   SOCRATES: It is surely clear that he would not have taught his boys what it costs
      money to teach, but have failed to teach them what costs nothing—making them
      good men—if that could be taught? Or was Thucydides perhaps an inferior person
      who had not many friends among the Athenians and the allies? He belonged to a
      great house; he had great influence in the city and among the other Greeks, so that if
      virtue could be taught he would have found the man who could make his sons good
      men, be it a citizen or a stranger, if he himself did not have the time because of his
e   public concerns. But, friend Anytus, virtue can certainly not be taught.
            ANYTUS: I think, Socrates, that you easily speak ill of people. I would advise
      you, if you will listen to me, to be careful. Perhaps also in another city, and certainly
95   here, it is easier to injure people than to benefit them. I think you know that yourself.
            SOCRATES: I think, Meno, that Anytus is angry, and I am not at all surprised. He
      thinks, to begin with, that I am slandering those men, and then he believes himself
      to be one of them. If he ever realizes what slander is, he will cease from anger, but
      he does not know it now. You tell me, are there not worthy men among your
      people?—Certainly.
b   SOCRATES: Well now, are they willing to offer themselves to the young as
      teachers? Do they agree they are teachers, and that virtue can be taught?
            MENO: No, by Zeus, Socrates, but sometimes you would hear them say that it
      can be taught, at other times, that it cannot.
            SOCRATES: Should we say that they are teachers of this subject, when they do
      not even agree on this point?—I do not think so, Socrates.
            SOCRATES: Further, do you think that these sophists, who alone profess to be so,
      are teachers of virtue?
c   MENO: I admire this most in Gorgias, Socrates, that you would never hear him
      promising this. Indeed, he ridicules the others when he hears them making this claim.
      He thinks one should make people clever speakers.
            SOCRATES: You do not think then that the sophists are teachers?
            MENO: I cannot tell, Socrates; like most people, at times I think they are, at other
      times I think that they are not.

---

[17] Not the historian but Thucydides the son of Melesias, an Athenian statesman who was an opponent of
    Pericles and who was ostracized in 440 B.C.

SOCRATES: Do you know that not only you and the other public men at times   d
think that it can be taught, at other times that it cannot, but that the poet Theognis[18]
says the same thing?—Where?

SOCRATES: In his elegiacs: "Eat and drink with these men, and keep their
company. Please those whose power is great, for you will learn goodness from the   e
good. If you mingle with bad men you will lose even what wit you possess." You see
that here he speaks as if virtue can be taught?—So it appears.

SOCRATES: Elsewhere, he changes somewhat: "if this could be done" he says,
"and intelligence could be instilled," somehow those who could do this "would
collect large and numerous fees," and further: "Never would a bad son be born of a
good father, for he would be persuaded by wise words, but you will never make a   96
bad man good by teaching." You realize that the poet is contradicting himself on the
same subject?—He seems to be.

SOCRATES: Can you mention any other subject of which those who claim to be
teachers not only are not recognized to be teachers of others but are not recognized
to have knowledge of it themselves, and are thought to be poor in the very matter   b
which they profess to teach? Or any other subject of which those who are recognized
as worthy teachers at one time say it can be taught and at other times that it cannot?
Would you say that people who are so confused about a subject can be effective
teachers of it?—No, by Zeus, I would not.

SOCRATES: If then neither the sophists nor the worthy people themselves are
teachers of this subject, clearly there would be no others?—I do not think there are.

SOCRATES: If there are no teachers, neither are there pupils?—As you say.   c
SOCRATES: And we agreed that a subject that has neither teachers nor pupils is not
teachable?—We have so agreed.

SOCRATES: Now there seem to be no teachers of virtue anywhere?—That is so.

SOCRATES: If there are no teachers, there are no learners?—That seems so.

SOCRATES: Then virtue cannot be taught?

MENO: Apparently not, if we have investigated this correctly. I certainly wonder,   d
Socrates, whether there are no good men either, or in what way good men come to be.

SOCRATES: We are probably poor specimens, you and I, Meno. Gorgias has not
adequately educated you, nor Prodicus me. We must then at all costs turn our
attention to ourselves and find someone who will in some way make us better. I say   e
this in view of our recent investigation, for it is ridiculous that we failed to see that
it is not only under the guidance of knowledge that men succeed in their affairs, and
that is perhaps why the knowledge of how good men come to be escapes us.

MENO: How do you mean, Socrates?

SOCRATES: I mean this: we were right to agree that good men must be
beneficent, and that this could not be otherwise. Is that not so?—Yes.

SOCRATES: And that they will be beneficent if they give us correct guidance in
our affairs. To this too we were right to agree?—Yes.   97

SOCRATES: But that one cannot guide correctly if one does not have
knowledge; to this our agreement is likely to be incorrect.—How do you mean?

---

[18] Theognis was a poet of the mid-sixth century B.C. The quotations below are of lines 33–36 and 434–38
(Diehl) of his elegies.

SOCRATES: I will tell you. A man who knew the way to Larissa, or anywhere else you like, and went there and guided others would surely lead them well and correctly?—Certainly.

b
e
SOCRATES: What if someone had had a correct opinion as to which was the way but had not gone there nor indeed had knowledge of it, would he not also lead correctly?—Certainly.

SOCRATES: And as long as he has the right opinion about that of which the other has knowledge, he will not be a worse guide than the one who knows, as he has a true opinion, though not knowledge.—In no way worse.

SOCRATES: So true opinion is in no way a worse guide to correct action than knowledge. It is this that we omitted in our investigation of the nature of virtue, when
c   we said that only knowledge can lead to correct action, for true opinion can do so also.—So it seems.

SOCRATES: So correct opinion is no less useful than knowledge?

MENO: Yes, to this extent, Socrates. But the man who has knowledge will always succeed, whereas he who has true opinion will only succeed at times.

SOCRATES: How do you mean? Will he who has the right opinion not always succeed, as long as his opinion is right?

MENO: That appears to be so of necessity, and it makes me wonder, Socrates, this
d   being the case, why knowledge is prized far more highly than right opinion, and why they are different.

SOCRATES: Do you know why you wonder, or shall I tell you?—By all means tell me.

SOCRATES: It is because you have paid no attention to the statues of Daedalus, but perhaps there are none in Thessaly.

MENO: What do you have in mind when you say this?

SOCRATES: That they too run away and escape if one does not tie them down
e   but remain in place if tied down.—So what?

SOCRATES: To acquire an untied work of Daedalus is not worth much, like acquiring a runaway slave, for it does not remain, but it is worth much if tied down, for his works are very beautiful. What am I thinking of when I say this? True opinions. For true opinions, as long as they remain, are a fine thing and all they do
98 is good, but they are not willing to remain long, and they escape from a man's mind, so that they are not worth much until one ties them down by (giving) an account of the reason why. And that, Meno my friend, is recollection, as we previously agreed. After they are tied down, in the first place they become knowledge, and then they remain in place. That is why knowledge is prized higher than correct opinion, and knowledge differs from correct opinion in being tied down.

MENO: Yes by Zeus, Socrates, it seems to be something like that.

b
SOCRATES: Indeed, I too speak as one who does not have knowledge but is guessing. However, I certainly do not think I am guessing that right opinion is a different thing from knowledge. If I claim to know anything else—and I would make that claim about few things—I would put this down as one of the things I know.—Rightly so, Socrates.

SOCRATES: Well then, is it not correct that when true opinion guides the course of every action, it does no worse than knowledge?—I think you are right in this too.

SOCRATES: Correct opinion is then neither inferior to knowledge nor less useful in directing actions, nor is the man who has it less so than he who has knowledge.—That is so.

SOCRATES: And we agreed that the good man is beneficent.—Yes.

SOCRATES: Since then it is not only through knowledge but also through right opinion that men are good, and beneficial to their cities when they are, and neither knowledge nor true opinion come to men by nature but are acquired—or do you think either of these comes by nature?—I do not think so.

SOCRATES: Then if they do not come by nature, men are not so by nature either.—Surely not.

SOCRATES: As goodness does not come by nature, we inquired next whether it could be taught.—Yes.

SOCRATES: We thought it could be taught, if it was knowledge?—Yes.

SOCRATES: And that it was knowledge if it could be taught?—Quite so.

SOCRATES: And that if there were teachers of it, it could be taught, but if there were not, it was not teachable?—That is so.

SOCRATES: And then we agreed that there were no teachers of it?—We did.

SOCRATES: So we agreed that it was neither teachable nor knowledge?—Quite so.

SOCRATES: But we certainly agree that virtue is a good thing?—Yes.

SOCRATES: And that which guides correctly is both useful and good?—Certainly.

SOCRATES: And that only these two things, true belief and knowledge, guide correctly, and that if a man possesses these he gives correct guidance. The things that turn out right by some chance are not due to human guidance, but where there is correct human guidance it is due to two things, true belief or knowledge.—I think that is so.

SOCRATES: Now because it cannot be taught, virtue no longer seems to be knowledge?—It seems not.

SOCRATES: So one of the two good and useful things has been excluded, and knowledge is not the guide in public affairs.—I do not think so.

SOCRATES: So it is not by some kind of wisdom, or by being wise, that such men lead their cities, those such as Themistocles and those mentioned by Anytus just now? That is the reason why they cannot make others be which makes them what they are.

MENO: It is likely to be as you say, Socrates.

SOCRATES: Therefore, if it is not through knowledge, the only alternative is that it is through right opinion that statesmen follow the right course for their cities. As regards knowledge, they are no different from soothsayers and prophets. They too say many true things when inspired, but they have no knowledge of what they are saying.—That is probably so.

SOCRATES: And so, Meno, is it right to call divine these men who, without any understanding, are right in much that is of importance in what they say and do?—Certainly.

d   SOCRATES: We should be right to call divine also those soothsayers and prophets whom we just mentioned, and all the poets, and we should call no less divine and inspired those public men who are no less under the gods' influence and possession, as their speeches lead to success in many important matters, though they have no knowledge of what they are saying.—Quite so.

SOCRATES: Women too, Meno, call good men divine, and the Spartans, when they eulogize someone, say "This man is divine."

e   MENO: And they appear to be right, Socrates, though perhaps Anytus here will be annoyed with you for saying so.

SOCRATES: I do not mind that; we shall talk to him again, but if we were right in the way in which we spoke and investigated in this whole discussion, virtue would be neither an inborn quality nor taught, but comes to those who possess it as a gift from the gods which is not accompanied by understanding, unless there is someone

100   among our statesmen who can make another into a statesman. If there were one, he could be said to be among the living as Homer said Tiresias was among the dead, namely, that "he alone retained his wits while the others flitted about like shadows."[19] In the same manner such a man would, as far as virtue is concerned, here also be the only true reality compared, as it were, with shadows.

b   MENO: I think that is an excellent way to put it, Socrates.

SOCRATES: It follows from this reasoning, Meno, that virtue appears to be present in those of us who may possess it as a gift from the gods. We shall have clear knowledge of this when, before we investigate how it comes to be present in men, we first try to find out what virtue in itself is. But now the time has come for me to go. You convince your guest friend Anytus here of these very things of which you have yourself been convinced, in order that he may be more amenable. If you succeed, you will also confer a benefit upon the Athenians.

[19] *Odyssey* x.494–95.

5

Meditations on First Philosophy in Which the Existence of God and the Distinction Between the Soul and the Body Are Demonstrated

17

MEDITATION ONE: Concerning Those Things That Can Be Called into Doubt

Several years have now passed since I first realized how numerous were the false opinions that in my youth I had taken to be true, and thus how doubtful were all those that I had subsequently built upon them. And thus I realized that once in my life I had to raze everything to the ground and begin again from the original foundations, if I wanted to establish anything firm and lasting in the sciences. But the task seemed enormous, and I was waiting until I reached a point in my life that was so timely that no more suitable time for undertaking these plans of action would come to pass. For this reason, I procrastinated for so long that I would henceforth be at fault, were I to waste the time that remains for carrying out the project by brooding over it. Accordingly, I have today suitably freed my mind of all cares, secured for myself a period of leisurely tranquillity, and am withdrawing into solitude. At last I will apply myself earnestly and unreservedly to this general demolition of my opinions.

Yet to bring this about I will not need to show that all my opinions are false, which is perhaps something I could never accomplish. But reason now persuades me that I should withhold my assent no less carefully from opinions that are not completely certain and indubitable than I would from those that are patently false. For this reason, it will suffice for the rejection of all of these opinions, if I find in each of them some reason for doubt. Nor therefore need I survey each opinion individually, a task that would be endless. Rather, because undermining the foundations will cause whatever has been built upon them to crumble of its own accord, I will attack straightaway those principles which supported everything I once believed.

Surely whatever I had admitted until now as most true I received either from the senses or through the senses. However, I have noticed that the senses are sometimes deceptive; and it is a mark of prudence never to place our complete trust in those who have deceived us even once.

But perhaps, even though the senses do sometimes deceive us when it is a question of very small and distant things, still there are many other matters concerning which one simply cannot doubt, even though they are derived from the very same senses: for example, that I am sitting here next to the fire, wearing my winter dressing gown, that I am holding this sheet of paper in my hands, and the like. But on what grounds could one deny that these hands and this entire body are mine? Unless perhaps I were to liken myself to the insane, whose brains are impaired by such an unrelenting vapor of black bile that they steadfastly insist that they are kings when they are utter paupers, or that they are arrayed in purple robes when they are naked, or that they have heads made of clay, or that they are gourds, or that they are

18

19

made of glass. But such people are mad, and I would appear no less mad, were I to take their behavior as an example for myself.

This would all be well and good, were I not a man who is accustomed to sleeping at night, and to experiencing in my dreams the very same things, or now and then even less plausible ones, as these insane people do when they are awake. How often does my evening slumber persuade me of such ordinary things as these: that I am here, clothed in my dressing gown, seated next to the fireplace—when in fact I am lying undressed in bed! But right now my eyes are certainly wide awake when I gaze upon this sheet of paper. This head which I am shaking is not heavy with sleep. I extend this hand consciously and deliberately, and I feel it. Such things would not be so distinct for someone who is asleep. As if I did not recall having been deceived on other occasions even by similar thoughts in my dreams! As I consider these matters more carefully, I see so plainly that there are no definitive signs by which to distinguish being awake from being asleep. As a result, I am becoming quite dizzy, and this dizziness nearly convinces me that I am asleep.

Let us assume then, for the sake of argument, that we are dreaming and that such particulars as these are not true: that we are opening our eyes, moving our head, and extending our hands. Perhaps we do not even have such hands, or any such body at all. Nevertheless, it surely must be admitted that the things seen during slumber are, as it were, like painted images, which could only have been produced in the likeness of true things, and that therefore at least these general things—eyes, head, hands, and the whole body—are not imaginary things, but are true and exist. For indeed when

20   painters themselves wish to represent sirens and satyrs by means of especially bizarre forms, they surely cannot assign to them utterly new natures. Rather, they simply fuse together the members of various animals. Or if perhaps they concoct something so utterly novel that nothing like it has ever been seen before (and thus is something utterly fictitious and false), yet certainly at the very least the colors from which they fashion it ought to be true. And by the same token, although even these general things—eyes, head, hands and the like—could be imaginary, still one has to admit that at least certain other things that are even more simple and universal are true. It is from these components, as if from true colors, that all those images of things that are in our thought are fashioned, be they true or false.

This class of things appears to include corporeal nature in general, together with its extension; the shape of extended things; their quantity, that is, their size and number; as well as the place where they exist; the time through which they endure, and the like.

Thus it is not improper to conclude from this that physics, astronomy, medicine, and all the other disciplines that are dependent upon the consideration of composite things are doubtful, and that, on the other hand, arithmetic, geometry, and other such disciplines, which treat of nothing but the simplest and most general things and which are indifferent as to whether these things do or do not in fact exist, contain something certain and indubitable. For whether I am awake or asleep, 2 plus 3 make 5, and a square does not have more than 4 sides. It does not seem possible that such obvious truths should be subject to the suspicion of being false.

Be that as it may, there is fixed in my mind a certain opinion of long standing,   21
namely that there exists a God who is able to do anything and by whom I, such as I
am, have been created. How do I know that he did not bring it about that there is no
earth at all, no heavens, no extended thing, no shape, no size, no place, and yet
bringing it about that all these things appear to me to exist precisely as they do now?
Moreover, since I judge that others sometimes make mistakes in matters that they
believe they know most perfectly, may I not, in like fashion, be deceived every time
I add 2 and 3 or count the sides of a square, or perform an even simpler operation, if
that can be imagined? But perhaps God has not willed that I be deceived in this way,
for he is said to be supremely good. Nonetheless, if it were repugnant to his goodness
to have created me such that I be deceived all the time, it would also seem foreign
to that same goodness to permit me to be deceived even occasionally. But we cannot
make this last assertion.

Perhaps there are some who would rather deny so a powerful a God, than believe
that everything else is uncertain. Let us not oppose them; rather, let us grant that
everything said here about God is fictitious. Now they suppose that I came to be what
I am either by fate, or by chance, or by a connected chain of events, or by some other
way. But because deceived and being mistaken appear to be a certain imperfection,
the less powerful they take the author of my origin to be, the more probable it will
be that I am so imperfect that I am always deceived. I have nothing to say in response
to these arguments. But eventually I am forced to admit that there is nothing among
the things I once believed to be true which it is not permissible to doubt—and not out
of frivolity or lack of forethought, but for valid and considered arguments. Thus I
must be no less careful to withhold assent henceforth even from these beliefs than I   22
would from those that are patently false, if I wish to find anything certain.

But it is not enough simply to have realized these things; I must take steps to keep
myself mindful of them. For long-standing opinions keep returning, and, almost
against my will, they take advantage of my credulity, as if it were bound over to them
by long use and the claims of intimacy. Nor will I ever get out of the habit of
assenting to them and believing in them, so long as I take them to be exactly what
they are, namely, in some respects doubtful, as has just now been shown, but
nevertheless highly probable, so that it is much more consonant with reason to
believe them than to deny them. Hence, it seems to me I would do well to deceive
myself by turning my will in completely the opposite direction and pretend for a time
that these opinions are wholly false and imaginary, until finally, as if with prejudices
weighing down each side equally, no bad habit should turn my judgment any further
from the correct perception of things. For indeed I know that meanwhile there is no
danger or error in following this procedure, and that it is impossible for me to indulge
in too much distrust, since I am now concentrating only on knowledge, not on action.

Accordingly, I will suppose not a supremely good God, the source of truth, but
rather an evil genius, supremely powerful and clever, who has directed his entire
effort at deceiving me. I will regard the heavens, the air, the earth, colors, shapes,
sounds, and all external things as nothing but the bedeviling hoaxes of my dreams,
with which he lays snares for my credulity. I will regard myself as not having hands,   23

or eyes, or flesh, or blood, or any senses, but as nevertheless falsely believing that I possess all these things. I will remain resolute and steadfast in this meditation, and even if it is not within my power to know anything true, it certainly is within my power to take care resolutely to withhold my assent to what is false, lest this deceiver, however powerful, however clever he may be, have any effect on me. But this undertaking is arduous, and a certain laziness brings me back to my customary way of living. I am not unlike a prisoner who enjoyed an imaginary freedom during his sleep, but, when he later begins to suspect that he is dreaming, fears being awakened and nonchalantly conspires with these pleasant illusions. In just the same way, I fall back of my own accord into my old opinions, and dread being awakened, lest the toilsome wakefulness which follows upon a peaceful rest must be spent thenceforward not in the light but among the inextricable shadows of the difficulties now brought forward.

6

MEDITATION TWO: Concerning the Nature of the Human Mind: That It Is Better Known Than the Body

Yesterday's meditation has thrown me into such doubts that I can no longer ignore them, yet I fail to see how they are to be resolved. It is as if I had suddenly fallen into a deep whirlpool; I am so tossed about that I can neither touch bottom with my foot, nor swim up to the top. Nevertheless I will work my way up and will once again attempt the same path I entered upon yesterday. I will accomplish this by putting aside everything that admits of the least doubt, as if I had discovered it to be completely false. I will stay on this course until I know something certain, or, if nothing else, until I at least know for certain that nothing is certain. Archimedes sought but one firm and immovable point in order to move the entire earth from one place to another. Just so, great things are also to be hoped for if I succeed in finding just one thing, however slight, that is certain and unshaken. 24

Therefore I suppose that everything I see is false. I believe that none of what my deceitful memory represents ever existed. I have no senses whatever. Body, shape, extension, movement, and place are all chimeras. What then will be true? Perhaps just the single fact that nothing is certain.

But how do I know there is not something else, over and above all those things that I have just reviewed, concerning which there is not even the slightest occasion for doubt? Is there not some God, or by whatever name I might call him, who instills these very thoughts in me? But why would I think that, since I myself could perhaps be the author of these thoughts? Am I not then at least something? But I have already denied that I have any senses and any body. Still I hesitate; for what follows from this? Am I so tied to a body and to the senses that I cannot exist without them? But I have persuaded myself that there is absolutely nothing in the world: no sky, no earth, no minds, no bodies. Is it then the case that I too do not exist? But doubtless I did exist, if I persuaded myself of something. But there is some deceiver or other who is supremely powerful and supremely sly and who is always deliberately deceiving me. Then too there is no doubt that I exist, if he is deceiving me. And let him do his best at deception, he will never bring it about that I am nothing so long as I shall think that I am something. Thus, after everything has been most carefully weighed, it must finally be established that this pronouncement "I am, I exist" is necessarily true every time I utter it or conceive it in my mind. 25

But I do not yet understand sufficiently what I am—I, who now necessarily exist. And so from this point on, I must be careful lest I unwittingly mistake something else for myself, and thus err in that very item of knowledge that I claim to be the most certain and evident of all. Thus, I will meditate once more on what I once believed myself to be, prior to embarking upon these thoughts. For this reason, then, I will set aside whatever can be weakened even to the slightest degree by the arguments brought forward, so that eventually all that remains is precisely nothing but what is certain and unshaken.

What then did I formerly think I was? A man, of course. But what is a man? Might I not say a "rational animal"? No, because then I would have to inquire what "animal" and "rational" mean. And thus from one question I would slide into many more difficult ones. Nor do I now have enough free time that I want to waste it on subtleties of this sort. Instead, permit me here to focus here on what came spontaneously and naturally into my thinking whenever I pondered what I was. Now it occurred to me first that I had a face, hands, arms, and this entire mechanism of bodily members: the very same as are discerned in a corpse, and which I referred to by the name "body." It next occurred to me that I took in food, that I walked about, and that I sensed and thought various things; these actions I used to attribute to the soul. But as to what this soul might be, I either did not think about it or else I imagined it a rarefied I-know-not-what, like a wind, or a fire, or ether, which had been infused into my coarser parts. But as to the body I was not in any doubt. On the contrary, I was under the impression that I knew its nature distinctly. Were I perhaps tempted to describe this nature such as I conceived it in my mind, I would have described it thus: by "body," I understand all that is capable of being bounded by some shape, of being enclosed in a place, and of filling up a space in such a way as to exclude any other body from it; of being perceived by touch, sight, hearing, taste, or smell; of being moved in several ways, not, of course, by itself, but by whatever else impinges upon it. For it was my view that the power of self-motion, and likewise of sensing or of thinking, in no way belonged to the nature of the body. Indeed I used rather to marvel that such faculties were to be found in certain bodies.

But now what am I, when I suppose that there is some supremely powerful and, if I may be permitted to say so, malicious deceiver who deliberately tries to fool me in any way he can? Can I not affirm that I possess at least a small measure of all those things which I have already said belong to the nature of the body? I focus my attention on them, I think about them, I review them again, but nothing comes to mind. I am tired of repeating this to no purpose. But what about those things I ascribed to the soul? What about being nourished or moving about? Since I now do not have a body, these are surely nothing but fictions. What about sensing? Surely this too does not take place without a body; and I seemed to have sensed in my dreams many things that I later realized I did not sense. What about thinking? Here I make my discovery: thought exists; it alone cannot be separated from me. I am; I exist—this is certain. But for how long? For as long as I am thinking; for perhaps it could also come to pass that if I were to cease all thinking I would then utterly cease to exist. At this time I admit nothing that is not necessarily true. I am therefore precisely nothing but a thinking thing; that is, a mind, or intellect, or understanding, or reason—words of whose meanings I was previously ignorant. Yet I am a true thing and am truly existing; but what kind of thing? I have said it already: a thinking thing.

What else am I? I will set my imagination in motion. I am not that concatenation of members we call the human body. Neither am I even some subtle air infused into these members, nor a wind, nor a fire, nor a vapor, nor a breath, nor anything I devise for myself. For I have supposed these things to be nothing. The assumption still stands; yet nevertheless I am something. But is it perhaps the case that these very things which I take to be nothing, because they are unknown to me, nevertheless are in fact no different from that me that I know? This I do not know, and I will not quarrel about it now. I can make a judgment only about things that are known to me. I know that I exist; I ask now who is this "I" whom I know? Most certainly, in the strict sense the knowledge of this "I" does not depend upon things whose existence I do not yet know. Therefore it is not dependent upon any of those things that I simulate in my imagination. But this word "simulate" warns me of my error. For I would indeed be simulating were I to "imagine" that I was something, because imagining is merely the contemplating of the shape or image of a corporeal thing. But I now know with certainty that I am and also that all these images—and, generally, everything belonging to the nature of the body—could turn out to be nothing but dreams. Once I have realized this, I would seem to be speaking no less foolishly were I to say: "I will use my imagination in order to recognize more distinctly who I am," than were I to say: "Now I surely am awake, and I see something true; but since I do not yet see it clearly enough, I will deliberately fall asleep so that my dreams might represent it to me more truly and more clearly." Thus I realize that none of what I can grasp by means of the imagination pertains to this knowledge that I have of myself. Moreover, I realize that I must be most diligent about withdrawing my mind from these things so that it can perceive its nature as distinctly as possible.

28

But what then am I? A thing that thinks. What is that? A thing that doubts, understands, affirms, denies, wills, refuses, and that also imagines and senses.

Indeed it is no small matter if all of these things belong to me. But why should they not belong to me? Is it not the very same "I" who now doubts almost everything, who nevertheless understands something, who affirms that this one thing is true, who denies other things, who desires to know more, who wishes not to be deceived, who imagines many things even against my will, who also notices many things which appear to come from the senses? What is there in all of this that is not every bit as true as the fact that I exist—even if I am always asleep or even if my creator makes every effort to mislead me? Which of these things is distinct from my thought? Which of them can be said to be separate from myself? For it is so obvious that it is I who doubt, I who understand, and I who will, that there is nothing by which it could be explained more clearly. But indeed it is also the same "I" who imagines; for although perhaps, as I supposed before, absolutely nothing that I imagined is true, still the very power of imagining really does exist, and constitutes a part of my thought. Finally, it is this same "I" who senses or who is cognizant of bodily things as if through the senses. For example, I now see a light, I hear a noise, I feel heat. These things are false, since I am asleep. Yet I certainly do seem to see, hear, and feel warmth. This cannot be false. Properly speaking, this is what in me is called "sensing." But this, precisely so taken, is nothing other than thinking.

29

From these considerations I am beginning to know a little better what I am. But it still seems (and I cannot resist believing) that corporeal things—whose images are formed by thought, and which the senses themselves examine—are much more distinctly known than this mysterious "I" which does not fall within the imagination.

And yet it would be strange indeed were I to grasp the very things I consider to be doubtful, unknown, and foreign to me more distinctly than what is true, what is known—than, in short, myself. But I see what is happening: my mind loves to wander and does not yet permit itself to be restricted within the confines of truth. So be it then; let us just this once allow it completely free rein, so that, a little while later, when the time has come to pull in the reins, the mind may more readily permit itself to be controlled.

Let us consider those things which are commonly believed to be the most distinctly grasped of all: namely the bodies we touch and see. Not bodies in general, mind you, for these general perceptions are apt to be somewhat more confused, but one body in particular. Let us take, for instance, this piece of wax. It has been taken quite recently from the honeycomb; it has not yet lost all the honey flavor. It retains some of the scent of the flowers from which it was collected. Its color, shape, and size are manifest. It is hard and cold; it is easy to touch. If you rap on it with your knuckle it will emit a sound. In short, everything is present in it that appears needed to enable a body to be known as distinctly as possible. But notice that, as I am speaking, I am bringing it close to the fire. The remaining traces of the honey flavor are disappearing; the scent is vanishing; the color is changing; the original shape is disappearing. Its size is increasing; it is becoming liquid and hot; you can hardly touch it. And now, when you rap on it, it no longer emits any sound. Does the same wax still remain? I must confess that it does; no one denies it; no one thinks otherwise. So what was there in the wax that was so distinctly grasped? Certainly none of the aspects that I reached by means of the senses. For whatever came under the senses of taste, smell, sight, touch, or hearing has now changed; and yet the wax remains.

Perhaps the wax was what I now think it is: namely that the wax itself never really was the sweetness of the honey, nor the fragrance of the flowers, nor the whiteness, nor the shape, nor the sound, but instead was a body that a short time ago manifested itself to me in these ways, and now does so in other ways. But just what precisely is this thing that I thus imagine? Let us focus our attention on this and see what remains after we have removed everything that does not belong to the wax: only that it is something extended, flexible, and mutable. But is it to be flexible and mutable? Is it what my imagination shows it to be: namely, that this piece of wax can change from a round to a square shape, or from the latter to a triangular shape? Not at all; for I grasp that the wax is capable of innumerable changes of this sort, even though I am incapable of running through these innumerable changes by using my imagination. Therefore this insight is not achieved by the faculty of imagination. What is it to be extended? Is this thing's extension also unknown? For it becomes greater in wax that is beginning to melt, greater in boiling wax, and greater still as the heat is increased. And I would not judge correctly what the wax is if I did not believe that it takes on an even greater variety of dimensions than I could ever grasp with the imagination. It remains then for me to concede that I do not grasp what this wax is through the imagination; rather, I perceive it through the mind alone. The point I am making refers to this particular piece of wax, for the case of wax in general is clearer still.

But what is this piece of wax which is perceived only by the mind? Surely it is the same piece of wax that I see, touch, and imagine; in short it is the same piece of wax I took it to be from the very beginning. But I need to realize that the perception of the wax is neither a seeing, nor a touching, nor an imagining. Nor has it ever been, even though it previously seemed so; rather it is an inspection on the part of the mind alone. This inspection can be imperfect and confused, as it was before, or clear and distinct, as it is now, depending on how closely I pay attention to the things in which the piece of wax consists.

But meanwhile I marvel at how prone my mind is to errors. For although I am considering these things within myself silently and without words, nevertheless I   32
seize upon words themselves and I am nearly deceived by the ways in which people commonly speak. For we say that we see the wax itself, if it is present, and not that we judge it to be present from its color or shape. Whence I might conclude straightaway that I know the wax through the vision had by the eye, and not through an inspection on the part of the mind alone. But then were I perchance to look out my window and observe men crossing the square, I would ordinarily say I see the men themselves just as I say I see the wax. But what do I see aside from hats and clothes, which could conceal automata? Yet I judge them to be men. Thus what I thought I had seen with my eyes, I actually grasped solely with the faculty of judgment, which is in my mind.

But a person who seeks to know more than the common crowd ought to be ashamed of himself for looking for doubt in common ways of speaking. Let us then go forward, inquiring on when it was that I perceived more perfectly and evidently what the piece of wax was. Was it when I first saw it and believed I knew it by the external sense, or at least by the so-called "common" sense, that is, the power of imagination? Or do I have more perfect knowledge now, when I have diligently examined both what the wax is and how it is known? Surely it is absurd to be in doubt about this matter. For what was there in my initial perception that was distinct? What was there that any animal seemed incapable of possessing? But indeed when I distinguish the wax from its external forms, as if stripping it of its clothing, and look at the wax in its nakedness, then, even though there can be still an error in my judgment, nevertheless I cannot perceive it thus without a human mind.

But what am I to say about this mind, that is, about myself? For as yet I admit   33
nothing else to be in me over and above the mind. What, I ask, am I who seem to perceive this wax so distinctly? Do I not know myself not only much more truly and with greater certainty, but also much more distinctly and evidently? For if I judge that the wax exists from the fact that I see it, certainly from this same fact that I see the wax it follows much more evidently that I myself exist. For it could happen that what I see is not truly wax. It could happen that I have no eyes with which to see anything. But it is utterly impossible that, while I see or think I see (I do not now distinguish these two), I who think am not something. Likewise, if I judge that the wax exists from the fact that I touch it, the same outcome will again obtain, namely that I exist. If I judge that the wax exists from the fact that I imagine it, or for any other reason, plainly the same thing follows. But what I note regarding the wax

applies to everything else that is external to me. Furthermore, if my perception of the wax seemed more distinct after it became known to me not only on account of sight or touch, but on account of many reasons, one has to admit how much more distinctly I am now known to myself. For there is not a single consideration that can aid in my perception of the wax or of any other body that fails to make even more manifest the nature of my mind. But there are still so many other things in the mind itself on the basis of which my knowledge of it can be rendered more distinct that it hardly seems worth enumerating those things which emanate to it from the body.

34   But lo and behold, I have returned on my own to where I wanted to be. For since I now know that even bodies are not, properly speaking, perceived by the senses or by the faculty of imagination, but by the intellect alone, and that they are not perceived through their being touched or seen, but only through their being understood, I manifestly know that nothing can be perceived more easily and more evidently than my own mind. But since the tendency to hang on to long-held beliefs cannot be put aside so quickly, I want to stop here, so that by the length of my meditation this new knowledge may be more deeply impressed upon my memory.

MEDITATION THREE: Concerning God, That He Exists

I will now shut my eyes, stop up my ears, and withdraw all my senses. I will also blot out from my thoughts all images of corporeal things, or rather, since the latter is hardly possible, I will regard these images as empty, false, and worthless. And as I converse with myself alone and look more deeply into myself, I will attempt to render myself gradually better known and more familiar to myself. I am a thing that thinks, that is to say, a thing that doubts, affirms, denies, understands a few things, is ignorant of many things, wills, refrains from willing, and also imagines and senses. For as I observed earlier, even though these things that I sense or imagine may perhaps be nothing at all outside me, nevertheless I am certain that these modes of thinking, which are cases of what I call sensing and imagining, insofar as they are merely modes of thinking, do exist within me.

In these few words, I have reviewed everything I truly know, or at least what so far I have noticed that I know. Now I will ponder more carefully to see whether perhaps there may be other things belonging to me that up until now I have failed to notice. I am certain that I am a thinking thing. But do I not therefore also know what is required for me to be certain of anything? Surely in this first instance of knowledge, there is nothing but a certain clear and distinct perception of what I affirm. Yet this would hardly be enough to render me certain of the truth of a thing, if it could ever happen that something that I perceived so clearly and distinctly were false. And thus I now seem able to posit as a general rule that everything I very clearly and distinctly perceive is true.

Be that as it may, I have previously admitted many things as wholly certain and evident that nevertheless I later discovered to be doubtful. What sort of things were these? Why, the earth, the sky, the stars, and all the other things I perceived by means of the senses. But what was it about these things that I clearly perceived? Surely the fact that the ideas or thoughts of these things were hovering before my mind. But even now I do not deny that these ideas are in me. Yet there was something else I used to affirm, which, owing to my habitual tendency to believe it, I used to think was something I clearly perceived, even though I actually did not perceive it all: namely, that certain things existed outside me, things from which those ideas proceeded and which those ideas completely resembled. But on this point I was mistaken; or, rather if my judgment was a true one, it was not the result of the force of my perception.

But what about when I considered something very simple and easy in the areas of arithmetic or geometry, for example that 2 plus 3 make 5, and the like? Did I not intuit them at least clearly enough so as to affirm them as true? To be sure, I did decide later on that I must doubt these things, but that was only because it occurred to me that some God could perhaps have given me a nature such that I might be deceived even about matters that seemed most evident. But whenever this preconceived opinion about the supreme power of God occurs to me, I cannot help admitting that, were he to wish it, it would be easy for him to cause me to err even in those matters that I think I intuit as clearly as possible with the eyes of the mind.

35

36

On the other hand, whenever I turn my attention to those very things that I think I perceive with such great clarity, I am so completely persuaded by them that I spontaneously blurt out these words: "let him who can deceive me; so long as I think that I am something, he will never bring it about that I am nothing. Nor will he one day make it true that I never existed, for it is true now that I do exist. Nor will he even bring it about that perhaps 2 plus 3 might equal more or less than 5, or similar items in which I recognize an obvious contradiction." And certainly, because I have no reason for thinking that there is a God who is a deceiver (and of course I do not yet sufficiently know whether there even is a God), the basis for doubting, depending as it does merely on the above hypothesis, is very tenuous and, so to speak, metaphysical. But in order to remove even this basis for doubt, I should at the first opportunity inquire whether there is a God, and, if there is, whether or not he can be a deceiver. For if I am ignorant of this, it appears I am never capable of being completely certain about anything else.

However, at this stage good order seems to demand that I first group all my thoughts into certain classes, and ask in which of them truth or falsity properly resides. Some of these thoughts are like images of things; to these alone does the word "idea" properly apply, as when I think of a man, or a chimera, or the sky, or an
37   angel, or God. Again there are other thoughts that take different forms: for example, when I will, or fear, or affirm, or deny, there is always some thing that I grasp as the subject of my thought, yet I embrace in my thought something more than the likeness of that thing. Some of these thoughts are called volitions or affects, while others are called judgments.

Now as far as ideas are concerned, if they are considered alone and in their own right, without being referred to something else, they cannot, properly speaking, be false. For whether it is a she-goat or a chimera that I am imagining, it is no less true that I imagine the one than the other. Moreover, we need not fear that there is falsity in the will itself or in the affects, for although I can choose evil things or even things that are utterly nonexistent, I cannot conclude from this that it is untrue that I do choose these things. Thus there remain only judgments in which I must take care not to be mistaken. Now the principal and most frequent error to be found in judgments consists in the fact that I judge that the ideas which are in me are similar to or in conformity with certain things outside me. Obviously, if I were to consider these ideas merely as certain modes of my thought, and were not to refer them to anything else, they could hardly give me any subject matter for error.

Among these ideas, some appear to me to be innate, some adventitious, and some produced by me. For I understand what a thing is, what truth is, what thought is, and I appear to have derived this exclusively from my very own nature. But say I am now hearing a noise, or looking at the sun, or feeling the fire; up until now I judged that
38   these things proceeded from certain things outside me, and finally, that sirens, hippogriffs, and the like are made by me. Or perhaps I can even think of all these ideas as being adventitious, or as being innate, or as fabrications, for I have not yet clearly ascertained their true origin.

But here I must inquire particularly into those ideas that I believe to be derived from things existing outside me. Just what reason do I have for believing that these ideas resemble those things? Well, I do seem to have been so taught by nature. Moreover, I do know from experience that these ideas do not depend upon my will, nor consequently upon myself, for I often notice them even against my will. Now, for example, whether or not I will it, I feel heat. It is for this reason that I believe this feeling or idea of heat comes to me from something other than myself, namely from heat of the fire by which I am sitting. Nothing is more obvious than the judgment that this thing is sending its likeness rather than something else into me.

I will now see whether these reasons are powerful enough. When I say here "I have been so taught by nature," all I have in mind is that I am driven by a spontaneous impulse to believe this, and not that some light of nature is showing me that it is true. These are two very different things. For whatever is shown me by this light of nature, for example, that from the fact that I doubt, it follows that I am, and the like, cannot in any way be doubtful. This is owing to the fact that there can be no other faculty that I can trust as much as this light and which could teach that these things are not true. But as far as natural impulses are concerned, in the past I have often judged myself to have been driven by them to make the poorer choice when it was a question of choosing a good; and I fail to see why I should place any greater faith in them in other matters.

Again, although these ideas do not depend upon my will, it does not follow that   39
they necessarily proceed from things existing outside me. For just as these impulses about which I spoke just now seem to be different from my will, even though they are in me, so too perhaps there is also in me some other faculty, one not yet sufficiently known to me, which produces these ideas, just as it has always seemed up to now that ideas are formed in me without any help from external things when I am asleep.

And finally, even if these ideas did proceed from things other than myself, it does not therefore follow that they must resemble those things. Indeed it seems I have frequently noticed a vast difference in many respects. For example, I find within myself two distinct ideas of the sun. One idea is drawn, as it were, from the senses. Now it is this idea which, of all those that I take to be derived from outside me, is most in need of examination. By means of this idea the sun appears to me to be quite small. But there is another idea, one derived from astronomical reasoning, that is, it is elicited from certain notions that are innate in me, or else is fashioned by me in some other way. Through this idea the sun is shown to be several times larger than the earth. Both ideas surely cannot resemble the same sun existing outside me; and reason convinces me that the idea that seems to have emanated from the sun itself from so close is the very one that least resembles the sun.

All these points demonstrate sufficiently that up to this point it was not a well-founded judgment, but only a blind impulse that formed the basis of my belief that things existing outside me send ideas or images of themselves to me through the sense organs or by some other means.

But still another way occurs to me for inquiring whether some of the things of   40
which there are ideas in me do exist outside me: insofar as these ideas are merely

modes of thought, I see no inequality among them; they all seem to proceed from me in the same manner. But insofar as one idea represents one thing and another idea another thing, it is obvious that they do differ very greatly from one another. Unquestionably, those ideas that display substances to me are something more and, if I may say so, contain within themselves more objective reality than those which represent only modes or accidents. Again, the idea that enables me to understand a supreme deity, eternal, infinite, omniscient, omnipotent, and creator of all things other than himself, clearly has more objective reality within it than do those ideas through which finite substances are displayed.

Now it is indeed evident by the light of nature that there must be at least as much [reality] in the efficient and total cause as there is in the effect of that same cause. For whence, I ask, could an effect get its reality, if not from its cause? And how could the cause give that reality to the effect, unless it also possessed that reality? Hence it follows that something cannot come into being out of nothing, and also that what is more perfect (that is, what contains in itself more reality) cannot come into being from what is less perfect. But this is manifestly true not merely for those effects whose reality is actual or formal, but also for ideas in which only objective reality is considered. For example, not only can a stone which did not exist previously not now begin to exist unless it is produced by something in which there is, either formally
41   or eminently, everything that is in the stone; nor heat be introduced into a subject which was not already hot unless it is done by something that is of at least as perfect an order as heat—and the same for the rest—but it is also true that there can be in me no idea of heat, or of a stone, unless it is placed in me by some cause that has at least as much reality as I conceive to be in the heat or in the stone. For although this cause conveys none of its actual or formal reality to my idea, it should not be thought for that reason that it must be less real. Rather, the very nature of an idea is such that of itself it needs no formal reality other than what it borrows from my thought, of which it is a mode. But that a particular idea contains this as opposed to that objective reality is surely owing to some cause in which there is at least as much formal reality as there is objective reality contained in the idea. For if we assume that something is found in the idea that was not in its cause, then the idea gets that something from nothing. Yet as imperfect a mode of being as this is by which a thing exists in the intellect objectively through an idea, nevertheless it is plainly not nothing; hence it cannot get its being from nothing.

Moreover, even though the reality that I am considering in my ideas is merely objective reality, I ought not on that account to suspect that there is no need for the same reality to be formally in the causes of these ideas, but that it suffices for it to be in them objectively. For just as the objective mode of being belongs to ideas by their very nature, so the formal mode of being belongs to the causes of ideas, at least to the first and preeminent ones, by their very nature. And although one idea can
42   perhaps issue from another, nevertheless no infinite regress is permitted here; eventually some first idea must be reached whose cause is a sort of archetype that contains formally all the reality that is in the idea merely objectively. Thus it is clear to me by the light of nature that the ideas that are in me are like images that can easily

fail to match the perfection of the things from which they have been drawn, but which can contain nothing greater or more perfect.

And the longer and more attentively I examine all these points, the more clearly and distinctly I know they are true. But what am I ultimately to conclude? If the objective reality of any of my ideas is found to be so great that I am certain that the same reality was not in me, either formally or eminently, and that therefore I myself cannot be the cause of the idea, then it necessarily follows that I am not alone in the world, but that something else, which is the cause of this idea, also exists. But if no such idea is found in me, I will have no argument whatsoever to make me certain of the existence of anything other than myself, for I have conscientiously reviewed all these arguments, and so far I have been unable to find any other.

Among my ideas, in addition to the one that displays me to myself (about which there can be no difficulty at this point), are others that represent God, corporeal and inanimate things, angels, animals, and finally other men like myself.

As to the ideas that display other men, or animals, or angels, I easily understand that they could be fashioned from the ideas that I have of myself, of corporeal things, and of God—even if no men (except myself), no animals, and no angels existed in   43
the world.

As to the ideas of corporeal things, there is nothing in them that is so great that it seems incapable of having originated from me. For if I investigate them thoroughly and examine each one individually in the way I examined the idea of wax yesterday, I notice that there are only a very few things in them that I perceive clearly and distinctly: namely, size, or extension in length, breadth, and depth; shape, which arises from the limits of this extension; position, which various things possessing shape have in relation to one another; and motion, or alteration in position. To these can be added substance, duration, and number. But as for the remaining items, such as light and colors, sounds, odors, tastes, heat and cold, and other tactile qualities, I think of these only in a very confused and obscure manner, to the extent that I do not even know whether they are true or false, that is, whether the ideas I have of them are ideas of things or ideas of non-things. For although a short time ago I noted that falsity properly so called (or "formal" falsity) is to be found only in judgments, nevertheless there is another kind of falsity (called "material" falsity) which is found in ideas whenever they represent a non-thing as if it were a thing. For example, the ideas I have of heat and cold fall so far short of being clear and distinct that I cannot tell from them whether cold is merely the privation of heat or whether heat is the privation of cold, or whether both are real qualities, or whether neither is. And because ideas can only be, as it were, of things, if it is true that cold is merely the absence of heat, then an idea that represents cold to me as something real and positive, will not   44
inappropriately be called false. The same holds for other similar ideas.

Assuredly I need not assign to these ideas an author distinct from myself. For if they were false, that is, if they were to represent non-things, I know by the light of nature that they proceed from nothing; that is, they are in me for no other reason than that something is lacking in my nature, and that my nature is not entirely perfect. If, on the other hand, these ideas are true, then because they exhibit so little reality to me that I cannot distinguish it from a non-thing, I see no reason why they cannot get their being from me.

As for what is clear and distinct in the ideas of corporeal things, it appears I could have borrowed some of these from the idea of myself. namely, substance, duration, number, and whatever else there may be of this type. For instance, I think that a stone is a substance, that is to say, a thing that is suitable for existing in itself, and likewise I think that I too am a substance. Despite the fact that I conceive myself to be a thinking thing and not an extended thing, whereas I conceive of a stone as an extended thing and not a thinking thing, and hence there is the greatest diversity between these two concepts, nevertheless they seem to agree with one another when considered under the rubric of substance. Furthermore, I perceive that I now exist and recall that I have previously existed for some time. And I have various thoughts and know how many of them there are. It is in doing these things that I acquire the ideas of duration and number, which I can then apply to other things. However, none of the other components out of which the ideas of corporeal things are fashioned (namely extension, shape, position, and motion) are contained in me formally, since I am merely a thinking thing. But since these are only certain modes of a substance, whereas I am a substance, it seems possible that they are contained in me eminently.

45

Thus there remains only the idea of God. I must consider whether there is anything in this idea that could not have originated from me. I understand by the name "God" a certain substance that is infinite, independent, supremely intelligent and supremely powerful, and that created me along with everything else that exists— if anything else exists. Indeed all these are such that, the more carefully I focus my attention on them, the less possible it seems they could have arisen from myself alone. Thus, from what has been said, I must conclude that God necessarily exists.

For although the idea of substance is in me by virtue of the fact that I am a substance, that fact is not sufficient to explain my having the idea of an infinite substance, since I am finite, unless this idea proceeded from some substance which really was infinite.

Nor should I think that I do not perceive the infinite by means of a true idea, but only through a negation of the finite, just as I perceive rest and darkness by means of a negation of motion and light. On the contrary, I clearly understand that there is more reality in an infinite substance than there is in a finite one. Thus the perception of the infinite is somehow prior in me to the perception of the finite, that is, my perception of God is prior to my perception of myself. For how would I understand that I doubt and that I desire, that is, that I lack something and that I am not wholly perfect, unless there were some idea in me of a more perfect being, by comparison with which I might recognize my defects?

Nor can it be said that this idea of God is perhaps materially false and thus can originate from nothing, as I remarked just now about the ideas of heat and cold, and the like. On the contrary, because it is the most clear and distinct and because it contains more objective reality than any other idea, no idea is in and of itself truer and has less of a basis for being suspected of falsehood. I maintain that this idea of a being that is supremely perfect and infinite is true in the highest degree. For

46

although I could perhaps pretend that such a being does not exist, nevertheless I could not pretend that the idea of such a being discloses to me nothing real, as was the case with the idea of cold which I referred to earlier. It is indeed an idea that is utterly clear and distinct; for whatever I clearly and distinctly perceive to be real and true and to involve some perfection is wholly contained in that idea. It is no objection that I do not comprehend the infinite or that there are countless other things in God that I can in no way either comprehend or perhaps even touch with my thought. For the nature of the infinite is such that it is not comprehended by a being such as I, who am finite. And it is sufficient that I understand this very point and judge that all those things that I clearly perceive and that I know to contain some perfection—and perhaps even countless other things of which I am ignorant—are in God either formally or eminently. The result is that, of all the ideas that are in me, the idea that I have of God is the most true, the most clear and distinct.

But perhaps I am something greater than I myself understand. Perhaps all these perfections that I am attributing to God are somehow in me potentially, although they do no yet assert themselves and are not yet actualized. For I now observe that my knowledge is gradually being increased, and I see nothing standing in the way of its being increased more and more to infinity. Moreover, I see no reason why, with my knowledge thus increased, I could not acquire all the remaining perfections of God. And, finally, if the potential for these perfections is in me already, I see no reason 47 why this potential would not suffice to produce the idea of these perfections.

Yet none of these things can be the case. First, while it is true that my knowledge is gradually being increased and that there are many things in me potentially that are not yet actual, nevertheless, none of these pertains to the idea of God, in which there is nothing whatever that is potential. Indeed this gradual increase is itself a most certain proof of imperfection. Moreover, although my knowledge may always increase more and more, nevertheless I understand that this knowledge will never by this means be actually infinite, because it will never reach a point where it is incapable of greater increase. On the contrary, I judge God to be actually infinite, so that nothing can be added to his perfection. Finally, I perceive that the objective being of an idea cannot be produced by a merely potential being (which, strictly speaking, is nothing), but only by an actual or formal being.

Indeed there is nothing in all these things that is not manifest by the light of nature to one who is conscientious and attentive. But when I am less attentive, and the images of sensible things blind the mind's eye, I do not so easily recall why the idea of a being more perfect than me necessarily proceeds from a being that really is more perfect. This being the case, it is appropriate to ask further whether I myself who have this idea could exist, if such a being did not exist.

From what source, then, do I derive my existence? Why, from myself, or from my parents, or from whatever other things there are that are less perfect than God. For nothing more perfect than God, or even as perfect as God, can be thought or imagined. 48

But if I got my being from myself, I would not doubt, nor would I desire, nor would I lack anything at all. For I would have given myself all the perfections of which I have some idea; in so doing, I myself would be God! I must not think that the things I lack could perhaps be more difficult to acquire than the ones I have now. On the contrary, it is obvious that it would have been much more difficult for me (that is, a thing or substance that thinks) to emerge out of nothing than it would be to acquire the knowledge of many things about which I am ignorant (these items of knowledge being merely accidents of that substance). Certainly, if I got this greater thing from myself, I would not have denied myself at least those things that can be had more easily. Nor would I have denied myself any of those other things that I perceive to be contained in the idea of God, for surely none of them seem to me more difficult to bring about. But if any of them were more difficult to bring about, they would certainly also seem more difficult to me, even if the remaining ones that I possess I got from myself, since it would be on account of them that I would experience that my power is limited.

Nor am I avoiding the force of these arguments, if I suppose that perhaps I have always existed as I do now, as if it then followed that no author of my existence need be sought. For because the entire span of one's life can be divided into countless parts, each one wholly independent of the rest, it does not follow from the fact that I existed a short time ago that I must exist now, unless some cause, as it were, creates me all over again at this moment, that is to say, which preserves me. For it is obvious to one who pays close attention to the nature of time that plainly the same force and action are needed to preserve anything at each individual moment that it lasts as would be required to create that same thing anew, were it not yet in existence. Thus conservation differs from creation solely by virtue of a distinction of reason; this too is one of those things that are manifest by the light of nature.

Therefore I must now ask myself whether I possess some power by which I can bring it about that I myself, who now exist, will also exist a little later on. For since I am nothing but a thinking thing—or at least since I am now dealing simply and precisely with that part of me which is a thinking thing—if such a power were in me, then I would certainly be aware of it. But I observe that there is no such power; and from this very fact I know most clearly that I depend upon some being other than myself.

But perhaps this being is not God, and I have been produced either by my parents or by some other causes less perfect than God. On the contrary, as I said before, it is obvious that there must be at least as much in the cause as there is in the effect. Thus, regardless of what it is that eventually is assigned as my cause, because I am a thinking thing and have within me a certain idea of God, it must be granted that what caused me is also a thinking thing and it too has an idea of all the perfections which I attribute to God. And I can again inquire of this cause whether it got its existence from itself or from another cause. For if it got its existence from itself, it is evident from what has been said that it is itself God, because, having the power of existing in and of itself, it unquestionably also has the power of actually possessing all the perfections of which it has in itself an idea—that is, all the perfections that I conceive to be in God. However, if it got its existence from another cause, I will once again inquire in similar fashion about this other cause: whether it got its existence from itself or from another cause, until finally I arrive at the ultimate cause, which will be God. For it is apparent enough that there can be no infinite regress here, especially

49

50

since I am not dealing here merely with the cause that once produced me, but also and most especially with the cause that preserves me at the present time.

Nor can one fancy that perhaps several partial causes have concurred in bringing me into being, and that I have taken the ideas of the various perfections I attribute to God from a variety of causes, so that all of these perfections are found somewhere in the universe, but not all joined together in a single being—God. On the contrary, the unity, the simplicity, that is, the inseparability of all those features that are in God is one of the chief perfections that I understand to be in him. Certainly the idea of the unity of all his perfections could not have been placed in me by any cause from which I did not also get the ideas of the other perfections; for neither could some cause have made me understand them joined together and inseparable from one another, unless it also caused me to recognize what they were.

Finally, as to my parents, even if everything that I ever believed about them were true, still it is certainly not they who preserve me; nor is it they who in any way brought me into being, insofar as I am a thinking thing. Rather, they merely placed certain dispositions in the matter which I judged to contain me, that is, a mind, which now is the only thing I take myself to be. And thus there can be no difficulty here concerning my parents. Indeed I have no choice but to conclude that the mere fact of my existing and of there being in me an idea of a most perfect being, that is, God, demonstrates most evidently that God too exists.

All that remains for me is to ask how I received this idea of God. For I did not draw it from the senses; it never came upon me unexpectedly, as is usually the case with the ideas of sensible things when these things present themselves (or seem to present themselves) to the external sense organs. Nor was it made by me, for I plainly can neither subtract anything from it nor add anything to it. Thus the only option remaining is that this idea is innate in me, just as the idea of myself is innate in me.   51

To be sure, it is not astonishing that in creating me, God should have endowed me with this idea, so that it would be like the mark of the craftsman impressed upon his work, although this mark need not be something distinct from the work itself. But the mere fact that God created me makes it highly plausible that I have somehow been made in his image and likeness, and that I perceive this likeness, in which the idea of God is contained, by means of the same faculty by which I perceive myself. That is, when I turn the mind's eye toward myself, I understand not only that I am something incomplete and dependent upon another, something aspiring indefinitely for greater and greater or better things, but also that the being on whom I depend has in himself all those greater things—not merely indefinitely and potentially, but infinitely and actually, and thus that he is God. The whole force of the argument rests on the fact that I recognize that it would be impossible for me to exist, being of such a nature as I am (namely, having in me the idea of God), unless God did in fact exist. God, I say, that same being the idea of whom is in me: a being having all those   52 perfections that I cannot comprehend, but can somehow touch with my thought, and a being subject to no defects whatever. From these considerations it is quite obvious that he cannot be a deceiver, for it is manifest by the light of nature that all fraud and deception depend on some defect.

But before examining this idea more closely and at the same time inquiring into other truths that can be gathered from it, at this point I want to spend some time contemplating this God, to ponder his attributes and, so far as the eye of my darkened mind can take me, to gaze upon, to admire, and to adore the beauty of this immense light. For just as we believe by faith that the greatest felicity of the next life consists solely in this contemplation of the divine majesty, so too we now experience that from the same contemplation, although it is much less perfect, the greatest pleasure of which we are capable in this life can be perceived.

MEDITATION FOUR: Concerning the True and the False

Lately I have become accustomed to withdrawing my mind from the senses, and I have carefully taken note of the fact that very few things are truly perceived   53
regarding corporeal things, although a great many more things are known regarding the human mind, and still many more things regarding God. The upshot is that I now have no difficulty directing my thought away from things that can be imagined to things that can be grasped only by the understanding and are wholly separate from matter. In fact the idea I clearly have of the human mind—insofar as it is a thinking thing, not extended in length, breadth, or depth, and having nothing else from the body—is far more distinct than the idea of any corporeal thing. And when I take note of the fact that I doubt, or that I am a thing that is incomplete and dependent, there comes to mind a clear and distinct idea of a being that is independent and complete, that is, an idea of God. And from the mere fact that such an idea is in me, or that I who have this idea exist, I draw the obvious conclusion that God also exists, and that my existence depends entirely upon him at each and every moment. This conclusion is so obvious that I am confident that the human mind can know nothing more evident or more certain. And now I seem to see a way by which I might progress from this contemplation of the true God, in whom, namely, are hidden all the treasures of the sciences and wisdom, to the knowledge of other things.

To begin with, I acknowledge that it is impossible for God ever to deceive me, for trickery or deception are always indicative of some imperfection. And although the ability to deceive seems to be an indication of cleverness or power, the will to deceive undoubtedly attests to maliciousness or weakness. Accordingly, deception is incompatible with God.

Next I experience that there is in me a certain faculty of judgment, which, like everything else that is in me, I undoubtedly received from God. And since he does   54
not wish to deceive me, he assuredly has not given me the sort of faculty with which I could ever make a mistake, when I use it properly.

No doubt regarding this matter would remain, but for the fact that it seems to follow from this that I am never capable of making a mistake. For if everything that is in me I got from God, and he gave me no faculty for making mistakes, it seems I am incapable of ever erring. And thus, so long as I think exclusively about God and focus my attention exclusively on him, I discern no cause of error or falsity. But once I turn my attention back on myself, I nevertheless experience that I am subject to countless errors. As I seek a cause of these errors, I notice that passing before me is not only a real and positive idea of God (that is, of a supremely perfect being), but also, as it were, a certain negative idea of nothingness (that is, of what is at the greatest possible distance from any perfection), and that I have been so constituted as a kind of middle ground between God and nothingness, or between the supreme being and non-being. Thus insofar as I have been created by the supreme being, there is nothing in me by means of which I might be deceived or be led into error; but insofar as I participate in nothingness or non-being, that is, insofar as I am not the supreme being and lack a great many things, it is not surprising that I make mistakes.

Thus I certainly understand that error as such is not something real that depends upon God, but rather is merely a defect. And thus there is no need to account for my errors by positing a faculty given to me by God for the purpose. Rather, it just so happens that I make mistakes because the faculty of judging the truth, which I got from God, is not, in my case, infinite.

55   Still this is not yet altogether satisfactory; for error is not a pure negation, but rather a privation or a lack of some knowledge that somehow ought to be in me. And when I attend to the nature of God, it seems impossible that he would have placed in me a faculty that is not perfect in its kind or that is lacking some perfection it ought to have. For if it is true that the more expert the craftsman, the more perfect the works he produces, what can that supreme creator of all things make that is not perfect in all respects? No doubt God could have created me such that I never erred. No doubt, again, God always wills what is best. Is it then better that I should be in error rather than not?

As I mull these things over more carefully, it occurs to me first that there is no reason to marvel at the fact that God should bring about certain things the reasons for which I do not understand. Nor is his existence therefore to be doubted because I happen to experience other things of which I fail to grasp why and how he made them. For since I know now that my nature is very weak and limited, whereas the nature of God is immense, incomprehensible, and infinite, this is sufficient for me also to know that he can make innumerable things whose causes escape me. For this reason alone the entire class of causes which people customarily derive from a thing's "end," I judge to be utterly useless in physics. It is not without rashness that I think myself capable of inquiring into the ends of God.

It also occurs to me that whenever we ask whether the works of God are perfect, we should keep in view not simply some one creature in isolation from the rest, but the universe as a whole. For perhaps something might rightfully appear very
56   imperfect if it were all by itself; and yet be most perfect, to the extent that it has the status of a part in the universe. And although subsequent to having decided to doubt everything, I have come to know with certainty only that I and God exist, nevertheless, after having taken note of the immense power of God, I cannot deny that many other things have been made by him, or at least could have been made by him. Thus I may have the status of a part in the universal scheme of things.

Next, as I focus more closely on myself and inquire into the nature of my errors (the only things that are indicative of some imperfection in me), I note that these efforts depend on the simultaneous concurrence of two causes: the faculty of knowing that is in me and the faculty of choosing, that is, the free choice of the will, in other words, simultaneously on the intellect and will. Through the intellect alone I merely perceive ideas, about which I can render a judgment. Strictly speaking, no error is to be found in the intellect when properly viewed in this manner. For although perhaps there may exist countless things about which I have no idea, nevertheless it must not be said that, strictly speaking, I am deprived of these ideas but only that I lack them in a negative sense. This is because I cannot adduce an argument to prove that God ought to have given me a greater faculty of knowing than he did. No matter how expert a craftsman I understand him to be, still I do not for that reason believe he ought to have bestowed on each one of his works all the perfections that he can put into some. Nor, on the other hand, can I complain that the will or free choice I have received from God is insufficiently ample or perfect, since I experience that it is limited by no boundaries whatever. In fact, it seems to be especially worth noting that no other things in me are so perfect or so great but that I understand that they can be still more perfect or greater. If, for example, I consider the faculty of understanding, I immediately recognize that in my case it is very small and quite limited, and at the very same time I form an idea of another much greater faculty of understanding—in fact, an understanding which is consummately great and infinite; and from the fact that I can form an idea of this faculty, I perceive that it pertains to the nature of God. Similarly, were I to examine the faculties of memory or imagination, or any of the other faculties, I would understand that in my case each of these is without exception feeble and limited, whereas in the case of God I understand each faculty to be boundless. It is only the will or free choice that I experience to be so great in me that I cannot grasp the idea of any greater faculty. This is so much the case that the will is the chief basis for my understanding that I bear a certain image and likeness of God. For although the faculty of willing is incomparably greater in God than it is in me, both by virtue of the knowledge and power that are joined to it and that render it more resolute and efficacious and by virtue of its object inasmuch as the divine will stretches over a greater number of things, nevertheless, when viewed in itself formally and precisely, God's faculty of willing does not appear to be any greater. This is owing to the fact that willing is merely a matter of being able to do or not do the same thing, that is, of being able to affirm or deny, to pursue or to shun; or better still, the will consists solely in the fact that when something is proposed to us by our intellect either to affirm or deny, to pursue or to shun, we are moved in such a way that we sense that we are determined to it by no external force. In order to be free I need not be capable of being moved in each direction; on the contrary, the more I am inclined toward one direction— either because I clearly understand that there is in it an aspect of the good and the true, or because God has thus disposed the inner recesses of my thought—the more freely do I choose that direction. Nor indeed does divine grace or natural knowledge ever diminish one's freedom; rather, they increase and strengthen it. However, the indifference that I experience when there is no reason moving me more in one direction than in another is the lowest grade of freedom; it is indicative not of any perfection in freedom, but rather of a defect, that is, a certain negation in knowledge. Were I always to see clearly what is true and good, I would never deliberate about what is to be judged or chosen. In that event, although I would be entirely free, I could never be indifferent.

But from these considerations I perceive that the power of willing, which I got from God, is not, taken by itself, the cause of my errors, for it is most ample as well as perfect in its kind. Nor is my power of understanding the cause of my errors. For since I got my power of understanding from God, whatever I understand I doubtless understand rightly, and it is impossible for me to be deceived in this. What then is the source of my errors? They are owing simply to the fact that, since the will extends further than the intellect, I do not contain the will within the same boundaries; rather, I also extend it to things I do not understand. Because the will is indifferent in regard to such matters, it easily turns away from the true and the good; and in this way I am deceived and I sin.

For example, during these last few days I was examining whether anything in the world exists, and I noticed that, from the very fact that I was making this examination, it obviously followed that I exist. Nevertheless, I could not help judging that what I understood so clearly was true; not that I was coerced into making this judgment because of some external force, but because a great light in my intellect gave way to a great inclination in my will, and the less indifferent I was, the more spontaneously and freely did I believe it. But now, in addition to my knowing that I exist, insofar as I am a certain thinking thing, I also observe a certain idea of corporeal nature. It happens that I am in doubt as to whether the thinking nature which is in me, or rather which I am, is something different from this corporeal nature, or whether both natures are one and the same thing. And I assume that as yet no consideration has occurred to my intellect to convince me of the one alternative rather than the other. Certainly in virtue of this very fact I am indifferent about whether to affirm or to deny either alternative, or even whether to make no judgment at all in the matter.

Moreover, this indifference extends not merely to things about which the intellect knows absolutely nothing, but extends generally to everything of which the intellect does not have a clear enough knowledge at the very time when the will is deliberating on them. For although probable guesses may pull me in one direction, the mere knowledge that they are merely guesses and not certain and indubitable proofs is all it takes to push my assent in the opposite direction. These last few days have provided me with ample experience on this point. For all the beliefs that I had once held to be most true I have supposed to be utterly false, and for the sole reason that I determined that I could somehow raise doubts about them.

But if I hold off from making a judgment when I do not perceive what is true with sufficient clarity and distinctness, it is clear that I am acting properly and am not committing an error. But if instead I were to make an assertion or a denial, then I am not using my freedom properly. Were I to select the alternative that is false, then obviously I will be in error. But were I to embrace the other alternative, it will be by sheer luck that I happen upon the truth; but I will still not be without fault, for it is manifest by the light of nature that a perception on the part of the intellect must always precede a determination on the part of the will. Inherent in this incorrect use of free will is the privation that constitutes the very essence of error: the privation, I say, present in this operation insofar as the operation proceeds from me, but not in the faculty given to me by God, nor even in its operation insofar as it depends upon him.

Indeed I have no cause for complaint on the grounds that God has not given me a greater power of understanding or a greater light of nature than he has, for it is of the essence of a finite intellect not to understand many things, and it is of the essence of a created intellect to be finite. Actually, instead of thinking that he has withheld from me or deprived me of those things that he has not given me, I ought to thank God, who never owed me anything, for what he has bestowed upon me.

Again, I have no cause for complaint on the grounds that God has given me a will that has a wider scope than my intellect. For since the will consists of merely one thing, something indivisible, as it were, it does not seem that its nature could withstand anything being removed from it. Indeed, the more ample the will is, the more I ought to thank the one who gave it to me.

Finally, I should not complain because God concurs with me in eliciting those acts of the will, that is those judgments, in which I am mistaken. For insofar as those acts depend on God, they are absolutely true and good; and in a certain sense, there is greater perfection in me in being able to elicit those acts than in not being able to do so. But privation, in which alone the defining characteristic of falsehood and wrongdoing is to be found, has no need whatever for God's concurrence, since a privation is not a thing, nor, when it is related to God as its cause, is it to be called a privation, but simply a negation. For it is surely no imperfection in God that he has given me the freedom to give or withhold my assent in those instances where he has not placed a clear and distinct perception in my intellect. But surely it is an imperfection in me that I do not use my freedom well and that I make judgments about things I do not properly understand. Nevertheless, I see that God could easily have brought it about that, while still being free and having finite knowledge, I should nonetheless never make a mistake. This result could have been achieved either by his endowing my intellect with a clear and distinct perception of everything about which I would ever deliberate, or by simply impressing the following rule so firmly upon my memory that I could never forget it: I should never judge anything that I do not clearly and distinctly understand. I readily understand that, considered as a totality, I would have been more perfect than I am now, had God made me that way. But I cannot therefore deny that it may somehow be a greater perfection in the universe as a whole that some of its parts are not immune to error, while others are, than if all of them were exactly alike. And I have no right to complain that the part God has wished me to play is not the principal and most perfect one of all.

Furthermore, even if I cannot abstain from errors in the first way mentioned above, which depends upon a clear perception of everything about which I must deliberate, nevertheless I can avoid error in the other way, which depends solely on my remembering to abstain from making judgments whenever the truth of a given matter is not apparent. For although I experience a certain infirmity in myself, namely that I am unable to keep my attention constantly focused on one and the same item of knowledge, nevertheless, by attentive and often repeated meditation, I can bring it about that I call this rule to mind whenever the situation calls for it, and thus I would acquire a certain habit of not erring.

Since herein lies the greatest and chief perfection of man, I think today's meditation, in which I investigated the cause of error and falsity, was quite profitable. Nor can this cause be anything other than the one I have described; for as often as I restrain my will when I make judgments, so that it extends only to those matters that the intellect clearly and distinctly discloses to it, it plainly cannot happen that I err. For every clear and distinct perception is surely something, and hence it cannot come from nothing. On the contrary, it must necessarily have God for its author: God, I say, that supremely perfect being to whom it is repugnant to be a deceiver. Therefore the perception is most assuredly true. Today I have learned not merely what I must avoid so as never to make a mistake, but at the same time what I must do to attain truth. For I will indeed attain it, if only I pay enough attention to all the things that I perfectly understand, and separate them off from the rest, which I apprehend more confusedly and more obscurely. I will be conscientious about this in the future.

MEDITATION FIVE: Concerning the Essence of Material Things, and   63
Again Concerning God, That He Exists

Several matters remain for me to examine concerning the attributes of God and myself, that is, concerning the nature of my mind. But perhaps I will take these up at some other time. For now, since I have noted what to avoid and what to do in order to attain the truth, nothing seems more pressing than that I try to free myself from the doubts into which I fell a few days ago, and that I see whether anything certain is to be had concerning material things.

Yet, before inquiring whether any such things exist outside me, I surely ought to consider the ideas of these things, insofar as they exist in my thought, and see which ones are distinct and which ones are confused.

I do indeed distinctly imagine the quantity that philosophers commonly call "continuous," that is, the extension of this quantity, or rather of the thing quantified in length, breadth, and depth. I enumerate the various parts in it. I ascribe to these parts any sizes, shapes, positions, and local movements whatever; to these movements I ascribe any durations whatever.

Not only are these things manifestly known and transparent to me, viewed thus in a general way, but also, when I focus my attention on them, I perceive countless particulars concerning shapes, number, movement, and the like. Their truth is so open and so much in accord with my nature that, when I first discover them, it seems   64
I am not so much learning something new as recalling something I knew beforehand. In other words, it seems as though I am noticing things for the first time that were in fact in me for a long while, although I had not previously directed a mental gaze upon them.

What I believe must be considered above all here is the fact that I find within me countless ideas of certain things, that, even if perhaps they do not exist anywhere outside me, still cannot be said to be nothing. And although, in a sense, I think them at will, nevertheless they are not something I have fabricated; rather they have their own true and immutable natures. For example, when I imagine a triangle, even if perhaps no such figure exists outside my thought anywhere in the world and never has, the triangle still has a certain determinate nature, essence, or form which is unchangeable and eternal, which I did not fabricate, and which does not depend on my mind. This is evident from the fact that various properties can be demonstrated regarding this triangle: namely, that its three angles are equal to two right angles, that its longest side is opposite its largest angle, and so on. These are properties I now clearly acknowledge, whether I want to or not, even if I previously had given them no thought whatever when I imagined the triangle. For this reason, then, they were not fabricated by me.

It is irrelevant for me to say that perhaps the idea of a triangle came to me from external things through the sense organs because of course I have on occasion seen triangle-shaped bodies. For I can think of countless other figures, concerning which

there can be no suspicion of their ever having entered me through the senses, and yet
65   I can demonstrate various properties of these figures, no less than I can those of the
triangle. All these properties are patently true because I know them clearly, and thus
they are something and not merely nothing. For it is obvious that whatever is true is
something, and I have already demonstrated at some length that all that I know clearly
is true. And even if I had not demonstrated this, certainly the nature of my mind is
such that nevertheless I cannot refrain from assenting to these things, at least while I
perceive them clearly. And I recall that even before now, when I used to keep my
attention glued to the objects of the senses, I always took the truths I clearly
recognized regarding figures, numbers, or other things pertaining to arithmetic,
geometry, or, in general, to pure and abstract mathematics to be the most certain of all.

But if, from the mere fact that I can bring forth from my thought the idea of
something, it follows that all that I clearly and distinctly perceive to belong to that
thing really does belong to it, then cannot this too be a basis for an argument proving
the existence of God? Clearly the idea of God, that is, the idea of a supremely perfect
being, is one I discover to be no less within me than the idea of any figure or number.
And that it belongs to God's nature that he always exists is something I understand
no less clearly and distinctly than is the case when I demonstrate in regard to some
figure or number that something also belongs to the nature of that figure or number.
Thus, even if not everything that I have meditated upon during these last few days
were true, still the existence of God ought to have for me at least the same degree of
66   certainty that truths of mathematics had until now.

However, this point is not wholly obvious at first glance, but has a certain look of
a sophism about it. Since in all other matters I have become accustomed to
distinguishing existence from essence, I easily convince myself that it can even be
separated from God's essence, and hence that God can be thought of as not existing.
But nevertheless, it is obvious to anyone who pays close attention that existence can
no more be separated from God's essence than its having three angles equal to two
right angles can be separated from the essence of a triangle, or than the idea of a
valley can be separated from the idea of a mountain. Thus it is no less[4] contradictory
to think of God (that is, a supremely perfect being) lacking existence (that is, lacking
some perfection), than it is to think of a mountain without a valley.

But granted I can no more think of God as not existing than I can think of a
mountain without a valley, nevertheless it surely does not follow from the fact that I
think of a mountain without a valley that a mountain exists in the world. Likewise,
from the fact that I think of God as existing, it does not seem to follow that God
exists, for my thought imposes no necessity on things. And just as one may imagine
a winged horse, without there being a horse that has wings, in the same way perhaps
I can attach existence to God, even though no God exists.

But there is a sophism lurking here. From the fact that I am unable to think of a
67   mountain without a valley, it does not follow that a mountain or a valley exists
anywhere, but only that, whether they exist or not, a mountain and a valley are
inseparable from one another. But from the fact that I cannot think of God except as

---

4   A literal translation of the Latin text (*non magis*) is "no more." This is obviously a misstatement on
Descartes's part, since it contradicts his own clearly stated views.

existing, it follows that existence is inseparable from God, and that for this reason he really exists. Not that my thought brings this about or imposes any necessity on anything; but rather the necessity of the thing itself, namely of the existence of God, forces me to think this. For I am not free to think of God without existence, that is, a supremely perfect being without a supreme perfection, as I am to imagine a horse with or without wings.

Further, it should not be said here that even though I surely need to assent to the existence of God once I have asserted that God has all perfections and that existence is one of these perfections, nevertheless that earlier assertion need not have been made. Likewise, I need not believe that all four-sided figures can be inscribed in a circle; but given that I posit this, it would then be necessary for me to admit that a rhombus can be inscribed in a circle. Yet this is obviously false. For although it is not necessary that I should ever happen upon any thought of God, nevertheless whenever I am of a mind to think of a being that is first and supreme, and bring forth the idea of God as it were from the storehouse of my mind, I must of necessity ascribe all perfections to him, even if I do not at that time enumerate them all or take notice of each one individually. This necessity plainly suffices so that afterwards, when I realize that existence is a perfection, I rightly conclude that a first and supreme being exists. In the same way, there is no necessity for me ever to imagine a triangle, but whenever I do wish to consider a rectilinear figure having but three angles, I must ascribe to it those properties on the basis of which one rightly infers that the three   68 angles of this figure are no greater than two right angles, even though I do not take note of this at the time. But when I inquire as to the figures that may be inscribed in a circle, there is absolutely no need whatever for my thinking that all four-sided figures are of this sort; for that matter, I cannot even fabricate such a thing, so long as I am of a mind to admit only what I clearly and distinctly understand. Consequently, there is a great difference between false assumptions of this sort and the true ideas that are inborn in me, the first and chief of which is the idea of God. For there are a great many ways in which I understand that this idea is not an invention that is dependent upon my thought, but is an image of a true and immutable nature. First, I cannot think of anything aside from God alone to whose essence existence belongs. Next, I cannot understand how there could be two or more Gods of this kind. Again, once I have asserted that one God now exists, I plainly see that it is necessary that he has existed from eternity and will endure for eternity. Finally, I perceive many other features in God, none of which I can remove or change.

But, whatever type of argument I use, it always comes down to the fact that the only things that fully convince me are those that I clearly and distinctly perceive. And although some of these things I thus perceive are obvious to everyone, while others are discovered only by those who look more closely and inquire carefully, nevertheless, once they have been discovered, they are considered no less certain than the others. For example, in the case of a right triangle, although it is not so readily apparent that the square of the hypotenuse is equal to the sum of the squares   69 of the other two sides as it is that the hypotenuse is opposite the largest angle, nevertheless, once the former has been ascertained, it is no less believed. However, as far as God is concerned, if I were not overwhelmed by prejudices and if the images of sensible things were not besieging my thought from all directions, I would certainly acknowledge nothing sooner or more easily than him. For what, in and of itself, is more manifest than that a supreme being exists, that is, that God, to whose essence alone existence belongs, exists?

And although I needed to pay close attention in order to perceive this, nevertheless I now am just as certain about this as I am about everything else that seems most certain. Moreover, I observe also that certitude about other things is so dependent on this, that without it nothing can ever be perfectly known.

For I am indeed of such a nature that, while I perceive something very clearly and distinctly, I cannot help believing it to be true. Nevertheless, my nature is also such that I cannot focus my mental gaze always on the same thing, so as to perceive it clearly. Often the memory of a previously made judgment may return when I am no longer attending to the arguments on account of which I made such a judgment. Thus, other arguments can be brought forward that would easily make me change my opinion, were I ignorant of God. And thus I would never have true and certain knowledge about anything, but merely fickle and changeable opinions. Thus, for example, when I consider the nature of a triangle, it appears most evident to me, steeped as I am in the principles of geometry, that its three angles are equal to two right angles. And so long as I attend to its demonstration I cannot help believing this to be true. But no sooner do I turn the mind's eye away from the demonstration, than, however much I still recall that I had observed it most clearly, nevertheless, it can easily happen that I entertain doubts about whether it is true, were I ignorant of God. For I can convince myself that I have been so constituted by nature that I might occasionally be mistaken about those things I believe I perceive most evidently, especially when I recall that I have often taken many things to be true and certain, which other arguments have subsequently led me to judge to be false.

But once I perceived that there is a God, and also understood at the same time that everything else depends on him, and that he is not a deceiver, I then concluded that everything that I clearly and distinctly perceive is necessarily true. Hence even if I no longer attend to the reasons leading me to judge this to be true, so long as I merely recall that I did clearly and distinctly observe it, no counterargument can be brought forward that might force me to doubt it. On the contrary, I have a true and certain knowledge of it. And not just of this one fact, but of everything else that I recall once having demonstrated, as in geometry, and so on. For what objections can now be raised against me? That I have been made such that I am often mistaken? But I now know that I cannot be mistaken in matters I plainly understand. That I have taken many things to be true and certain which subsequently I recognized to be false? But none of these were things I clearly and distinctly perceived. But I was ignorant of this rule for determining the truth, and I believed these things perhaps for other reasons, which I later discovered were less firm. What then remains to be said? That perhaps I am dreaming, as I recently objected against myself, in other words, that everything I am now thinking of is no truer than what occurs to someone who is asleep? Be that as it may, this changes nothing; for certainly, even if I were dreaming, if anything is evident to my intellect, then it is entirely true.

And thus I see plainly that the certainty and truth of every science depends exclusively upon the knowledge of the true God, to the extent that, prior to my becoming aware of him, I was incapable of achieving perfect knowledge about anything else. But now it is possible for me to achieve full and certain knowledge about countless things, both about God and other intellectual matters, as well as about the entirety of that corporeal nature which is the object of pure mathematics.

10

MEDITATION SIX: Concerning the Existence of Material Things, and the Real Distinction between Mind and Body

It remains for me to examine whether material things exist. Indeed I now know that they can exist, at least insofar as they are the object of pure mathematics, since I clearly and distinctly perceive them. For no doubt God is capable of bringing about everything that I am capable of perceiving in this way. And I have never judged that God was incapable of something, except when it was incompatible with my perceiving it distinctly. Moreover, from the faculty of imagination, which I notice I use while dealing with material things, it seems to follow that they exist. For to anyone paying very close attention to what imagination is, it appears to be simply a certain application of the knowing faculty to a body intimately present to it, and which therefore exists.

72

To make this clear, I first examine the difference between imagination and pure intellection. So, for example, when I imagine a triangle, I not only understand that it is a figure bounded by three lines, but at the same time I also envisage with the mind's eye those lines as if they were present; and this is what I call "imagining." On the other hand, if I want to think about a chiliagon, I certainly understand that it is a figure consisting of a thousand sides, just as well as I understand that a triangle is a figure consisting of three sides, yet I do not imagine those thousand sides in the same way, or envisage them as if they were present. And although in that case, because of force of habit I always imagine something whenever I think about a corporeal thing, I may perchance represent to myself some figure in a confused fashion, nevertheless this figure is obviously not a chiliagon. For this figure is really no different from the figure I would represent to myself, were I thinking of a myriagon or any other figure with a large number of sides. Nor is this figure of any help in knowing the properties that differentiate a chiliagon from other polygons. But if the figure in question is a pentagon, I surely can understand its figure, just as was the case with the chiliagon, without the help of my imagination. But I can also imagine a pentagon by turning the mind's eye both to its five sides and at the same time to the area bounded by those sides. At this point I am manifestly aware that I am in need of a peculiar sort of effort on the part of the mind in order to imagine, one that I do not employ in order to understand. This new effort on the part of the mind clearly shows the difference between imagination and pure intellection.

73

Moreover, I consider that this power of imagining that is in me, insofar as it differs from the power of understanding, is not required for my own essence, that is, the essence of my mind. For were I to be lacking this power, I would nevertheless undoubtedly remain the same entity I am now. Thus it seems to follow that the power of imagining depends upon something distinct from me. And I readily understand that, were a body to exist to which a mind is so joined that it may apply itself in order, as it were, to look at it any time it wishes, it could happen that it is by means of this very body that I imagine corporeal things. As a result, this mode of thinking may differ from pure intellection only in the sense that the mind, when it understands, in a sense turns toward itself and looks at one of the ideas that are in it;

whereas when it imagines, it turns toward the body, and intuits in the body something that conforms to an idea either understood by the mind or perceived by sense. To be sure, I easily understand that the imagination can be actualized in this way, provided a body does exist. And since I can think of no other way of explaining imagination that is equally appropriate, I make a probable conjecture from this that a body exists. But this is only a probability. And even though I may examine everything carefully, nevertheless I do not yet see how the distinct idea of corporeal nature that I find in my imagination can enable me to develop an argument which necessarily concludes that some body exists.

74   But I am in the habit of imagining many other things, over and above that corporeal nature which is the object of pure mathematics, such as colors, sounds, tastes, pain, and the like, though not so distinctly. And I perceive these things better by means of the senses, from which, with the aid of the memory, they seem to have arrived at the imagination. Thus I should pay the same degree of attention to the senses, so that I might deal with them more appropriately. I must see whether I can obtain any reliable argument for the existence of corporeal things from those things that are perceived by the mode of thinking that I call "sense."

First of all, to be sure, I will review here all the things I previously believed to be true because I had perceived them by means of the senses and the causes I had for thinking this. Next I will assess the causes why I later called them into doubt. Finally, I will consider what I must now believe about these things.

So first, I sensed that I had a head, hands, feet, and other members that comprised this body which I viewed as part of me, or perhaps even as the whole of me. I sensed that this body was found among many other bodies, by which my body can be affected in various beneficial or harmful ways. I gauged what was opportune by means of a certain sensation of pleasure, and what was inopportune by a sensation of pain. In addition to pain and pleasure, I also sensed within me hunger, thirst, and other such appetites, as well as certain bodily tendencies toward mirth, sadness, anger, and other such affects. And externally, besides the extension, shapes, and

75   motions of bodies, I also sensed their hardness, heat, and other tactile qualities. I also sensed light, colors, odors, tastes, and sounds, on the basis of whose variety I distinguished the sky, the earth, the seas, and the other bodies, one from the other. Now given the ideas of all these qualities that presented themselves to my thought, and which were all that I properly and immediately sensed, still it was surely not without reason that I thought I sensed things that were manifestly different from my thought, namely, the bodies from which these ideas proceeded. For I knew by experience that these ideas came upon me utterly without my consent, to the extent that, wish as I may, I could not sense any object unless it was present to a sense organ. Nor could I fail to sense it when it was present. And since the ideas perceived by sense were much more vivid and explicit and even, in their own way, more distinct than any of those that I deliberately and knowingly formed through meditation or that I found impressed on my memory, it seemed impossible that they came from myself. Thus the remaining alternative was that they came from other things. Since I had no knowledge of such things except from those same ideas

themselves, I could not help entertaining the thought that they were similar to those
ideas. Moreover, I also recalled that the use of the senses antedated the use of reason.
And since I saw that the ideas that I myself fashioned were not as explicit as those
that I perceived through the faculty of sense, and were for the most part composed
of parts of the latter, I easily convinced myself that I had absolutely no idea in the
intellect that I did not have beforehand in the sense faculty. Not without reason did
I judge that this body, which by a certain special right I called "mine," belongs more
to me than did any other. For I could never be separated from it in the same way I
could be from other bodies. I sensed all appetites and feelings in and on behalf of it.
Finally, I noticed pain and pleasurable excitement in its parts, but not in other bodies
external to it. But why should a certain sadness of spirit arise from some sensation
or other of pain, and why should a certain elation arise from a sensation of
excitement, or why should that peculiar twitching in the stomach, which I call
hunger, warn me to have something to eat, or why should dryness in the throat warn
me to take something to drink, and so on? I plainly had no explanation other than
that I had been taught this way by nature. For there is no affinity whatsoever, at least
none I am aware of, between this twitching in the stomach and the will to have
something to eat, or between the sensation of something causing pain and the
thought of sadness arising from this sensation. But nature also seems to have taught
me everything else as well that I judged concerning the objects of the senses, for I
had already convinced myself that this was how things were, prior to my assessing
any of the arguments that might prove it.

Afterwards, however, many experiences gradually weakened any faith that I had
in the senses. Towers that had seemed round from afar occasionally appeared square
at close quarters. Very large statues mounted on their pedestals did not seem large to
someone looking at them from ground level. And in countless other such instances I
determined that judgments in matters of the external senses were in error. And not
just the external senses, but the internal senses as well. For what can be more
intimate than pain? But I had sometimes heard it said by people whose leg or arm
had been amputated that it seemed to them that they still occasionally sensed pain in
the very limb they had lost. Thus, even in my own case it did not seem to be entirely
certain that some bodily member was causing me pain, even though I did sense pain
in it. To these causes for doubt I recently added two quite general ones. The first was
that everything I ever thought I sensed while awake I could believe I also sometimes
sensed while asleep, and since I do not believe that what I seem to sense in my
dreams comes to me from things external to me, I saw no reason why I should hold
this belief about those things I seem to be sensing while awake. The second was that,
since I was still ignorant of the author of my origin (or at least pretended to be
ignorant of it), I saw nothing to prevent my having been so constituted by nature that
I should be mistaken even about what seemed to me most true. As to the arguments
that used to convince me of the truth of sensible things, I found no difficulty
responding to them. For since I seemed driven by nature toward many things about
which reason tried to dissuade me, I did not think that what I was taught by nature
deserved much credence. And even though the perceptions of the senses did not

76

77

depend on my will, I did not think that we must therefore conclude that they came from things distinct from me, since perhaps there is some faculty in me, as yet unknown to me, that produces these perceptions.

But now, having begun to have a better knowledge of myself and the author of my origin, I am of the opinion that I must not rashly admit everything that I seem to derive from the senses; but neither, for that matter, should I call everything into doubt.

78

First, I know that all the things that I clearly and distinctly understand can be made by God such as I understand them. For this reason, my ability clearly and distinctly to understand one thing without another suffices to make me certain that the one thing is different from the other, since they can be separated from each other, at least by God. The question as to the sort of power that might effect such a separation is not relevant to their being thought to be different. For this reason, from the fact that I know that I exist, and that at the same time I judge that obviously nothing else belongs to my nature or essence except that I am a thinking thing, I rightly conclude that my essence consists entirely in my being a thinking thing. And although perhaps (or rather, as I shall soon say, assuredly) I have a body that is very closely joined to me, nevertheless, because on the one hand I have a clear and distinct idea of myself, insofar as I am merely a thinking thing and not an extended thing, and because on the other hand I have a distinct idea of a body, insofar as it is merely an extended thing and not a thinking thing, it is certain that I am really distinct from my body, and can exist without it.

Moreover, I find in myself faculties for certain special modes of thinking, namely the faculties of imagining and sensing. I can clearly and distinctly understand myself in my entirety without these faculties, but not vice versa: I cannot understand them clearly and distinctly without me, that is, without a substance endowed with understanding in which they inhere, for they include an act of understanding in their formal concept. Thus I perceive them to be distinguished from me as modes from a thing. I also acknowledge that there are certain other faculties, such as those of moving from one place to another, of taking on various shapes, and so on, that, like sensing or imagining, cannot be understood apart from some substance in which they inhere, and hence without which they cannot exist. But it is clear that these faculties, if in fact they exist, must be in a corporeal or extended substance, not in a substance endowed with understanding. For some extension is contained in a clear and distinct concept of them, though certainly not any understanding. Now there clearly is in me a passive faculty of sensing, that is, a faculty for receiving and knowing the ideas of sensible things; but I could not use it unless there also existed, either in me or in something else, a certain active faculty of producing or bringing about these ideas. But this faculty surely cannot be in me, since it clearly presupposes no act of understanding, and these ideas are produced without my cooperation and often even against my will. Therefore the only alternative is that it is in some substance different from me, containing either formally or eminently all the reality that exists objectively in the ideas produced by that faculty, as I have just noted above. Hence this substance is either a body, that is, a corporeal nature, which contains formally all that is contained objectively in the ideas, or else it is God, or some other creature

79

more noble than a body, which contains eminently all that is contained objectively in the ideas. But since God is not a deceiver, it is patently obvious that he does not send me these ideas either immediately by himself, or even through the mediation of some creature that contains the objective reality of these ideas not formally but only eminently. For since God has given me no faculty whatsoever for making this determination, but instead has given me a great inclination to believe that these ideas   80
issue from corporeal things, I fail to see how God could be understood not to be a deceiver, if these ideas were to issue from a source other than corporeal things. And consequently corporeal things exist. Nevertheless, perhaps not all bodies exist exactly as I grasp them by sense, since this sensory grasp is in many cases very obscure and confused. But at least they do contain everything I clearly and distinctly understand—that is, everything, considered in a general sense, that is encompassed in the object of pure mathematics.

As far as the remaining matters are concerned, which are either merely particular (for example, that the sun is of such and such a size or shape, and so on) or less clearly understood (for example, light, sound, pain, and the like), even though these matters are very doubtful and uncertain, nevertheless the fact that God is no deceiver (and thus no falsity can be found in my opinions, unless there is also in me a faculty given me by God for the purpose of rectifying this falsity) offers me a definite hope of reaching the truth even in these matters. And surely there is no doubt that all that I am taught by nature has some truth to it; for by "nature," taken generally, I understand nothing other than God himself or the ordered network of created things which was instituted by God. By my own particular nature I understand nothing other than the combination of all the things bestowed upon me by God.

There is nothing that this nature teaches me more explicitly than that I have a body that is ill-disposed when I feel pain, that needs food and drink when I suffer hunger or thirst, and the like. Therefore, I should not doubt that there is some truth in this.

By means of these sensations of pain, hunger, thirst, and so on, nature also   81
teaches that I am present in my body not merely in the way a sailor is present in a ship, but that I am most tightly joined and, so to speak, commingled with it, so much so that I and the body constitute one single thing. For if this were not the case, then I, who am only a thinking thing, would not sense pain when the body is injured; rather, I would perceive the wound by means of the pure intellect, just as a sailor perceives by sight whether anything in his ship is broken. And when the body is in need of food or drink, I should understand this explicitly, instead of having confused sensations of hunger and thirst. For clearly these sensations of thirst, hunger, pain, and so on are nothing but certain confused modes of thinking arising from the union and, as it were, the commingling of the mind with the body.

Moreover, I am also taught by nature that various other bodies exist around my body, some of which are to be pursued, while others are to be avoided. And to be sure, from the fact that I sense a wide variety of colors, sounds, odors, tastes, levels of heat, and grades of roughness, and the like, I rightly conclude that in the bodies from which these different perceptions of the senses proceed there are differences corresponding to the different perceptions—though perhaps the latter do not resemble the former. And from the fact that some of these perceptions are pleasant while others are unpleasant, it is plainly certain that my body, or rather my whole self, insofar as I am comprised of a body and a mind, can be affected by various beneficial and harmful bodies in the vicinity.

82   Granted, there are many other things that I seem to have been taught by nature; nevertheless it was not really nature that taught them to me but a certain habit of making reckless judgments. And thus it could easily happen that these judgments are false: for example, that any space where there is absolutely nothing happening to move my senses is empty; or that there is something in a hot body that bears an exact likeness to the idea of heat that is in me; or that in a white or green body there is the same whiteness or greenness that I sense; or that in a bitter or sweet body there is the same taste, and so on; or that stars and towers and any other distant bodies have the same size and shape that they present to my senses, and other things of this sort. But to ensure that my perceptions in this matter are sufficiently distinct, I ought to define more precisely what exactly I mean when I say that I am "taught something by nature." For I am taking "nature" here more narrowly than the combination of everything bestowed on me by God. For this combination embraces many things that belong exclusively to my mind, such as my perceiving that what has been done cannot be undone, and everything else that is known by the light of nature. That is not what I am talking about here. There are also many things that belong exclusively to the body, such as that it tends to move downward, and so on. I am not dealing with these either, but only with what God has bestowed on me insofar as I am composed of mind and body. Accordingly, it is this nature that teaches me to avoid things that produce a sensation of pain and to pursue things that produce a sensation of pleasure, and the like. But it does not appear that nature teaches us to conclude anything, besides these things, from these sense perceptions unless the intellect has first conducted its own inquiry regarding things external to us. For it seems to belong

83   exclusively to the mind, and not to the composite of mind and body, to know the truth in these matters. Thus, although a star affects my eye no more than does the flame from a small torch, still there is no real or positive tendency in my eye toward believing that the star is no larger than the flame. Yet, ever since my youth, I have made this judgment without any reason for doing so. And although I feel heat as I draw closer to the fire, and I also feel pain upon drawing too close to it, there is not a single argument that persuades me that there is something in the fire similar to that heat, any more than to that pain. On the contrary, I am convinced only that there is something in the fire that, regardless of what it finally turns out to be, causes in us those sensations of heat or pain. And although there may be nothing in a given space that moves the senses, it does not therefore follow that there is no body in it. But I see that in these any many other instances I have been in the habit of subverting the order of nature. For admittedly I use the perceptions of the senses (which are properly given by nature only for signifying to the mind what things are useful or harmful to the composite of which it is a part, and to that extent they are clear and distinct enough), as reliable rules for immediately discerning what is the essence of

bodies located outside us. Yet they signify nothing about that except quite obscurely and confusedly.

I have already examined in sufficient detail how it could happen that my judgments are false, despite the goodness of God. But a new difficulty now arises regarding those very things that nature shows me are either to be sought out or avoided, as well as the internal sensations where I seem to have detected errors, as for example, when someone is deluded by a food's pleasant taste to eat the poison hidden inside it. In this case, however, he is driven by nature only toward desiring the thing in which the pleasurable taste is found, but not toward the poison, of which he obviously is unaware. I can only conclude that this nature is not omniscient. This is not remarkable, since man is a limited thing, and thus only what is of limited perfection befits him.

84

But we not infrequently err even in those things to which nature impels us. Take, for example, the case of those who are ill and who desire food or drink that will soon afterwards be injurious to them. Perhaps it could be said here that they erred because their nature was corrupt. However, this does not remove our difficulty, for a sick man is no less a creature of God than a healthy one, and thus it seems no less inconsistent that the sick man got a deception-prone nature from God. And a clock made of wheels and counterweights follows all the laws of nature no less closely when it has been badly constructed and does not tell time accurately than it does when it completely satisfies the wish of its maker. Likewise, I might regard a man's body as a kind of mechanism that is outfitted with and composed of bones, nerves, muscles, veins, blood, and skin in such a way that, even if no mind existed in it, the man's body would still exhibit all the same motions that are in it now except for those motions that proceed either from a command of the will or, consequently, from the mind. I easily recognize that it would be natural for this body, were it, say, suffering from dropsy and experiencing dryness in the throat (which typically produces a thirst sensation in the mind), and also so disposed by its nerves and other parts to take something to drink, the result of which would be to exacerbate the illness. This is as natural as for a body without any such illness to be moved by the same dryness in the throat to take something to drink that is useful to it. And given the intended purpose of the clock, I could say that it deviates from its nature when it fails to tell the right time. And similarly, considering the mechanism of the human body in terms of its being equipped for the motions that typically occur in it, I may think that it too is deviating from its nature, if its throat were dry when having something to drink is not beneficial to its conservation. Nevertheless, I am well aware that this last use of "nature" differs greatly from the other. For this latter "nature" is merely a designation dependent on my thought, since it compares a man in poor health and a poorly constructed clock with the ideas of a healthy man and of a well-made clock, a designation extrinsic to the things to which it is applied. But by "nature" taken in the former sense, I understand something that is really in things, and thus is not without some truth.

85

When we say, then, in the case of the body suffering from dropsy, that its "nature" is corrupt, given the fact that it has a parched throat and yet does not need something to drink, "nature" obviously is merely an extrinsic designation. Nevertheless, in the case of the composite, that is, of a mind joined to such a body, it is not a mere designation, but a true error of nature that this body should be thirsty when having something to drink would be harmful to it. It therefore remains to inquire here how the goodness of God does not prevent "nature," thus considered, from being deceptive.

Now my first observation here is that there is a great difference between a mind and a body, in that a body, by its very nature, is always divisible. On the other hand, the mind is utterly indivisible. For when I consider the mind, that is, myself insofar as I am only a thinking thing, I cannot distinguish any parts within me; rather, I understand myself to be manifestly one complete thing. Although the entire mind seems to be united to the entire body, nevertheless, were a foot or an arm or any other bodily part to be amputated, I know that nothing has been taken away from the mind on that account. Nor can the faculties of willing, sensing, understanding, and so on be called "parts" of the mind, since it is one and the same mind that wills, senses, and understands. On the other hand, there is no corporeal or extended thing I can think of that I may not in my thought easily divide into parts; and in this way I understand that it is divisible. This consideration alone would suffice to teach me that the mind is wholly diverse from the body, had I not yet known it well enough in any other way.

My second observation is that my mind is not immediately affected by all the parts of the body, but only by the brain, or perhaps even by just one small part of the brain, namely, by that part where the "common" sense is said to reside. Whenever this part of the brain is disposed in the same manner, it presents the same thing to the mind, even if the other parts of the body are able meanwhile to be related in diverse ways. Countless experiments show this, none of which need be reviewed here.

My next observation is that the nature of the body is such that whenever any of its parts can be moved by another part some distance away, it can also be moved in the same manner by any of the parts that lie between them, even if this more distant part is doing nothing. For example, in the cord ABCD, if the final part D is pulled, the first part A would be moved in exactly the same manner as it could be, if one of the intermediate parts B or C were pulled, while the end part D remained immobile. Likewise, when I feel a pain in my foot, physics teaches me that this sensation took place by means of nerves distributed throughout the foot, like stretched cords extending from the foot all the way to the brain. When these nerves are pulled in the foot, they also pull on the inner parts of the brain to which they extend, and produce a certain motion in them. This motion has been constituted by nature so as to affect the mind with a sensation of pain, as if it occurred in the foot. But because these nerves need to pass through the shin, thigh, loins, back, and neck, to get from the foot to the brain, it can happen that even if it is not the part in the foot, but merely one of the intermediate parts that is being struck, the very same movement will occur in the brain that would occur, were the foot badly injured. The inevitable result will be that the mind feels the same pain. The same opinion should hold for any other sensation.

My final observation is that, since any given motion occurring in that part of the brain immediately affecting the mind produces but one sensation in it, I can think of no better arrangement than that it produces the one sensation that, of all the ones it

is able to produce, is most especially and most often conducive to the maintenance
of a healthy man. Moreover, experience shows that all the sensations bestowed on us
by nature are like this. Hence there is absolutely nothing to be found in them that
does not bear witness to God's power and goodness. Thus, for example, when the
nerves in the foot are agitated in a violent and unusual manner, this motion of theirs   88
extends through the marrow of the spine to the inner reaches of the brain, where it
gives the mind the sign to sense something, namely, the pain as if it is occurring in
the foot. This provokes the mind to do its utmost to move away from the cause of the
pain, since it is seen as harmful to the foot. But the nature of man could have been
so constituted by God that this same motion in the brain might have indicated
something else to the mind: for example, either the motion itself as it occurs in the
brain, or in the foot, or in some place in between, or something else entirely different.
But nothing else would have served so well the maintenance of the body. Similarly,
when we need something to drink, a certain dryness arises in the throat that moves
the nerves in the throat, and, by means of them, the inner parts of the brain. And this
motion affects the mind with a sensation of thirst, because in this entire affair nothing
is more useful for us to know than that we need something to drink in order to
maintain our health; the same holds in the other cases.

From these considerations it is utterly apparent that, notwithstanding the immense
goodness of God, the nature of man, insofar as it is composed of mind and body,
cannot help being sometimes mistaken. For if some cause, not in the foot but in some
other part through which the nerves extend from the foot to the brain, or perhaps
even in the brain itself, were to produce the same motion that would normally be
produced by a badly injured foot, the pain will be felt as if it were in the foot, and
the senses will naturally be deceived. For since an identical motion in the brain can
only bring about an identical sensation in the mind, and it is more frequently the case
that this motion is wont to arise on account of a cause that harms the foot than on
account of some other thing existing elsewhere, it is reasonable that the motion   89
should always show pain to the mind as something belonging to the foot rather than
to some other part. And if dryness in the throat does not arise, as is normal, from
drink's contributing to bodily health, but from a contrary cause, as happens in the
case of someone with dropsy, then it is far better that it should deceive on that
occasion than that it should always be deceptive when the body is in good health.
The same holds for the other cases.

This consideration is most helpful, not only for my noticing all the errors to which
my nature is liable, but also for enabling me to correct or avoid them without
difficulty. To be sure, I know that all the senses set forth what is true more frequently
than what is false regarding what concerns the welfare of the body. Moreover, I can
nearly always make use of several of them in order to examine the same thing.
Furthermore, I can use my memory, which connects current happenings with past
ones, and my intellect, which now has examined all the causes of error. Hence I
should no longer fear that those things that are daily shown me by the senses are
false. On the contrary, the hyperbolic doubts of the last few days ought to be rejected
as ludicrous. This goes especially for the chief reason for doubting, which dealt with

my failure to distinguish being asleep from being awake. For I now notice that there is a considerable difference between these two; dreams are never joined by the memory with all the other actions of life, as is the case with those actions that occur when one is awake. For surely, if, while I am awake, someone were suddenly to appear to me and then immediately disappear, as occurs in dreams, so that I see neither where he came from nor where he went, it is not without reason that I would judge him to be a ghost or a phantom conjured up in my brain, rather than a true man. But when these things happen, and I notice distinctly where they come from, where they are now, and when they come to me, and when I connect my perception of them without interruption with the whole rest of my life, I am clearly certain that these perceptions have happened to me not while I was dreaming but while I was awake. Nor ought I have even the least doubt regarding the truth of these things, if, having mustered all the senses, in addition to my memory and my intellect, in order to examine them, nothing is passed on to me by one of these sources that conflicts with the others. For from the fact that God is no deceiver, it follows that I am in no way mistaken in these matters. But because the need to get things done does not always permit us the leisure for such a careful inquiry, we must confess that the life of man is apt to commit errors regarding particular things, and we must acknowledge the infirmity of our nature.

90